THE INVISIBLE
PALESTINIANS

PUBLIC CULTURES OF THE MIDDLE EAST AND NORTH AFRICA

Paul A. Silverstein, Susan Slyomovics,

and Ted Swedenburg, editors

THE INVISIBLE PALESTINIANS

The Hidden Struggle for Inclusion in Jewish Tel Aviv

—ɯ—

ANDREAS HACKL

INDIANA UNIVERSITY PRESS

This book is a publication of

Indiana University Press
Office of Scholarly Publishing
Herman B Wells Library 350
1320 East 10th Street
Bloomington, Indiana 47405 USA

iupress.org

Manufactured in the United States of America

First printing 2022

Cover photo: *Samar, Saja, and Beagle on the roof of Samar's apartment building, Tel Aviv, 2015*. Credit: Iris Hassid, author and photographer of *A Place of Our Own* (Amsterdam: Schilt Publishing & Gallery, 2020).

Cataloging information is available from the Library of Congress.

ISBN 978-0-253-06082-2 (hdbk.)
ISBN 978-0-253-06083-9 (pbk.)
ISBN 978-0-253-06084-6 (web PDF)

CONTENTS

ACKNOWLEDGMENTS

THIS BOOK IS A STORY about Tel Aviv told from the perspective of the Palestinians. At the same time, it is a story about the Palestinians narrated through the prism of Tel Aviv. It is also a story about hopes and the shattering of hopes, about aspirations and their denial, about desires and fears, ambition and discrimination, movement and restriction. The book is the culmination of around eight years of work and this journey naturally passed through a variety of stages. About two years of ethnographic research were followed by a year of writing up the material as a doctoral thesis in social anthropology at the University of Edinburgh. But the many rounds of rewriting and rethinking the collected materials certainly did not end there; it continued into the crafting of various publications for academic journals and other outlets. In between, there were countless exchanges and thought-provoking conversations with colleagues and friends. Looking back at this journey naturally demands a proper acknowledgment of the people and institutions that helped me shape this research into the book it has now become.

Transforming the initial idea into actual research was made possible by the Austrian Academy of Sciences, which generously funded my work on Palestinians in Israel with a Doctoral Fellowship. I spent the initial stages of the research at the Department of Sociology and Anthropology at Tel Aviv University, from where I began to explore the lives and challenges of Palestinian citizens of Israel in the city. Under the knowledgeable and inspiring supervision of Dan Rabinowitz, I gradually developed my ideas into a mature research project, while benefiting from the support and critical input of numerous other Palestinian and Israeli scholars and research students in Tel Aviv and beyond. While unable to name all of them, I would like to thank, in particular, Khaled

Furani, Yehouda Shenhav, Ofra Goldstein-Gidoni, Amalia Sa'ar, Natalia Gut-kowski, and Maisalon Dallashi for their support and critical input. I was lucky to have been included in a generous transnational doctoral program, which was coordinated by the Institute for European Ethnology at the Ludwig Maximil-ian University of Munich. The program facilitated international meetings, con-ferences, and exchanges with fellow doctoral researchers and faculty members that shaped the course of my research and offered an invaluable social network of friends and colleagues.

Most importantly, I am eternally indebted to all the Palestinians and Israelis I have met in the course of my research, who have shared their valuable time, their ideas, and their experiences with me. Although I would like to name each of them individually, this would undermine the book's aim of safeguarding their privacy and anonymity. Some of the people I have known during the re-search behind this book will always be dear friends to me. They have not only a special place in this book but also a special place in my heart.

The intensive two years of research on Palestinian Tel Aviv behind this book were preceded and paralleled by my work as a journalist and foreign corre-spondent based in Jerusalem. Here I owe special thanks to my editors of the Austrian newspaper *Wiener Zeitung* and the Sunday edition of the *Neue Zürcher Zeitung* in Switzerland. Although most of the knowledge contained in this book emerged from two years of intensive research on the ground, most of the think-ing and writing about it happened elsewhere. The University of Edinburgh was the perfectly supportive and inspiring environment I needed to mold the many stories and insights I had gained into a concrete form. Here I am particularly indebted to my PhD supervisor and mentor, Toby Kelly; my second supervisor, Jamie Furniss; my internal examiner, Jonathan Spencer; alongside many others within and beyond the social anthropology subject area at Edinburgh's School of Social and Political Science. Beyond Edinburgh, I would like to express my gratitude to my external PhD examiner Lori Allen, who provided important critical input on my doctoral thesis. Much of the writing and thinking that transformed this early thesis into the current book form happened during the three years of teaching and research between the end of my PhD and the Lec-tureship I was eventually offered in 2019. A postdoctoral fellowship by the UK's Economic and Social Research Council (ESRC) had allowed me to return to Israel/Palestine in 2017 for two months of additional research on Palestinians from the West Bank who worked in Israel. Here I am grateful for the support, expertise, and office space the East Jerusalem office of the International Labour Organization provided during this brief research visit. Thanks to an ESRC New

Investigator Grant held between 2019 and 2021, I was then able to dedicate some of this time to completing the manuscript.

However, the final version of the book would not be what it is without the critical reviews of two anonymous readers. I am grateful for their thoughtful comments, their honest critique, and their many suggestions for improving the manuscript. Many others, however, read and commented on parts of the manuscript in the long course of its production. Without naming everyone individually, I thank all of them for their time and their valuable input. Ultimately, there is clearly much more to a book than the written word: the cover image was kindly provided by the photographer Iris Hassid, with additional design input by Indiana University Press, and the maps were created by Marie Storrar at the University of Edinburgh.

Moreover, I would like to thank my partner, Kate, for her continuous support, motivation, and encouragement as well as my parents and the rest of my family for always believing in what I do. Finally, I would like to dedicate this book to my dear friend Rima, who inspired and shaped this research more than anyone else.

This leaves me with a final thought about how I see the role of this book and its wider relevance. Although it is rooted in serious academic research, I hope that the stories and ideas that live within it will appeal to a wide readership. Like any work of nonfiction writing, this book offers a necessarily partial and incomplete picture. For some, it may raise at least as many questions as it tries to answer. Perhaps it is precisely this lack of completeness that will make these pages feel real, alive, and relevant to a wide range of themes and lived experiences.

Andreas Hackl
Edinburgh, October 2021

THE INVISIBLE
PALESTINIANS

ISRAEL AND THE OCCUPIED PALESTINIAN TERRITORY

Acre

Occupied Golan Heights (Syria)

Haifa

Tiberias

Nazareth

Umm el-Fahm

Jenin

Baqa al-Gharbiyyeh

Tulkarm

Tubas

Taibe

Qalqiliya

Nablus

Salfit

Tel Aviv-Jaffa

West Bank

Ramallah

Jericho

Ashdod

1949 Armistice (Green Line)

Jerusalem

Jordan

Bethlehem

Gaza Strip

Hebron

Israel

1949 Armistice (Green Line)

Be'er Sheva

JORDAN RIVER

Settlements*

West Bank Barrier

—— Constructed

·········· Under Construction

·········· Projected

ISRAEL AND THE OCCUPIED PALESTINIAN TERRITORY

Taibe

Qalqiliya

Nablus

Salfit

West Bank

Ramallah

Jericho

No Man's
Land

1949 Armistice (Green Line)

Jerusalem

Bethlehem

Settlements*

West Bank Barrier
——— Constructed
············· Under Construction
·········· Projected

Hebron

*Due to size restrictions in this map, the settlements visible here are only those in the Seam Zone between the Separation Barrier and the official West Bank boundary. Jewish settlements are in reality scattered throughout the West Bank, with at least 132 official settlements, 135 unofficially established outposts, and a population of 441,600 settlers by 2021. Map design: School of Social and Political Science, University of Edinburgh.

Sources: UN-OCHA, Peace Now, "Settlement Watch," accessed April 25, 2021, https://peacenow.org.il/en/settlements-watch/settlements-data/population.

INTRODUCTION

—ᴠᴠ—

USING THE SETTLER CITY

Immersive Invisibility and the Palestinian Struggle for Urban Access in Tel Aviv

VERY FEW NEWCOMERS TO TEL Aviv University realize that it stands in the place of a former Palestinian village called al-Sheikh Muwannis. The university's buildings are too white, its architecture too modern. But, before it, the village had been there, with its citrus groves and about two thousand inhabitants, until the Arab-Israeli War of 1948 forced the last residents to abandon their homes and flee. The newly founded state of Israel then took back, or "redeemed," as it was called, their lands and turned the area into a neighborhood of the fast-expanding Jewish city of Tel Aviv. One remaining mansion of the former village was transformed into a university clubhouse. Some seventy years after the villagers' exile from their homes, the number of Palestinians who enrolled at Tel Aviv University roughly equaled the original indigenous population of al-Sheikh Muwannis. Had these young students, who were now Palestinian citizens of Israel, returned to reclaim this ancestral Palestinian land from the Jewish city that has since occupied it? Not, at least, in any straightforward way: most of them came to make use of Tel Aviv by accessing its many professional and educational opportunities, even though this urban space has overwritten Palestinian history and its remnants.

Many of the students had come to embark on careers as doctors, engineers, or lawyers. As they became temporary residents in Tel Aviv, some hoped to enjoy the relative freedom and anonymity this big city provided. Yet, they soon discovered that the city does not offer them these freedoms without reserve. These Palestinian citizens carry the burden of Palestine's tragically lost past in the very place that symbolizes the success of the Zionist project that brought about that loss.[1] It is, therefore, tremendously difficult to live as Palestinians

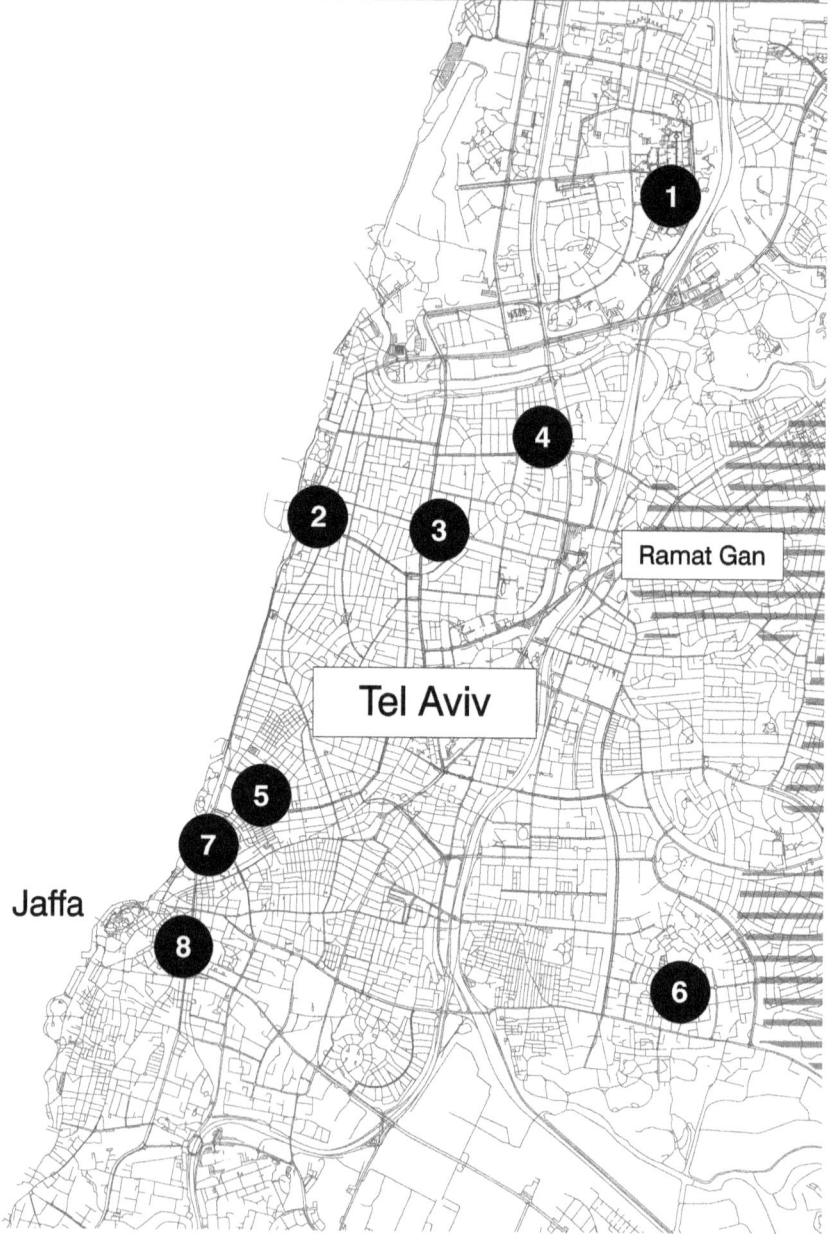

MAP OF TEL AVIV AND JAFFA

1

4

2 3

Ramat Gan

Tel Aviv

5

7

Jaffa

8

6

in Tel Aviv, where their ambivalent experience in the city involves balancing between their ethnonational identity and its ongoing erasure.

One day I met a group of students selling Arabic-language books from a folding table just outside the university campus. They hoped to remind their fellow students that Palestinian history and Arabic literature still existed, since all their teaching was in Hebrew and no conventional bookshop in the city stocked Arabic books. As the young generation of middle-class Palestinian *citizens* of Israel, they felt a sense of political responsibility, perhaps, especially, because they studied at an Israeli university. Who, if not these students, could define what it meant to be Palestinian in the foremost modern Jewish city? Selling Arabic books on campus was their way of expressing a sense of political identity and cultural heritage. But the path toward successful professional careers in Israel required that they adapt and modify how they were perceived publicly to evade the recurring stigmatization of their Palestinian identity.

At the time of Tel Aviv's early years as the First Hebrew City, the students' grandparents had grown up in a Palestine where Arabic was still the main language spoken. Even in 1947, Palestine was home to six hundred thousand Jews as compared with a majority of 1.3 million Palestinians.[2] Jerusalem, Haifa, Acre, and the port city of Jaffa were the major urban centers of Palestine in

---

Map legend. 1. Tel Aviv University: Some three thousand Palestinian citizens had studied at Tel Aviv University by 2018, making up around 14.5 percent of all its students. The campus was partly built on lands that were once home to the Palestinian village of al-Sheikh Muwannis. 2. 'Abd al Nabi cemetery: Jaffa's Muslim cholera victims lie buried in this old cemetery, which is hidden away behind shrubbery next to Tel Aviv's seaside Hilton Hotel. Historically a property of the Islamic waqf, it was illegally sold to an Israeli investment company and confiscated. 3. al-Mas'udiyya: A former Palestinian village, also referred to as Summayl. 4. al-Jammasin al-Gharbi: A former Palestinian village in the location of today's Bavli neighborhood. 5. Hassan Bek Mosque: The mosque was built in 1916 at the northern boundary of Palestinian Jaffa. It still operates today and serves Palestinians from Tel Aviv and Jaffa as a place of worship and a refuge. 6. Salame: A former Palestinian village near today's Ramat Gan area. A number of houses from the original village still remain today. 7. al-Manshiyye: A former Palestinian neighborhood of Jaffa at the southern boundary of today's Tel Aviv. 8. Clock tower: The old clock tower once marked Jaffa's commercial and cultural center. Today, it is perceived by many Jaffans as the symbolic boundary between a centerless Jaffa and Tel Aviv. Map design: School of Social and Political Science, University of Edinburgh.

Source: Zochrot.

an interconnected Arab region. After decades of intensive Jewish settlement, the Arab-Israeli War of 1948 eventually displaced some seven hundred and fifty thousand Palestinians from their homes. In addition to the destruction of hundreds of rural villages, Tel Aviv's ascent coincided with the destruction of Palestinian urbanism: 95 percent of Palestinians from Jaffa, Haifa, Acre, and other cities were forced to leave their hometowns, many of which were soon repopulated by Jewish immigrants.[3] Some mixed towns were officially turned into Israeli cities but still had Arab residents in them.

After the majority of the Palestinian urban population had been exiled, Tel Aviv encompassed the former port city of Jaffa as a gentrified suburb with a mixed Jewish-Arab population. Yet, the city does not recognize itself as mixed, despite the municipality's hyphenated official name being Tel Aviv-Yafo. We will see that the boundary between Jaffa and Tel Aviv signifies a mutual distancing between Jaffa's native Palestinian community and those Palestinian newcomers who are immersed in Jewish Tel Aviv. While Jaffa continues to be associated with an "Arab" community and a national Palestinian past, Tel Aviv, for most Jews, has come to symbolize the success of the modern Zionist project in opposition to Palestine and the Palestinians.

Focusing on those Palestinians who are immersed in Jewish Tel Aviv sets this book apart from previous work on Jewish-Arab relations in cities, which studied recognized mixed spaces such as Jaffa, Haifa, and Acre, alongside smaller Israeli development towns.[4] The story of Palestinian Tel Aviv also differs from that of other cities with colonial heritage in the Middle East. These so-called dual cities often featured parallel colonial and native neighborhoods, architecture, and infrastructures.[5] Settler-colonial Tel Aviv, in contrast, has not only enveloped but completely overwritten Palestinian history and identity with an essentially Jewish Israeli and self-consciously "liberal" city.

Tel Aviv's liberalism combines the nonrecognition of a Palestinian presence with a promise of urban freedoms, resulting in a contradictory space of *conditional* inclusion: Palestinians' ostensible access to the universal qualities of urban life is made conditional on their ongoing political and collective invisibility. This leads to what I call *immersive invisibility*: a set of practices that allow individuals to immerse themselves in an urban space and its economy despite being stigmatized as categorical outsiders. The Palestinians who do so must strike an "invisibility bargain," which prescribes that their presence in the city will be accepted only as long as they bring economic benefits and maintain political and social invisibility.[6] Such a regime of conditional inclusion precludes equal urban citizenship and, ultimately, undermines Palestinians' "right to the city" both as individuals and as a collective.[7]

For all that, Tel Aviv has become the unlikely destination for a growing number of Palestinian citizens of Israel who make a seemingly radical choice: to move from mixed and Arab towns elsewhere in Israel to live, work, and study in this Jewish metropolis. This choice often leads to a difficult balancing act between the pursuit of opportunities in the city and the visibility of their Palestinian identity, whose history the city denies. One of the students who distributed Arabic books on campus later told me about his search for an internship as a lawyer in Tel Aviv. To increase his chances, he intentionally scaled down his political activism, censored his Facebook profile, and avoided wearing the kaffiyeh—the iconic Palestinian scarf—in public. Others hid necklaces containing Arabic letters or concealed political symbols before entering their workplaces, where they were almost always the only, or one of very few, "Arab" employees. Many avoided talking in Arabic at Hebrew-speaking workplaces and on public transportation during their commutes, as trains or buses were often filled with armed Israeli soldiers in uniform.

This book examines this complex urban immersion of Palestinian citizens of Israel along with the comings and goings of Palestinian labor commuters from the occupied West Bank, who do not enjoy the privilege of citizenship in Israel and are confined to restrictive work permits that limit the extent to which they can participate in city life. Their urban invisibility is, therefore, less of a flexible choice than a forced condition of the underlying Israeli labor regime, which draws on an available pool of cheap workers from the territory it colonizes and occupies.[8] Although the larger part of the book focuses on Palestinian citizens of Israel, who make up some 21 percent of the country's population, the reasons for including labor commuters from the West Bank are rooted in their significant and long-standing presence in Tel Aviv's workplaces.

A NOTE ON SCOPE AND TERMINOLOGY

While clarifying the important differences between citizens and noncitizens wherever possible, I intentionally use, more generally, the terms *Palestinians in Tel Aviv* and *Palestinian Tel Aviv* to refer to the combined urban presence of citizens and noncitizens. This approach reflects the shared senses of identity and history among differently situated members of the Palestinian people, as an indigenous group that has been subject to a settler-colonial divide-and-rule politics. To mirror their frequent usage in Israel, the terms *"Arab"* and *"Arabs"* are mostly used in quotation marks while *Arab Israelis* or *Israeli Arabs* are rejected to avoid serving the implicit colonial logic of erasing indigenous solidarity and intentionally misrecognizing the affinity with and linkage to Palestine as a territory.[9]

Israel's intentional division of Palestinian Arabs has also targeted the different religious groups among Palestinian citizens of Israel, which include a majority of Muslims alongside sizable Christian and Druze minorities as well as a Bedouin Arab minority. These groups have all been subject to the political strategy of divide and conquer through which the Israeli state has aimed to co-opt collaborating elites and single out minorities as loyal and as "good Arabs" who are disconnected from the wider Palestinian community and nation.[10] Emphasizing the distinctiveness of these minorities over their similarities is, therefore, a sensitive issue. While Israel conceives of Christian and Druze citizens as distinct from Muslims, the Palestinian nation attempts to see them as Palestinians.[11] Although a detailed examination of these complex ethnic and religious dynamics is beyond the scope of this book, at times, I touch on these specifics when they become relevant.

TEL AVIV AS A SETTLER-COLONIAL BUBBLE

This book shows how a historical process of settler-colonial elimination and exclusion of indigenous people lives on within the false liberalism of a settler city. Traces of this exclusion are already evident in one of the city's nicknames, the Bubble. People have invoked this label to refer to a liberal city that is seemingly unaffected by recurring conflict, violence, and religious or political extremism. Along these lines, many Jewish residents and foreign visitors perceive it largely as a likable, innovative, and liberal Mediterranean metropolis. Implicitly, the Bubble suggests that Tel Aviv is far away from and largely untouched by Palestinians and Arabs. As Yonatan Mendel wrote, in his essay "Fantasising Israel" on the occasion of Tel Aviv's centennial, this seemingly "most 'liberal' and 'tolerant' city in Israel, as its residents like to imagine it, is not only 100 years old, but almost 100 per cent Arab-free."[12] This "fantasy" of an Arab-free modern Jewish metropolis is rooted in a colonial logic of erasure that continues to haunt the city's self-proclaimed liberalism.

Settler colonialism already played a crucial role in the nineteenth-century consolidation of liberal thought. Its colonial roots gave liberalism a built-in incapacity to respect the unfamiliar.[13] Indeed, liberal colonialism has involved a tense encounter between abstract universal ideas, such as equality and citizenship, and the concrete lifeworlds of indigenous Others. What is true for the settler colonies in America and Australia, which formed part of the British Empire, also applies to Zionist settler colonialism in Palestine: the colonists were considered already civilized, and they constructed a racialized difference to the local peoples they encountered and later dispossessed, creating a power-ful "mix of intraracial egalitarianism and interracial exclusion."[14] This becomes evident in the exclusive Jewish Israeli character of Tel Aviv's liberalism, which distinguishes itself from Palestine and everything Palestinian, making the city's liberal characteristics and its economy accessible to Palestinian citizens only under certain conditions of invisibility.

Jewish settler colonialism in Palestine nonetheless differs from conventional exploitation colonies, where expatriate colonial elites governed large subject populations for a European state or empire. Although aided by the politics of the late British empire, the Zionists had no straightforward mother state. They framed Jewish settlement as the homecoming of a diaspora and in reaction to centuries of antisemitism and persecution. The founders and early residents of Tel Aviv were mostly Eastern European immigrants and refugees who arrived with vastly disparate possessions.[15] Even so, these Jewish settlers came "to stay." They were primarily concerned with the construction of a new society in Pal-estine, which required the expropriation of land and the structural elimination of native sovereignty as part of ongoing colonization.[16]

Although necessarily incomplete, this process of elimination can involve a variety of strategies, such as coercive assimilation, strategic exclusion, and forms of integrative pacification.[17] This latter dimension of *integrative pacifica-tion* seeks to erase indigenous political solidarity and identity through co-opting and including natives as subordinates, not simply excluding them. Turning those remaining Palestinians who could not be expelled after Israel's creation in 1948 into "Arab" minority citizens was one way in which Israel attempted to do that. The invisible inclusion of Palestinians in Tel Aviv is yet another.

The Palestinian experience of Tel Aviv allows us to understand how the historical objective of colonial domination and elimination is realized through the ongoing processes of urban incorporation and enforced invisibility today. In this sense, settler colonialism does not necessarily derive its reproductive force from repressions or violence but from "its ability to produce forms of life that make settler-colonialism's constitutive hierarchies seem natural."[18] This includes the incorporation of indigenous people into an urban space that naturalized such a hierarchy, which becomes evident in the daily lives of Pal-estinians and Palestinian citizens in Tel Aviv.

PRESENT-ABSENT: PALESTINIANS AS EXILES IN TEL AVIV

A brief glance into history helps us understand how the contemporary pres-sures on Palestinians to manage their visibility in Tel Aviv are rooted in the long-standing colonial restructuring of this space. When Jewish families gathered there, in 1909, to lay the cornerstones of the first modern Hebrew city, this urban project evolved in strong opposition to Palestine. It also intensified Jewish colonization and instantiated the Jews as a people belonging to the modern urban space.[19] Tel Aviv's emergence and spread were bound up with Israel's wider history of violence and colonial expropriation. When Israel was established in 1948, it could absorb the remaining Palestinian Arabs without fear of losing an overall Jewish majority, thanks to the coerced flight and expulsion of hundreds of thousands of Palestinians who lived in the territory the Zionist forces captured.[20]

The state then extended to those indigenous Palestinians who remained within its newly imposed boundaries a discrete set of limited rights and duties, which only the dominant Jewish settler community could determine, and it placed them under military rule and surveillance for two decades.[21] Palestinian citizenship in Israel remains a means of colonial domination and subjugation in a state defined as Jewish. Indeed, as the Israeli prime minister Benjamin Netanyahu stated in 2019: "Israel is not a state of all its citizens. According to the basic nationality law we passed, Israel is the nation-state of the Jewish people—and only it."[22]

Today's Palestinians in Israel, about 21 percent of its population, are for the most part the descendants of those 150,000–160,000 Palestinian Arabs who had remained in or managed to return to Israel between 1948 and 1950.[23] They became citizens of the very state that forced them, by use of compulsory displacement, expulsion, and prevention of return, into exile from their homeland.[24] As families lost their original villages, they soon became referred to as present absentees in new towns. They were sometimes forced to live only a few miles away from their confiscated lands. Although within the boundaries of the newly founded state of Israel, they were considered absent in legal terms because their property had been transferred to state ownership so Jewish immigrants could move into abandoned homes.[25] They were unable to return home although they were still there.[26] Many other displaced Palestinians became "proximate exiles" in neighboring Arab states or in the West Bank, East Jerusalem, and the Gaza Strip.[27]

The term *present absentee* not only stands for this expropriation but also expresses a wider contradiction that stands metaphorically for the predicament of the Palestinians who remained in Israel and, even more so, for the Palestinians in Tel Aviv: they are present yet invisible, unrecognized as people who are indigenous to the land this city was built on. Theirs is a form of political invisibility in plain sight. Urban marginalization and invisibility form part of what it means to be a nation when one's territory has been taken, to live in continuous "exile at home."[28] The tragedy behind their unrecognized presence in the city is reflected in the need for a kind of "chosen" exile or absence.[29] This includes situational choices to remain invisible in certain ways, concealing aspects of one's identity in response to the discrimination and racism encountered. Such chosen invisibility is fueled by the aspiration to leave one's stigma behind, if only in certain situations, in order to pass as an unmarked person and access the socioeconomic opportunities and liberal qualities of the city. The problem is that this aspiration often remains unfulfilled.

Tel Aviv does not live up to its promise of being a liberal safe haven of urban coexistence away from the tribulations of conflict and religious or political extremism, as is implicitly suggested by the nickname the Bubble. The Palestinian experience challenges the idea that this modern liberal city has a capacity to transcend differences or conflicts between ethnonational minorities and majorities.[30] On a fundamental level, this questions the feasibility of pragmatic coexistence in a city like Tel Aviv, all the while colonization of Palestinian lands and a violent conflict are ongoing.

Yet, despite this, Tel Aviv continues to attract a diversity of Palestinian citizens and Palestinian labor commuters from the West Bank, who are largely dispersed and disconnected individuals without much communal infrastructure or a recognizable collective presence in this city. This is very different from the mixed Arab-Jewish town of Jaffa, the former Palestinian port city that now serves as Tel Aviv's gentrified and Orientalized southern suburb. Jaffa features the "contrived coexistence" between clearly delineated communities, characterized by Jewish spaces within Arab spaces and Palestinian spaces within Israeli ones.[31] The Palestinians in Jaffa have a recognized and identifiable "community." Within modern Tel Aviv, however, the Palestinians' journeys have carved countless isolated and fragmented trajectories onto a hidden and submerged layer of this urban space. As these journeys are often impermanent, dispersed, and noncollective, they make it very easy for a Palestinian presence within Tel Aviv not to be recognized.

The chronic nonrecognition of Palestinian Tel Aviv as a social reality builds on an enduring structure of settler-colonial "replacement" that permanently reshapes the relation between indigenous people and urban space.[32] Since Jewish Tel Aviv has historically attempted to replace and erase everything Palestinian within it, merely recognizing the Palestinians' existence as a significant urban minority today would upset the city's very identity. In the words of the city's long-term mayor Ron Khuldai, "Tel Aviv is not a mixed city. Indeed, we have a small Arab minority of 4 percent but it would be problematic to consider it as a mixed city."[33] Most Palestinians in Tel Aviv do not even appear in these official

4 percent because the city counts only Israeli citizens, among them only those who are registered residents, and, consequently, does not enumerate commuters, students, and many others living outside of Jaffa.[34] In a similar vein, labor force surveys of Arab citizens show the locations only of official residences, not of work locations.[35] This lack of definite numbers only deepens their betweenness as present absentees who are physically there, even while not being counted. They are present absentees.

THE INVISIBLE PALESTINIANS

The city's built-in opposition to recognizing a Palestinian presence is one of the everyday problems for Palestinian citizens of Israel who come to Tel Aviv in search of work, education, and urban life. These citizens are both middle class and working class, lawyers and software engineers, bus drivers and construction workers, artists, activists, and students; some are commuters, and others are long-term residents. They are men and women, married and unmarried, frequently between their early twenties and early forties, but they also include older generations of employees. In one way or another, they all use tactics of invisibility to control how they are perceived both by Jewish Israeli employers, colleagues, neighbors, landlords, and security guards and by other Palestinians who might deem their immersion into Tel Aviv controversial.

The exclusive liberalism of Tel Aviv combines with a reluctance among Palestinians to immerse themselves too deeply in the city. Their dilemma is similar to that of indigenous people in other settler-colonial cities, who are either stigmatized as outsiders by members of the settler majority or delegitimized for losing their identity by those who criticize them for integrating. They are not only structurally invisible to the settler state but also marginalized by their own communities as a result of the prevailing discourses about cultural and political authenticity.[36] Indeed, activists sometimes refer to Palestinians in Tel Aviv as *Aravivim*—a term that combines the Hebrew words *Aravim* (Arabs) and *Tel Avivim* (Tel Avivians). The fact that it is used in Hebrew, rather than Arabic, hints at the accusation that immersion in Tel Aviv brings with it a perceived loss of authentic Palestinian identity and political integrity. Their immersion in Tel Aviv was criticized as early as 1929, when political activists compared Palestinians who took part in the city's international fair to those Arabs who visited Tel Aviv's nightclubs for pursuing "foul objectives."[37]

Categorically unable to belong in Tel Aviv *as Palestinians*, and sometimes hoping to live in a politically more familiar environment, perhaps owning a house with land, many Palestinian citizens leave Tel Aviv at some point during their urban journey: back to their hometowns, to a mixed Jewish-Arab city such as Haifa, or even to Ramallah in the occupied West Bank where they live among Palestinians without Israeli citizenship. As Muhammad Jabali, a well-known cultural activist and former Tel Aviv resident put it in a conversation with me: "For Palestinians, the role of urban space in Tel Aviv is not to be seen. We came to Tel Aviv to be anonymous, as a collective. People don't think about conquering Tel Aviv back . . . Palestinians in Tel Aviv don't want to be marked . . . but most reach a breaking point after two years, two years is enough to realize that they can't blend in here."

We see throughout the book that this "breaking point" comes in different forms and shades, prompting some to leave and yet others to stay on despite a lack of recognition and belonging. One part of their tragedy is that even their intentional nonbelonging, such as the hope of wandering the city as an anonymous and unmarked urbanite, is often inaccessible to them.

This contrasts the common assumption that modern urban life creates a positive sense of invisibility and *anonymity*. The Palestinian citizens do not experience urban anonymity the same way many Jewish Israeli urbanites do. For the Palestinians, urban anonymity is chronically unstable and insecure. Failure to comply with racial profiling and requests for identification can have dangerous consequences, as the Arab supermarket worker Abu Alqian experienced in Tel Aviv in 2016 when he was viciously beaten by off-duty police officers, ostensibly for "failing to identify himself." He worked at both the supermarket and a Burger King in the city to pay for his education. One of the violent police officers reportedly called him "a dirty Arab."[38] "To be Arab in Tel Aviv is not easy," wrote one Arab journalist and activist in response, capturing the daily struggle of being an "Arab" in Tel Aviv:[39] "The difficulty of renting an apartment, the fear of speaking Arabic publicly in case they'll think I'm a terrorist roaming freely around Tel Aviv and, at the same time, concern that the next knife assailant will stab you because you look Israeli; the fear of not making it past the bouncers at the entrance to a nightclub; the sinking feeling in the pit of your stomach just before entering Ben Gurion International Airport, on the way to an invasive security check prior to the vacation of your dreams."

Palestinian citizens who hope to enjoy a sense of anonymity in this Jewish city often realize that it remains conditional on the partial invisibility of their identity. At the same time, they must be ready to identify themselves if called upon. The consequence is that Palestinian citizens cannot easily belong to this city and call it home without suppressing a part of who they are. Even if they do blend in and qualify as "good Arabs," they will always remain potentially "bad."[40] The many barriers to full inclusion mean that most of them experience

Tel Aviv like a *journey* on the way to a pragmatic goal or simply for the journey's sake: making money, building a career, obtaining a university degree, or exploring urban life. To them, Tel Aviv is a city that is *used* rather than a real home, because the prospect of equal urban citizenship remains foreclosed.

TACTICS OF IMMERSIVE INVISIBILITY

Although thousands of Palestinian workers fill Tel Aviv's construction sites and restaurants, the city is also home to a growing number of middle- and upper-class professionals who pursue ambitious careers. The marketing professional Farah,[41] a long-standing Palestinian resident of Tel Aviv, told me that she often preferred *not* to meet "other Arabs." Many were the only Palestinian employees in their companies or the only Arab residents in their buildings. She added, "Here in Tel Aviv, we Arabs don't know each other. . . . We are anonymous together."

In the context of Palestinian Tel Aviv, retaining anonymity in this way also becomes a question of safety, especially for unmarried Palestinian women and members of the LGBT community. To them, "enjoying" Tel Aviv requires caution, because meeting the wrong person at the wrong time can lead to unwanted gossip and even threats. Accessing "liberal" Tel Aviv comes at a cost for the young generation of Palestinian citizens of Israel who explore urban nightlife and live out their gender identity in ways that are not always possible in their hometowns. They struggle for individual agency and control while managing the visibility of several aspects of identity and practice, which serves two major purposes: to reconcile their political identity with immersion into a city that fends off this identity, and to reconcile such urban immersion—sometimes deemed illegitimate—with cultural norms and senses of political solidarity among Palestinians who may oppose it. This dual need for controlling visibility goes back to the underlying double bind of their contradictory immersion in the city. Living in a condition of dual exile, they are unrecognized twice over, as Palestinians within Tel Aviv and as Tel Avivians among Palestinians. As if on a tightrope between two unstable worlds, they are both unable to reconcile the worlds into a stable balance and prevented from ever fully arriving at the other end.

Tactics of invisibility and concealment become useful tools for this walk on a tightrope. Such situational concealment, in a variety of settings, has long been part of social relationships. Stigmatized minorities who want to access jobs, education, and urban life often leave specific aspects of their identity "backstage."[42] They use forms of "social camouflage" to blend into a potentially hostile environment.[43] But not everyone is able to control his or her visibility in such empowering ways, as the example above of the beaten Arab supermarket employee made clear. While cities often force the urban poor into the invisibility of informal spaces,[44] minorities of gender, culture, and religion cannot always control what kind of visibility they command in public.[45] Invisibility thus has different qualities for different people. Its effects can be "self-voicing" or a process of "being silenced."[46]

In addition to gender, the central factor that determines these qualities among Palestinians in Tel Aviv is citizenship or legal status. Unlike Palestinian *citizens* of Israel, Palestinians from the occupied West Bank can only access this city on restrictive work permits. Israeli authorities often deny them on "security" grounds in a permit regime of "bureaucratic occupation."[47] This selective regime forces tens of thousands to enter Israel illegally and hide underground. For educated middle- and upper-class *citizens* who have the right background to be successful in Tel Aviv and blend into workplaces and urban life, immersive invisibility can be like a shielding dive under water. The problem is that they must keep on diving if invisibility remains a precondition for their urban access and economic success.

The Palestinians' ambivalent experience with urban inclusion is in contrast to modern liberal cities that have a capacity to resolve differences and allow for the enhanced inclusion of diverse groups.[48] Although the city of Tel Aviv offers jobs and opportunities, its self-proclaimed "liberal" lifestyle demands a kind of apolitical civility from Palestinians. As a social lubricant that flattens differences in modern cities,[49] civility encourages individual self-restraint and mutual respect over possible disagreements.[50] This can involve, for instance, a silent agreement between colleagues at work not to talk about politics or the expectation that individuals will restrain their opinions and refrain from expressing aspects of their identity that are controversial. Civility thus acquires a very political dimension in this context of ethnonational conflict and settler colonialism. Although modern cities often flatten differences between individuals as anonymous urban strangers, this difference-eroding aspect of civility does not transcend the differences between friends and enemies, or between the colonizers and the colonized. This is particularly so during times of heightened political tensions and recurring polarizations, which regularly infect otherwise civil relations in Tel Aviv with antagonism and alterity.

Palestinian citizens are, thus, unable to be recognized as both civil *and* visibly Palestinian simultaneously because Tel Aviv makes the recognition of one dependent on the absence of the other. From the viewpoint of Tel Aviv's regime of urban inclusion, to be Palestinian and political is to be "uncivil."

Middle-class professionals may be able to immerse themselves in the city and live a successful professional life there, but the anonymity and privacy of some spaces is accessible to them only as long as they do not violate the parameters of "respect" imposed by dominant Israeli expectations. As visible *Palestinians*, they cannot enjoy the city's "impersonal" qualities in the same way Jewish Israelis can. To borrow from Richard Sennett's words, they are always the type of stranger who is "synonymous with the outsider."[51] This further invalidates the idea that individuality protects and shields urbanites from the destructive forces of modern cities.[52] In the settler-colonial city of Tel Aviv, urban individualism does not work too well for the Palestinians: their individualism is always racialized and subject to scrutiny.

USING THE CITY: A HIDDEN STRUGGLE FOR URBAN ACCESS

The Palestinian citizens' tendency to use the city in pragmatic ways is driven by an implicit liberal promise that economic self-sufficiency and success may lead to civic entitlements and a form of "economic citizenship."[53] The dilemma is that such economic citizenship imposes political and cultural invisibility on Palestinians in Tel Aviv: the conditions for accessing the economic dimension of the city foreclose the prospect of urban citizenship, for which greater freedom to express one's identity and difference is required.[54] In light of this estrangement, the class positions of individual Palestinians are experienced differently in Tel Aviv than in Arab towns and larger mixed cities with a strong Palestinian community, such as Haifa.

Within the constraints of this restricted urban inclusion, the tactics of invisibility that people adopt can become a resource for accessing "the 'neoliberal city' under the illiberal state."[55] These tactics include a large variety of practices, some of them obvious, such as the decision not to wear the Palestinian kaffiyeh or jewelry with Arabic letters on it. In one way or another, they must rid themselves of their obvious stigma, their Palestinian identity, as the psychologist Ilham told me at Tel Aviv University. She referred to the routine of hiding her necklace of Arabic lettering during therapy practice with Jewish patients and added: "I didn't want to bring *it* up; it gets really complicated and difficult."

These tactics of immersive invisibility form alternative pathways into a city. They are quiet articulations of urban citizenship that are very different from collective actions and strategic expressions of minority difference that aim to "transform the city."[56] What is often cited as a "politics of recognition" is, in this context, no longer how best to understand such power struggles between indigenous peoples and settler-colonial majorities.[57] Rather, these struggles take place in the subtle, often pragmatic, and largely hidden challenges of daily life. Although overt political activism is widespread among university students and activists in Jaffa, most Palestinian citizens of Israel follow their pursuits in Tel Aviv as an unseen urban minority. Indeed, people with "wrong" group membership must sometimes seek invisibility to participate quietly in cities and move around freely, instead of building a visible "case of identity."[58] The powerless cannot always produce a visible presence to claim rights to the city.[59] Tactics of immersive invisibility work well for those who merely *use a city* but not for those who seek a home in it. The Palestinians do not reclaim Tel Aviv with grand collective strategies; they make use of it from within.

This approach of using a city reflects one of citizenship's emerging uncertain forms.[60] Palestinian citizens of Israel have long pushed into Jewish Israeli cities where housing, education, public services, and jobs are better than in the often underfunded Arab municipalities.[61] The question of how they use Israeli urban space has received far less attention than the various "struggles for visibility" Palestinians have mounted at home and in exile.[62] Unlike urban "mobilisation and rallies" that can change and define the meanings of modern citizenship,[63] I argue that individual struggles for urban access and inclusion constitute a hidden and overlooked battleground of urban citizenship. The insights I provide throughout this book offer a new take on key questions about how marginalized minorities can manage their conditional access to urban spaces despite stigmatization and an underlying ethnonational conflict with settler-colonial history.

Palestinians and Palestinian citizens have long been engaged in overt and visible resistance practices against Israeli policies of colonization, occupation, and discrimination, with a rich history of nonviolent civil action.[64] This includes the politics and activism of Palestinian citizens who have struggled for space as they negotiate and disrupt the settler-colonial order they live in, which seeks to contain and discipline indigenous spaces and unruly populations while "re-articulating the spaces these 'others' inhabit, as empty or dangerous, marginal or illegitimate in order to efface or displace them."[65] The forms of resistance Sharri Plonski has unpacked represent a whole range of methods that the Palestinians have devised for challenging the limits of Zionist space. Rather than seeking to contrast or invalidate the significance of popular resistance, I argue that the Palestinians' invisible struggles for inclusion and access in Tel Aviv provide an important complementary perspective on how indigenous peoples use and navigate settler-colonial spaces. The Palestinian trajectory of quietly using Tel Aviv represents an overlooked struggle for access to urban space amid ongoing settler-colonial attempts at indigenous erasure. This struggle may involve accommodating practices and invisible compromises, but these concessions are no less difficult than overt resistance.

METHODOLOGY AND RESEARCH BACKGROUND

The fieldwork I conducted for this book was set in a particular time period of only moderate escalations in the Israeli-Palestinian conflict, interrupted by the significant disruption of the events leading to the 2014 Gaza conflict. The main part of the research included more than two years of continuous ethnography in Tel Aviv between 2012 and 2014, with a two-month follow-up visit in 2017. My positionality in this field was mostly that of a "familiar" outsider—an Austrian anthropologist who spoke Arabic and some Hebrew and had lived in the region for a few years. The main languages I used in conversations and interviews were Arabic and English, while intermediate knowledge of Hebrew helped me grasp everyday situations and understand group conversations in a mix of languages. In the two years before the research for this book began, and to a certain degree throughout its duration, I also worked as a freelance journalist and later as a foreign correspondent for newspapers in Austria and Switzerland. This dual role required a certain amount of moving in and out of different professional identities. Some weeks I spent most days reporting news or researching background stories for features in the papers' weekend editions. Other weeks I dedicated most of my time and energy to the Palestinians in Tel Aviv. This ethnographic research, over time, naturally involved emerging friendships and close relationships with people. It greatly benefited my critical perspective on Tel Aviv that I learned to understand it through the eyes and experiences of Palestinian friends and research participants, while also living and working in the city for more than two years. To protect the anonymity of my interlocutors, I use pseudonyms throughout the book except in cases where people's status as an official or public person requires the use of the real name.

In part because my friendships and closer contacts emerged mostly with people in their twenties or thirties, many of the Palestinians I introduce throughout this book are relatively young. This generational bias of the population I encountered in the city has another more relevant reason: Tel Aviv was a city many Palestinian citizens of Israel explored and used early on in their lives, as students, young professionals, or workers in construction and hospitality who hoped to save up money. They usually did so before settling down and having a family, which most likely happened elsewhere in the country. Only a few Palestinians I knew decided to make Tel Aviv their permanent home.

On the other hand, those who commuted between Tel Aviv and their hometowns for the purpose of work comprised a wider range of ages. This included Palestinian labor commuters from the West Bank and Palestinian citizens who worked in semiskilled jobs in the fields of construction, hospitality, or transportation.

Most Palestinians I met at the time of the research and in the subsequent years were politically disillusioned about decades of failed peace processes and the deepening of Israel's violent differential rule, labeled by some as a permanent "one-state condition."[66] Meanwhile, this disillusionment with promises of unfulfilled civic equality among Palestinians within Israel went hand in hand with a growing emphasis on the deeper struggles for historical justice among some sections of political activists.[67] But the state's flawed democratic system had no appetite for any such depth and repeatedly sidelined the collective interests of Palestinian citizens. The Joint List Alliance, which predominantly represented Palestinian citizens, mobilized Arab voters to turn out in unusually high numbers in the spring 2020 elections and claimed fifteen seats in the Knesset. But, after initial coalition talks, the Palestinians were once again excluded from decision-making and politics when the two main rivals representing the Jewish voters announced a "national unity government" in April. Jewish Israeli lawmakers had publicly opposed any government reliance on the Arab minority, as they "cannot trust important political decisions to people whose sympathies may be with the other side."[68] This chronic mistrust, among the political elites, of the Jewish majority may have further deepened the resigned mood among Palestinian citizens of Israel, many of whom prioritized pragmatic thinking and socioeconomic survival. The decision to make use of Tel Aviv despite unfulfilled equality and systematic discrimination forms part of this trajectory.

As a multisited urban ethnography, this anthropological research involved an ongoing process of mapping Palestinian Tel Aviv that accompanied the data collection through interviews, observations, and participation in daily life. Largely invisible as an urban collective, and little discussed in public and academic discourse, the Palestinians in Tel Aviv had first to be found and their main constituents and problems had to be identified. This was three to four years before the release of Maysaloun Hamoud's influential film *Bar Bahar* (*In Between*) in 2016, which portrayed, for the first time, the complicated and largely unrecognized lives of Palestinian women living in Tel Aviv. Until then, the phenomenon of a Palestinian Tel Aviv was mostly not talked about in the Israeli and Palestinian public.

Among educated Palestinian citizens of Israel who lived in Tel Aviv, the city's main university provided a clear entry point for my research. At other times, bicycle rides through neighborhoods and visits to cafés, shops, and restaurants led to acquaintances with gardeners, cleaners, waiters, and chefs; likewise, taking bus rides and hanging around construction sites led to acquaintances with bus drivers and construction workers. This first pillar of the selection process of research participants had a spatial dimension, in the sense that I identified particular places and areas of Tel Aviv where Palestinians could be found. Alongside these regular urban explorations, another pillar of the selection process was "problem-centered" and followed a number of key themes of Palestinian Tel Aviv that emerged over time: university life, work and professional life, leisure and nightlife, commuting practices, art and political activism, and gender and the LGBT community. Other subfields emerged with the occurrence of Israeli national holidays and contentious memorial days and, toward the end of fieldwork, with the outbreak of the 2014 Gaza conflict and its repercussions in Tel Aviv. In the sense of these explorations, the research had specific people in a very particular urban space as its focus at a particular historical period.

At the same time, the depth and breadth of the ethnography allows for a wide-ranging contribution to the understanding of invisibility and conditional inclusion in settler-colonial cities. This discussion joins an ongoing debate about the interaction of the colonial and the neoliberal city in the Middle East and around the world.[69] Moreover, each chapter follows a logical sequence that tells its own overarching story: from initial arrival in the city into the sphere of pragmatic work, education, and leisure; from there into the contentious dynamics of art and political activism; and, ultimately, into the experience of conflict and polarization that unmasks the ostensibly liberal bubble of Tel Aviv and reveals the circular recurrence of antagonism and alterity.

OVERVIEW OF CHAPTERS

At the beginning of the book's sequence of urban inclusion, chapter 1 explores Palestinian mobility into Tel Aviv. Conceptualized as a journey, their often circular and impermanent trajectories highlight the role of unequal geography and mobility in the production of an invisible urban minority with a fluctuating presence. These journeys are explored through different layers of mobility and urban arrival: commuting practices, the search for work, and the circular movements of Palestinians from the West Bank. The journeys of Palestinian citizens of Israel are thus juxtaposed with the commute of a Palestinian software engineer who lives in the West Bank city of Nablus but works in Tel Aviv. This dual perspective of citizens and noncitizens shows how Israel's political economy distributes mobility differentially, effectively constructing a complex net of limited pathways into the city that coproduce the Palestinians' invisibility, disconnection, and dispersion in this urban space.

Chapters 2 and 3 expand the idea of the journey to explore how Palestinians make use of urban opportunities in higher education and professional life, often with the help of tactical invisibility. Although this increases their access to the city and its economy, the requirements of invisible immersion simultaneously preclude the realization of equal urban citizenship. The built-in conditions and glass ceilings that define such limited immersion are discussed in two interlinked fields: higher education and work life. Chapter 2 looks at Palestinian students' diverse pathways through university toward graduation and into first job applications. The university plays a key role in the process of conditional inclusion, as students learn to mediate the visibility of their political activism under pressure to become recognized as "good Arabs," who are hardworking, politically docile, and exceptionally smart. At the same time, female students' immersion in the city's social and leisure spaces often results in complicated double lives as they balance between their families' expectations and their individual urban explorations.

Chapter 3 enters the world of the highly successful Palestinian middle and upper class in Tel Aviv, who enjoy the city's anonymity but also suffer from a sense of "loneliness" as Palestinians. This largely middle-class world coexists with another dimension of the city: the Palestinian working class that toils in the city's restaurants and construction sites, who experience invisibility not necessarily by choice but due to structural constraint. Although Palestinian class formation in Tel Aviv takes divergent paths, the settler-colonial dimension of this ostensibly "liberal" economy effectively racializes citizenship and class mobility on multiple levels. Alongside the categorical invisibility of the working class, it also fosters a disconnected sense of anonymity among the middle and upper classes as part of their conditional access to careers in the city.

Cities are not only a space of professional careers and labor; they also tend to offer spaces of leisure and fun that are closely tied to patterns of consumption and work life. Tel Aviv is certainly no exception with innumerable cafés and public beaches, parks, and a vibrant nightlife. Chapter 4 explores the controversial activities of fun and leisure among Palestinians in Tel Aviv and neighboring Jaffa. Some even carve out underground spaces for Palestinian fun and conviviality, such as regular LGBT parties. For all its fun, the sphere of leisure and urban life involves a highly politicized and tense experience for Palestinians in this city, not least because they must carefully calibrate their visibility in relation to both Jewish Israelis and other Palestinians who might deem playing in Tel Aviv illegitimate. Although rarely discussed as such, the freedom to have fun and enjoy leisure visibly and collectively emerges as a key component of urban inclusion and citizenship from their ambivalent experience.

Chapter 5 takes a step back from Palestinians' pragmatic use of the city and their ordinary life in it. We get to know three Palestinian artists: the contemporary artist Anisa Ashkar, the writer Raji Bathish, and the actor and musician Mira Awad. Having lived and worked in Tel Aviv, these three artists creatively engaged the contradictions of their urban immersion in their public artwork. Although Palestinian art becomes a critical tool for making marginalized perspectives and aspects of the Palestinian experience in Tel Aviv visible, Israeli liberalism nevertheless seeks to appropriate these artists and their artwork and utilizes their symbolic value for political purposes. As they juggle various senses of identity in their ambivalent urban lives, they experience an unresolved tension between aspects of Palestinian identity and culture, on the one hand, and the cultural and political character of the settler city, on the other.

Chapter 6 then explores the political dimensions of Palestinian life in Tel Aviv and Jaffa, which includes occasional protests and other public events, along with guided tours about the hidden history of Palestinian displacement and destruction in the city. These public political practices disrupt the normalized invisibility of Palestinian Tel Aviv and often trigger fierce reactions and opposition from the public. As these protests are often concerned with national issues, while the historical tours focus on a collective Palestinian past, they do not see the realities of Palestinians in Tel Aviv through this prism of national politics and history. Maybe, ironically, some Palestinian activism, therefore, coproduces the invisibility and ostensible illegitimacy of Palestinians within Tel Aviv. This becomes particularly clear in the political activism of Jaffa, which connects the local communal struggle to indigenous history and Palestinian nationalism all the while constructing a rigid boundary vis-à-vis Tel Aviv. The Palestinians within Jewish Israeli Tel Aviv are not considered to be part of Palestinian political space or national history. As dual exiles, they are unrecognized by other Palestinians and by the city.

One of the reasons why Palestinians in Tel Aviv are unrecognized twice over is their pragmatic urban immersion that deliberately avoids politics and the visibility of their ethnonational identity. Chapter 7 offers an ethnographic critique of the idea that such pragmatic urban immersion is feasible and represents a sustainable form of civil coexistence. I show how the bubble of liberal Tel Aviv frequently bursts under the impact of recurring violent and nationalist events. Among these events were the violent and polarized summer of 2014, including the Gaza conflict, as well as Israeli nationalist rituals, such as Remembrance Day and Independence Day. Experiencing the tribulations of living as a Palestinian in Tel Aviv during these tense and dangerous times helps us see how antagonism and alterity dissolve the unwritten agreement of depoliticized urban relations between Palestinians and Jewish Israelis in the city. This last chapter should be read as an important critical commentary on the flawed idea that the Palestinians' immersive invisibility in Tel Aviv offers a sustainable positive experience that benefits all: as relations between classmates and colleagues turn into relations between friends and enemies, between "us" and "them," the recurrence of antagonism and conflict unmasks the liberal bubble of Tel Aviv and shows its exclusive settler-colonial face.

The conclusion begins by situating the invisibility of Palestinian Tel Aviv in the framework of settler colonialism as an ongoing structure of elimination and indigenous erasure. Although each chapter in this book offers its own unique conceptual insight, together they provide the assemblage of experiences and analysis that underpins my argument: that the colonial elimination of indigenous identity and sovereignty lives on through the conditional urban inclusion of Palestinians in a "liberal" settler city. The conclusion then provides a succinct summary of the main findings that proceeds chronologically through the seven chapters, which shows that the complexity and diversity of the Palestinian experience with Tel Aviv ultimately goes deeper and wider than the overall argument of the book. As the first comprehensive ethnography of Palestinian Tel Aviv, this book can be seen as a piece of contemporary history and as an indication of current and future trends. The final part of the conclusion situates the Palestinians' journeys in this city against the backdrop of the wider context of Israel/Palestine, asking: What does Tel Aviv tell us about the Palestinians, and what do the Palestinians tell us about Tel Aviv?

NOTES

1. Where "Palestinian citizens" is used in this book, it refers to Palestinian citizens of Israel.

2. Pappé, *Forgotten Palestinians*, 17.

3. Monterescu, *Jaffa*, 2.

4. Monterescu, *Jaffa*; Rabinowitz and Monterescu, "Reconfiguring the 'Mixed Town'"; Rabinowitz, *Overlooking Nazareth*; Blatman-Thomas, "Commuting for Rights"; Torstrick, *Limits of Coexistence*.

5. J. Abu-Lughod, "Tale of Two Cities."

6. Pugh, "Negotiating Identity and Belonging."

7. Harvey, "Right to the City"; Lefebvre, *Urban Revolution*.

8. Berda, *Living Emergency*; Farsakh, *Palestinian Labour Migration to Israel*.

9. Rabinowitz and Abu-Baker, *Coffins on Our Shoulders*, 43–44.

10. Firro, "Reshaping Druze Particularism in Israel."

11. Sa'ar, "Carefully on the Margins."

12. Mendel, "Fantasising Israel."

13. Bell, "Dream Machine"; Mehta, *Liberalism and Empire*.

14. Bell, "Dream Machine," 39.

15. Mann, *Place in History*, xii.

16. Wolfe, "Settler Colonialism and Elimination of the Native," 388.

17. Hugill, "What Is a Settler-Colonial City?"

18. Coulthard, *Red Skin, White Masks*, 152.

19. Mann, *Place in History*, xii–xiii; Levine, *Overthrowing Geography*.

20. Robinson, *Citizen Strangers*, 70; Peteet, "Problematizing a Palestinian Diaspora," 627.

21. Robinson, *Citizen Strangers*, 3.

22. Tatour, "Citzenship as Domination," 9.

23. Pappé, *Forgotten Palestinians*, 11; Robinson, *Citizen Strangers*, 1.

24. Morris, *Birth of the Palestinian Refugee Problem*, 589.

25. Although often present, in terms of their legal ownership, "present absentees" were henceforth considered absent by the Custodian for Absentees' Property. This Absentees' Property Law was the main legal instrument Israel used to take possession of the lands and properties belonging to the internally displaced and to Palestinian refugees.

26. Kimmerling, "Zionism and Territory."

27. Peteet, "Unsettling the Categories of Displacement."

28. Hackl, "Key Figure of Mobility."

29. Hobbs, *Chosen Exile*.

30. Sassen, "Global City"; Sassen, "Urban Capabilities."

31. Monterescu, *Jaffa*, 6.

32. Edmonds, "Settler Colonialism's Urban Strategies," 4; Veracini, *Settler Colonialism*.

33. Monterescu, *Jaffa*, 126.

34. According to an email from the Tel Aviv municipality's Center for Economic and Social Research in 2014, Israel's Central Bureau of Statistics (CBS) counted only 18,500 "Arabs" in the greater Tel Aviv area but about 15,000 of these were registered residents of Arab neighborhoods in Jaffa. Although there are numbers for Arab students at Tel Aviv University, these are often not registered residents.

35. The Labor Force Survey of CBS in 2018 registered an Arab labor force of only 6,800 who were officially residents of the Tel Aviv District and 56,000 who were residents in the wider Central District (CBS website, accessed 5 September 2020, https://www.cbs.gov.il/he/publications/doclib/2020/lfs18_1782/t08_01 .pdf). Upon request for data showing the number of Palestinian citizens whose location of work was in Tel Aviv, the CBS stated no such data were available.

36. Gagné and Trépied, "Colonialism, Law, and the City."

37. Azaryahu, *Tel Aviv*, 47.

38. Zikri and Kubovich, "Arab Worker Freed to House Arrest."
39. Dacca, "What It's Really Like."
40. Kanaaneh, *Surrounded.*
41. All names are pseudonyms to ensure the anonymity of research participants, except in selected cases where the full names are stated, for example, in the case of public figures, officials, and well-known activists.
42. Goffman, *Presentation of Self in Everyday Life.*
43. Brighenti and Castelli, "Social Camouflage."
44. Wacquant, *Urban Outcasts,* 240.
45. Bayat, *Life as Politics,* 17; Ghorashi, "From Absolute Invisibility to Extreme Visibility."
46. Sözer, *Managing Invisibility,* 10.
47. Berda, *Living Emergency,* 12.
48. Sassen, "Urban Capabilities," 85–87.
49. Sennett, *Fall of Public Man.*
50. Calhoun, "Virtue of Civility," 256.
51. Sennett, *Fall of Public Man,* 48.
52. Simmel, "Metropolis and Mental Life."
53. Sa'ar, *Economic Citizenship,* 22.
54. Blokland et al., "Urban Citizenship and Right to the City," 656.
55. Bayat, "Politics in the City-Inside-Out," 110.
56. Blokland et al., "Urban Citizenship and Right to the City"; Harvey, *Rebel Cities.*
57. See Taylor, "Politics of Recognition."
58. Agier, "Between War and City," 333; Bayat, *Life as Politics.*
59. Sassen, "Urban Capabilities," 90.
60. Holston and Appadurai, "Introduction," 4.
61. Wesley, *State Practices and Zionist Images.*
62. Feldman, "Refusing Invisibility."
63. Holston and Appadurai, "Introduction," 2.
64. Rabinowitz and Abu-Baker, *Coffins on Our Shoulders;* King, *Quiet Revolution;* Hackl, "Orchestra of Civil Resistance."
65. Plonski, *Palestinian Citizens of Israel,* 4–5.
66. Azoulay and Ophir, *One-State Condition.*
67. Jamal, *Arab Minority Nationalism in Israel.*
68. Halbfinger, "Israel Faces a Defining Question."
69. J. Abu-Lughod, "Tale of Two Cities"; Babb, "'Managua Is Nicaragua'"; El-Kazaz and Mazur, "Introduction to Special Section."

ONE

—᙭—

A JOURNEY WITHOUT ARRIVAL?

Palestinian Mobility into the Jewish City

JUST AS SETTLER-COLONIAL CITIES HAVE a difficult relationship with their surroundings, so too does Tel Aviv: created by pioneers as a modern Jewish space, in contrast to Palestine and its southern neighbor Jaffa, it emerged in an Arab region as an essentially non-Arab place. The destruction of Palestinian urbanism and the displacement of Palestinians from the wider area of today's Tel Aviv enabled its emergence as a space that seemed to have no Arab history and characteristics. Colonizers often frame cities in such a way, as places that are not indigenous.[1] As it was nicknamed the "First Hebrew City," many Jews learned to imagine Tel Aviv as a place that lay outside of everything Palestinian. While we can say that some Palestinians have always worked and spent time in this settler city, their urban presence is not only invisible in space but also in memory, as this presence appears to have little transgenerational continuity. The Palestinians mostly come and go, some because they are legally prevented from putting down roots, such as labor commuters from the West Bank, and others because they do not want to stay in a city that feels hostile and foreign. Not only did most of them begin their journey into Tel Aviv fairly recently; they also seemed to never fully arrive.

Their suspended arrival resembles some of the so-called arrival cities around the world, where marginalized newcomers often fail to acquire a sense of urban citizenship and upward mobility.[2] Among Palestinians in Tel Aviv, a limiting regime of mobility conflates with self-limiting dispositions to create a different kind of arrival city for Palestinian citizens of Israel and for Palestinian labor commuters from the West Bank, who are subject to a restrictive legal regime. Their combined experiences show how the Israeli state has long used different legal statuses and various identification cards as bordering mechanisms that produce uneven mobility based on ethnonational and geographic distinctions.[3]

Yet, despite these differences in status and class, Palestinian citizens of Israel and Palestinian labor commuters from the West Bank experience similar patterns of circular mobility and urban invisibility in relation to Tel Aviv. As both groups approach the city primarily as a temporary space, this is mirrored by how the city approaches them: as temporary guests rather than urban citizens who are allowed to belong to this place. "Palestinian Tel Aviv" thus entails a highly unstable presence of a diversity of individuals who approach the city primarily as a *journey* for pragmatic reasons of work or education. These journeys rarely translate into long-term residence in the city.

In a way, all large cities experience a fluctuation in the comings and goings of newcomers. Because Tel Aviv is also the quintessential Jewish city, this fluctuation gains an ethnonational dimension. The Palestinians' commutes and shallow immersion help maintain the city's essentialized Jewish character. Their restricted mobility within and beyond the city, therefore, becomes a crucial component in their conditional inclusion as an invisible and unrecognized urban minority. By looking at these connections and movements we can understand better how access to this city is hierarchized along ethnonational lines.[4] Who can become mobile toward a city and by what means defines who can become a recognized part of it. It is not only much harder for Palestinians to feel at home in Tel Aviv than it is for most Jewish Israelis but also much more difficult to get there in the first place. These two aspects of urban marginalization are interconnected, the one determining the other.

This complex relationship between mobility and equality is best described through *mobility equity*: differently situated people often have very different capacities to turn geographic mobility into social upward mobility, depending on class background, gender identity, or ethnic identity.[5] We will see that Palestinian citizens of Israel, along with Palestinian labor commuters from the West Bank, have varying *capacities* and *potentials* to move in spatial and social terms when it comes to accessing Tel Aviv.[6] This mobility inequity between Palestinian and Jewish citizens is inherent in a highly unequal geography caused by territorial fragmentation between Arabs and Jews in Israel.[7] Palestinians are concentrated in the periphery of the economy and experience discrimination on public transportation and in Tel Aviv's labor market. Most live in relatively poor municipalities with few employment opportunities and industries. They have suffered from a long-standing lack of adequate access to public transportation.[8] All these relative disadvantages form part of a rationalized *regime* that regulates and governs the mobility of some people differently from others,[9] especially in relation to the region's major globalized metropolis. Because Tel Aviv is a key urban space for social mobility and professional advancement, the Palestinians' restricted mobility in geographic terms ultimately translates into limited mobility in social terms.

PALESTINIAN CITIZENS BETWEEN
MARGINALIZATION AND CIRCULATION

Unequal mobilities are full of contradictions: although Palestinian citizens of Israel lack adequate access to effective public transportation, they make up a significant share of Tel Aviv's bus drivers. Their selective inclusion and mobilization inside and outside of the city made it possible. The company Dan, which runs the bus services in greater Tel Aviv, sends shuttle services into the hometowns of some 140 Palestinians so they can drive the city's residents to work on time. "There are ten of these shuttle busses between the north and Tel Aviv every day," a human resources manager at Dan told me. He admitted that Jewish workers who live outside of Tel Aviv usually did not need any such shuttles because they simply come by bus or train. He added: "There is a train connection every night and they can come easily, but Arabs from their towns would not get here by public transport, they would need three or four hours. There is no good public transportation." Some changes to that situation have been underway, with a new train line linking the Galilee region to the main coastal line toward Tel Aviv, for the first time, in addition to new bus routes through towns previously circumvented by Israel's national carrier.[10]

Although they face a lack of mobility in their own towns, Palestinian bus drivers are pulled into Tel Aviv for work. According to Omar, who I met as he drove one of Dan's buses, "There was a lack of bus drivers about six years ago and this gap was mostly filled with Arabs from the north." Speaking during the holy month of Ramadan, when many of the drivers fasted and could be seen praying on carpets in parking lots or behind their parked buses, Omar said that he could never imagine living in Tel Aviv, because to him it was "the heart of Israel." At the same time, moving in and out all the time was exhausting: "I am moving 240 kilometers each day to get here and then I am driving in the bus. Each way home is one and a half hours. There are busses that are organized which bring us to work and back home. I get up at half past 8 and will be back around 12 at night. It's hard in Ramadan now." Even if he wanted to, he could not participate in the city's life, saying, "I can't take part in anything in Tel Aviv. The time is dead, I don't have any time. And getting a room is too expensive."

This makes clear that improving transportation alone is unlikely to improve Palestinian citizens' access to Tel Aviv in a more sustainable way. Their community has suffered from political marginalization, widespread poverty, low education levels, limited geographic distribution, and inadequate resource allocation on the part of the public sector as well as discrimination and the difficulties of getting to work.[11] This overall situation has limited their capacity to move into Tel Aviv and make use of its economic opportunities. Even for those middle-class professionals who have the necessary skills and aspirations, commuting resembles an ongoing uphill struggle for rights and social mobility.[12]

An added problem is that permanently living in Tel Aviv is not only expensive but also unrecognized as a viable option among most Palestinian citizens. While young men often have houses built for them in their parent's towns, waiting to be used once they marry, unmarried women can find it particularly difficult to justify living in Tel Aviv. Overall, resettling in Tel Aviv remains an unusual thing to do even for those who have the means to rent or buy property there. As parents expect their children to return home after university or work, the wider community considers holding onto a family's land a primary objective. Commuting into Israeli cities has nonetheless become a dominant response to their overall marginalization and lacking employment opportunities in their hometowns. For those who found a job or enrolled at a university, the real challenges of the journey of Tel Aviv often began soon after arrival.

These challenges have little to do with the distance of travel because even the blockaded and impoverished Gaza Strip is little more than an hour car drive away from Tel Aviv. Many places in the West Bank would be a short trip away if it were not for the long queues at Israel's military checkpoints and the difficulties of obtaining a work permit. Within the small country of Israel, almost all Palestinian citizens could *potentially* reach Tel Aviv as daily commuters. The real challenge lies in this *potentiality*, which too many Palestinians struggle to realize even if they wanted to. Take the one place that is closer to Tel Aviv than any other Palestinian town or neighborhood: Jaffa. Even from such close proximity—essentially forming one interconnected built-up space— Palestinian citizens face major obstacles on their journeys into Tel Aviv. This is especially so among Palestinian women from low socioeconomic backgrounds who have lived in Jaffa or other nearby towns. As socioeconomic, cultural, and political sources of immobilization intersect, powerful boundaries manifest themselves among some people while they are entirely invisible to others.

MOVING BEYOND JAFFA: GENDERED IMMOBILITY AND THE FEAR OF TEL AVIV

Jaffa has always had an ambivalent relationship with Tel Aviv. It was the port city many prestate Jewish immigrants saw upon their arrival. Yet, Tel

Aviv grew quickly and eventually conquered and encompassed Jaffa under one municipality in 1950. Long neglected as a "dilapidated South Side," Jaffa has gradually been redeveloped and is now increasingly gentrified with a luxury real estate market and weekend leisure "tourism" from Tel Aviv and abroad.[13] Consequently, the inequalities between locals and wealthy newcomers widen. How can Jaffa's Palestinians make use of Tel Aviv as it increasingly enters Jaffa?

The answer to this question is not simple and requires an analysis both of factors external to the Palestinian community and of many internal dynamics. The case of Palestinian women from Jaffa is particularly revealing as it shows how the racialized exclusion of Palestinians from Tel Aviv combines with class- and gender-related obstacles to urban mobility and boundary crossing. For some Palestinian women from working-class households with low educational backgrounds, the iconic clock tower of Jaffa marks a rigid boundary that is difficult to cross. "This clock-tower is the border for them. Everything beyond is Tel Aviv," said Bushra, who, when I met her, helped women in Jaffa searching for jobs in the surrounding Jewish metropolitan area. Sitting in a café next to the clock tower square, she explained that some of the women felt so insecure about Tel Aviv that she had to accompany them to their job interviews, unless their husbands insisted on doing so themselves.

Bushra worked for an NGO called Arus al-Bahr, which translates to "Bride of the Sea"—one of the nicknames of Jaffa. Their offices were a twenty-minute walk south of the clock tower. During one of my visits, Safa, the NGO's founder, opened the door and welcomed me in. She was born in Jaffa in 1975. When Israel conquered the town in 1948, her maternal family fled toward Gaza; only some were allowed to return. Safa was, in many ways, a pioneer among Palestinian women in Jaffa because she attended a Jewish school in Tel Aviv from the age of sixteen, which proved to be an important stepping-stone into a successful career. Her parents had hoped this would make it easier for her to go to a university. Her story remains an exception, she explained, adding that many of the women she tried to help were talking about working in Tel Aviv as if it were another country.

Most of these women were married with children and came from low socioeconomic backgrounds and educational levels. Some were never formally employed before. Asked if they wanted to work in Tel Aviv, "for most, the first reaction is: 'It's not for me, I am scared,'" said Safa after a meeting with some of the women at their office. According to her, they often feared that Jewish Israelis would not accept them as they were and "that they will stare at us." Those who wear a headscarf knew that they would be discriminated against in Tel Aviv's job market because of that alone. Safa's plan was to conquer these fears and overcome obstacles in order to improve the mobility of the women into Tel Aviv and its economy, saying, "I try to give them dreams, to help them to see their own potential." She wanted to help them make their journeys across a powerful yet invisible border between Jaffa and Tel Aviv: "A lot of women are scared to be attacked in Tel Aviv. One woman told me recently that the furthest place she would work in is the clock-tower in Jaffa. I asked her why, and she said that she heard about one woman being attacked *there* [in Tel Aviv] . . . There are also fears about being looked at, that they are not good enough in Hebrew, that they are wearing the veil and that it would be strange."

The clock tower marks both the end of a cultural and political safety zone and the beginning of a space perceived as hostile and foreign. Even Safa emphasized that Jaffa "is not like in Tel Aviv," adding, "There [in Tel Aviv], we always feel like a minority and have to feel like guests, even if we are actually from here." Yet, Safa also admitted that "if a woman here wants to advance, she has to go to these Jewish places in Tel Aviv. She simply has to deal with it." Work-seeking women in Jaffa had little alternative but to search in Tel Aviv and the Jewish suburban sprawl around it.

Although the two sides of the city are spatially proximate, the barriers between Jaffa and Tel Aviv are manifest for local Palestinian women. Bushra, who was thirty-nine at the time of our first meeting, used to be one of Safa's first success stories. Seven years back, she worked in the client-intake section of an insurance company in central Tel Aviv. "Because I was wearing this," she said, pointing at her headscarf, "the only jobs I could find in Tel Aviv were on the phone; no one else would have accepted me with a *hijab* in Tel Aviv." When Bushra joined Arus al-Bahr as a project manager, she had already finished her degree in counseling at a college in Tel Aviv. "Jaffa is small and they know my story. I am a living proof to them for what can be done."

The perceived rigid boundary between Jaffa and Tel Aviv is also reflected in the story of Asma Agbaria, a prominent socialist politician and political activist who grew up in Jaffa. Her own story of encountering Tel Aviv began in 1991 when she went to Tel Aviv University to study literature and philosophy at the age of nineteen. At the time, she was religious and wore a headscarf, saying that there was "always tension, you feel difference, or even a feeling of inferiority." To get to Tel Aviv University, she would travel north by bus for about an hour through heavy traffic. Recalling those first regular bus rides through Tel Aviv, Agbaria said: "You go out to another world, suddenly you see another world of strangers. These people of Tel Aviv didn't come to Jaffa . . . my own daily tourism through Tel Aviv was very shocking."

Agbaria said that as a young student she never got off the bus along the way, going only from Jaffa to the university and back. The space in between, the actual city of Tel Aviv, appeared to her as "a big gap"—a scary, unknown place she did not want to fall into. She knew how to write Hebrew but had little self-confidence expressing herself, saying: "I didn't really know how to talk. I was scared from this world. I felt the gap between me and the Jews. They knew how to express themselves, and after all it was their state." At the same time, the more she left Jaffa, the less she fitted in there, as she explained: "After some time in Tel Aviv, it is very hard afterwards to confront your own society. While Israel discriminates against you, you are also part of a very traditional society that is threatened by any sort of change. In this confrontation, you have to confront two societies, not only one. So many people just give up."

Accessing Tel Aviv and feeling at ease there remained an ongoing struggle for most women from Jaffa decades after Agbaria's time as a student, including for those women who had already found a job. On the same bus line that once took Asma Agbaria from Jaffa to Tel Aviv University, I met Basma, who worked as a cleaner on campus. Basma's daily bus route took a full hour through the mess of Tel Aviv's traffic.

"They should introduce an express bus between Jaffa and here. So many of us work here, the campus is full of Arab workers," she lamented. She ended up at the cleaning company because she felt uncomfortable applying for jobs where they could reject her because of the headscarf. In cleaning, it seemed, appearances mattered less. She had plenty of experiences with rejections, and, most of the time, the real answer was concealed by the wording "we already found someone." As access to Tel Aviv is racialized and hierarchized, with Palestinians facing disadvantages, so, too, are jobs hierarchized. Cleaners, builders, kitchen staff—the majority of Palestinian jobs in Tel Aviv remain at the bottom of the earnings pyramid. Another thing is apparent: working-class Palestinians, and, especially, women wearing headscarves, are offered jobs that are not public facing but hidden away from the city, all in line with the settler colonial aim of erasing a visible Palestinian presence within Tel Aviv.

As Ami Katz, who headed the Jaffa section of the municipality, said in a meeting in his office: "There is this unseen border dividing Jaffa from Tel Aviv; for any Muslim Arab woman in Jaffa, working in Tel Aviv is like working in the Antarctic." Coming from a powerful white male politician, this sounds like a problematic generalization. Yet, there is some truth to it beyond the women's own views of Tel Aviv being foreign, as it underscores that there is a structural and ethnonational element to their exclusion. He admits that for himself and many others, namely Jewish Israelis, such a border did not really exist anymore.

Tel Aviv had long ago absorbed Jaffa and gentrified it. According to Katz, the municipality tried, among other initiatives, to improve the mobility of local Palestinians in Jaffa through the opening of a youth center for men and women between the ages of eighteen and thirty-five. One of his goals was, indeed, to include more of them in quality jobs, but invisible and rigid borders were difficult to deconstruct.

Take one of Bushra's clients, the thirty-seven-year-old Reem, who was born in the Gaza Strip and has lived with her husband and six children in Jaffa for years under the terms of a residence permit that did not allow her to work until recently. She had been in Jaffa for twelve years at the time we met, and her Hebrew was still weak. She joined Arus al-Bahr to find a better job and to gain confidence. "I need to learn how to express myself better, how to survive in Tel Aviv," she told me in a meeting. Whenever she gets a new job offer in Tel Aviv, however, she needs someone to accompany her, saying that she doubts she can find the street the business is on and is scared to get lost. Overall, she faces a number of intersecting challenges: legal restrictions, language problems, socioeconomic problems, and gender-specific concerns. Many of the women have to fight for recognition among their husbands and family members at the same time as they are fighting for professional opportunities and against discrimination. Their experiences show how socioeconomic factors combine with political and cultural ones into a gender-differentiated regime that limits their mobility into Tel Aviv and its economy. Although Palestinian women in Israel often handle the pressures of increasing their income and becoming self-supportive, the expectations of an implicit "gender contract" add that, in addition to participating in the workforce, they must keep domestic care work as their first priority.[14]

This became evident when I met Haneen, another of Bushra's former clients at Arus al-Bahr. She had graduated in tourism studies but worked at another company's telephone hotline for years because the working hours fitted her parental responsibilities better. Balancing her individual aims with the responsibilities for her husband and children was an additional struggle, one that most women at Arus al-Bahr faced. "This balancing takes a lot of energy from me. This is why I don't have much energy for political issues," she said. Still, political issues constantly surfaced for Palestinians working in Tel Aviv. Haneen had just had an interview for a job at the hotline of the Israel Electric Company. One question at the interview unsettled her: "They asked me . . . if I did the army. So I checked the box for 'no.' But then there was a sub-question, asking 'why?' I wrote down 'because I am Arab.'" While Palestinian citizens of Israel are officially exempt from compulsory Israeli military service, employers sometimes use requirements or consideration of army service to indirectly discriminate against them.[15]

Obstacles to geographic and urban mobility, in terms of crossing a threshold that marks the boundary between Palestinian and Jewish space, are followed by fears of discrimination that impede professional and social mobility. Among Palestinians in Israel, *mobility equity* remains widely unrealized because of discriminatory obstacles to "upward" movement in socioeconomic terms and in space.[16] The exclusive Jewish Israeli labor market, in addition to problems with transport and mobility, combines with the gendered and class-based experiences of limiting spatial boundaries. What is an easy stroll past a clock tower for some can symbolize a rigid boundary for others. A gendered perspective is crucial in the analysis of Palestinian mobility in relation to Tel Aviv because their community or family often police such mobility. This is true for women from poor households in Jaffa and for young middle-class women from Israel's north, some of whom need the excuse of studying at university to be allowed to reside in the city. "Mobility is a real issue, also because young Arabs are only expected to go out of town for a specific purpose," said Farah, the Palestinian marketing expert who lived in Tel Aviv long term. This meant that women often had to justify their aspirations to live or work in Tel Aviv, unlike most men.

Women's constraints on geographic and social mobility are determined, in part, by social norms, responsibilities, gender roles, and considerations about female safety, but these underlying factors translate into female disadvantages in the labor market.[17] Mobility is deeply gendered and this includes differences in people's competence to recognize and make use of access, the appropriation of a particular choice, including the power to imagine other places and potential lives and follow such imaginings.[18] Initiatives such as Arus al-Bahr not only become mediators between a marginalized Palestinian population and Jewish Israeli urban space; they also become cooperative spheres for mutual support that inspire imagination and combat fear of the cultural and political Other. In workshops and trainings, women reconfigure what is considered to be possible and impossible in terms of their mobility and access to the Jewish city.

Class and gender are important factors that influence Palestinian mobility toward Tel Aviv in spatial and social terms, and yet, there is an ethnonational dimension to their urban exclusion that affects all Palestinians in one way or another. Experiences of discrimination and difficulties in finding highly skilled jobs have inspired some to praise the remote outsourcing of work from Tel Aviv's companies into their home areas as a perfect solution. Why bother with Palestinians moving into Tel Aviv, if you can bring Tel Aviv's work to them?

FROM COMMUTES TO TELECOMMUTES: OUTSOURCING
HIGH-TECH WORK TO PALESTINIAN CITIZENS

Amid the obstacles that stand between Palestinians and their access to the economy of Tel Aviv, it is no surprise that outsourcing remote work into Arab residential areas has come into fashion. Proponents of this trajectory seek to mobilize the product of people's work rather than the workers.[19] Although business process outsourcing, sometimes called telecommuting, has been around for decades, the rise of digital labor and an increasingly vibrant IT sector, in many parts of the world, have turned it into a global phenomenon.[20] Tel Aviv has been at the heart of this development, and it is frequently heralded for its vibrant tech-driven economy. Outsourcing is usually associated with the "Third World" and emerged at a time when capital mobility created new conditions for the mobility of labor.[21] That this framework is readily applied to Palestinian citizens of Israel highlights the deeply rooted inequalities that define their peripheral position as compared with the Jewish Israeli core of the economy.

On a side note, outsourcing has been applied to the West Bank, too, with the city of Ramallah featuring a growing number of technology start-ups. Even before digital outsourcing, Israeli production has often been outsourced into Palestinian agriculture and borderland industrial parks.[22] These are long-standing colonial patterns of utilizing the economic benefits of inequality, set against a wider backdrop of ethnoregionalism, which allocates particular places for Jews and Arabs following a rigid hierarchy. Palestinian mobility unsettles these static categories: core-periphery relations in the political economy draw more and more Palestinians into Jewish cities and towns for both low- and high-skilled work.[23]

Because friction may accompany this urban inclusion, outsourcing is promoted as a logical alternative. According to advocates of "Arab high tech" in Israel, the numbers of Palestinian citizens working in Israeli technology companies had risen steadily from a mere 350 in 2008 to about 6,600 people, or 4.5 percent of employees in the sector, by 2019.[24] Other studies put the figure lower, stating that "Arabs with Israeli citizenship account for only 1.4% when it comes to lucrative technology jobs in the local market."[25] One of the driving forces behind outsourcing software services into Palestinian towns in Israel is Inas Said, a founder of Galil Software in Nazareth.

We met for an interview, in June 2014, at a shopping mall next to the highway north of Tel Aviv, which made it easier for him to spare the time because he was constantly on the road. His idea behind building the company, which called itself "Israel's premier onshore outsourcing option," was to form an incubator in which a real high-tech environment could be simulated through outsourcing software development and research to Palestinians in Israel. According to Said, they planned to incubate a mass of engineers in a safe environment rather than providing potentially risky opportunities for a few in Israeli cities. As outsourcing is usually associated with sending jobs overseas to people who are otherwise excluded from the labor market, it lowers the costs of production and often evades regulatory standards and legal constraints.[26] Here, it serves the purpose of evading the constraints of Palestinian immersion into Tel Aviv's tech-driven economy. With Palestinian mobility toward Tel Aviv fragmented and restricted, the mobility of labor outruns the mobility of workers in ways that drive a restructuring of space-labor relations.

Mobilizing work rather than workers serves the indirect purpose of maintaining the existing division between the Jewish Israeli city of Tel Aviv and the Palestinian periphery. It not only precludes Palestinian access to Tel Aviv as an urban space but also evades the need for mobility altogether, ostensibly in response to Palestinians' own difficulty with integrating into the IT sector. Outsourcing into the city of Nazareth was meant to create spatial proximity and "cultural familiarity" between workers and their environment, according to Said. This refers to the idea that Palestinians had cultural reasons to remain resident in their hometowns, instead of living and working in Tel Aviv. Reasons cited by Said and the Palestinian professionals themselves included the need for Arabic-speaking schooling, the importance of landownership in Palestinian society, the high costs of living in Tel Aviv, and the estrangement of living in the midst of a Jewish Israeli city. Against this backdrop, *incubating* Palestinian citizens "at home" becomes a self-fulfilling prophecy that justifies spatial limitations because urban inclusion is considered to be too difficult.

NGOs such as Tsofen have spearheaded the movement to bring more Palestinian citizens into high tech. With strong links to Israeli and international industries, they have tried to promote the inclusion of Arab engineers into the sector while also pushing the outsourcing agenda as an alternative or even as a temporary stepping-stone. According to Smadar Nehab, a cofounder of the organization I first met in 2012, individual Palestinian citizens find integration into Israeli high-tech companies "almost impossible," which is where "onshore outsourcing" comes in. According to her, "The reason for doing high-tech in the [Arab areas in the] North is that it's an environment that is accepting them."

Among the stated obstacles to the integration of individual Palestinian citizens into the Israeli high-tech industry were that it tends to be homogeneous and that "there is a chasm between Arabs and Jews, they don't know each other; there are stereotypes, there is hatred." Moreover, Palestinian citizens also lacked networks of Jewish Israeli university graduates, many of which are forged during the mandatory army service, from which they are exempt. Adding anti-Arab prejudice among employers and language barriers, the obstacles seem indeed significant.

Despite these obstacles and the available alternative of outsourcing, Palestinian software engineers continue to search for jobs in Tel Aviv. Thirty-five-year-old Ramzi, one of Tsofen's former trainees and an Israeli citizen, preferred working in Tel Aviv rather than being tied to an incubator closer to his hometown of Sakhnin. It was clear that despite its difficulties, the Palestinian journey into Tel Aviv was somehow exciting and challenging: journeys are not only about rational movements from A to B; they also entail the possibility of transformation and change. Many of the Palestinian employees' hometowns are small and tightly knit communities. Living there is one thing but working nearby may be too much "cultural familiarity" for some of the young Palestinian middle class in Israel.

Meeting Ramzi outside his office in Tel Aviv, an interesting controversy emerged that highlighted the confining logic behind the outsourcing approach. Ramzi told me about a friend who had been previously "incubated" as an early career software engineer in Nazareth; then he had the opportunity of being hired by a more promising company in the Tel Aviv area. During the interview, his friend learned that one of Galil Software's managers had told the potential new employers in a reference that the candidate was not yet ready to leave Nazareth, "because of his family and other issues related to Arab culture," Ramzi recounted. As Said had told me in our interview, Arab engineers would often not succeed in Israeli companies "because of issues relating to culture."

Although the benefits of developing industries closer to Palestinian citizens' hometowns are clear, it should not undermine their freedom to move and access job opportunities in the Tel Aviv area. As Palestinian engineers contribute programming services to Israeli and international firms in the center of the political economy, the product of their work is mobilized while employees stay put. Those who invest in outsourcing may, indeed, have an interest in keeping Palestinian talents incubated, rather than offering them economic freedom, mobility, and inclusion. According to Said, "The goal is *not* to migrate into Tel Aviv, because if you do that, there is no more incentive for companies to come up North." The implicit assumption is that even those who make it into Tel Aviv eventually come back anyway: "When they get to the point where they have to weigh their career versus their family, they came back to us."

Onshore incubating in this context of inequality between a Palestinian periphery and a Jewish urban core has a particular significance. It promotes a confining form of economic development among members of a minority that conveniently fits into existing ethnonational divisions and socioeconomic inequalities. As it precludes Palestinian mobility into Tel Aviv, remote work and outsourcing help maintain the categorical invisibility of Palestinian citizens in the urban core of Israel's economy. The difficult and often tense experiences of commuting are another reason for some to stay at home, while others keep on moving and face stigmatization on a daily basis.

DO NOT SPEAK ARABIC: RESPONDING TO IMMOBILIZATION AND STIGMATIZATION

The perceived settler-colonial goal of eliminating a visible Palestinian presence from Tel Aviv extends into the tense experiences of commuting, during which the Palestinians need to employ tactics of invisibility in response to stigmatization and immobilization. Ramzi, who lived in Sakhnin, spent four hours a day on public transportation on top of ten working hours. However, the main problem with commuting as a Palestinian in Israel is not time, as Ramzi explained: "Recently on the train, there were a lot of people around me. Then my phone rang and I picked up, spoke in Arabic. They all stared at me and I felt how they went one step away from me. When I approached the guard in front of the train station while talking Arabic on the phone they always check me and ask me a few questions. If I don't (speak Arabic), they don't."

On a normal day, any person moving around Israel may experience a number of routine security checks. Yet, the practice of racial screening and profiling mainly affects Palestinians, and such "screening" forms an integral part of a limiting mobility regime.[27] As a preventive response, Ramzi avoided speaking Arabic at the station and in crowded trains or buses, which are often filled with soldiers in uniform and subject to frequent security checks. A history of violence and prejudice turned spotting "suspicious" people on buses into traits of good Israeli citizenship,[28] stigmatizing Palestinian citizens in a large number of everyday situations.[29] Tactics of invisibility—such as not speaking Arabic—help evade situational immobilization when travelers cross "thresholds" between social and spatial territories.[30] Moving from an Arab town into Jewish Tel Aviv crosses such a threshold, whether by entering a train station, sitting on a bus, or coping with inadequate public transportation. The overall tension Palestinians experience on public transportation becomes even worse during times of political polarization and violence.

Speaking on July 9, 2014, during the heated times of the Gaza conflict, Ramzi told me about another unsettling experience on the train to Tel Aviv. Once again, he talked on the phone in Arabic. Sitting beside him was an Israeli soldier in uniform. "He played a video on his phone loudly, a video of Michael Ben-Ari, the extremist Member of Parliament. The gun on his legs pointed towards me the whole trip," said Ramzi, inside an open workspace in central Tel Aviv, where his office was located. Trying to blend in might help him avoid direct stigmatization, but there is no escaping the estrangement and tension he feels as a Palestinian. In addition to their rides on transportation involving unsettling situations, Palestinian citizens are also treated differently at the entrances and gateways into train or bus stations, and, especially, at the international airport.

Many middle-class Palestinian citizens of Israel who can afford plane tickets may move in and out of Tel Aviv through the airport several times a year. Many of those who work in Tel Aviv travel internationally for their jobs, as artists, musicians, lawyers, or academics. As the main international gateway, Tel Aviv's Ben Gurion Airport exemplifies how Palestinian citizens' international mobility is regulated. To most, these international journeys in and out of Tel Aviv underscore their second-class citizenship and the vulnerability of being a Palestinian individual in a Jewish state.

A regular scenario circulated among Palestinians I knew in Tel Aviv: they were singled out and interrogated, strip searched, provoked, lost their temper, or missed their flights. Indeed, Israeli airport security staff racially profile Palestinian citizens routinely.[31] Such measures ensure citizen identification and help states control and regulate mobility. At the airport, more than anywhere else, passports and identity documents reveal the *illiberality* of the state and its differential treatment of some citizens: "a presumption of their bearers' guilt when called upon to identify themselves" indicates the state's fundamental suspicion that people will lie when asked who or what they are.[32] The need for documentation at the airport undermines Palestinians' ability to respond to immobilization with tactics of situational concealment.

One tactical response nevertheless became evident when I approached the checkpoint at the airport's outer rim in a taxi with a friend, a former Tel Aviv University student. The guards looked into her vehicle and asked a few routine questions in Hebrew, especially, "Where did you just come from?" She answered in fluent Hebrew, "We came from Tel Aviv," which eased the way. Another time, however, she drove her sister to the airport, saying she had come from Umm el-Fahm, a Palestinian town in Israel. They had to step out of the car, which was searched thoroughly, and almost missed their flight after a heated dispute and lengthy interrogation.

Although protesting on-site is always an option, passing unrecognized as a Palestinian avoids delay and is often more useful. Such tactical invisibility aids social navigation within a "force field"—a regime of mobility that moves around them and demands careful maneuvering.[33] Israel's mobility regime polices the movements and spatial access of Palestinian citizens on the basis of their identity, which is as true *within* Tel Aviv as it is for journeys in and out of the city.

Although the city of Tel Aviv has the appearance of a very open, free-flowing city to the uninformed urban visitor, its space and movements are regulated differentially for "Arabs." As the Tel Aviv University student Amira recounted one experience: "From what I wear, my accent, and in conversations . . . , the guards at the gates of university always think I am not Arab. But recently they began to request student cards from everyone. They always said hello and were friendly. But when they see my card and my family name, they realize I am Arab and ask me to open my bag. But before it was as if I was VIP, no one expected that I am Arab."

Here, the mobilizing effects of tactical invisibility ended with the requirement to present ID cards that reveal her family name, just like at the airport. "VIP" usually refers to mobile people with access to exclusive places. In this case, it suggests that VIP means not being visibly Palestinian. Although tactics of invisibility allow Palestinian citizens to respond to such discrimination as they move through Israeli space, this flexibility is often limited by racial profiling.

The commutes and journeys of Palestinian citizens of Israel highlight the multiple layers of systematic and situational immobilization of affected individuals and the responses they developed to it. This has become evident on three levels: traveling through the airport at the international level, commuting between hometowns and the city on the national level, and daily mobility within the city on an urban level. In their own way, each of these layers of limited mobility contributes to the ongoing invisibility of Palestinians in relation to Tel Aviv.

So far, we have explored the mobility of Palestinian citizens from varying class backgrounds and different locations within Israel. We now look at the journeys of Palestinians who live in the West Bank under Israeli occupation. Although they cannot immerse in Tel Aviv in the way Palestinian citizens of Israel can, many labor commuters from the West Bank end up working in the area of Greater Tel Aviv. How their mobility into Tel Aviv is regulated and restricted contributes to their marginalized and invisible presence within the city.

MOBILE EXCLUSION: TEL AVIV AND
THE WEST BANK COMMUTE

There are important differences between Palestinian citizens of Israel and Palestinian labor commuters who live in the West Bank when it comes to their mobility toward Tel Aviv. Palestinian labor commuting from the West Bank into Tel Aviv began, in 1967, soon after Israel occupied the West Bank alongside the Gaza Strip and East Jerusalem. After a period of initial openness, the state established a wide infrastructure of segregation and a restrictive permit regime.[34] Yet, despite segregation and restrictions, mobility across the border has been equally ubiquitous. Even the strongest symbol of segregation—the Israeli Separation Barrier—shows that the power of separation depends on a limited amount of contact and regulated exchange to remain sustainable.[35]

As Israel issues entry permits and regulates all crossings into the West Bank and numerous checkpoints within it, it becomes the primary regulator of Palestinian mobility: it has the power to open and close access for laborers as needed, depending on economic requirements and the wider political situation. They serve as a disposable, flexible, and dependent "industrial reserve army" of labor.[36] In 2019, some 127,000 workers from the West Bank were employed in Israel and the settlements, which provided the livelihood of some estimated 650,000 people in the occupied territory. Two-thirds of these laborers worked in construction and most crossed in and out of Israel on a daily or weekly basis. They have little alternative: unemployment in the occupied Palestinian territory was about 27 percent in 2019, one of the highest recorded rates in the world.[37]

The individual journeys from the West Bank are important indicators for the way Israel and its major city Tel Aviv incorporate those Palestinians who are not citizens, helping us see how the underlying mobility regime imposes a colonial hierarchy of movement and urban inclusion. One very unusual Tel Aviv employee was Raed from the West Bank city of Nablus, who had a background as a software engineer and found his way into the city's competitive high-tech sector. When I first met him, he said the main reason for working in Tel Aviv was not the money, but the opportunity "to get to know this world." The use of "world" here referred to the city of Tel Aviv and its high-tech economy, as well as its social life and the people he worked with.

The opportunity to work as a software engineer in Tel Aviv was made possible by a special program that offered internships to Palestinians in Israeli companies, which could then decide whether to keep them as employees. Raed's company decided to keep him. But his capacity to be mobile toward Tel Aviv remained highly conditional on a work permit that had to be renewed every three months and, sometimes, every month. This resulted in recurring periods of being stuck and waiting in his home city of Nablus. Such enforced waiting is in itself part of Israel's mobility regime for Palestinians.[38]

One day, I joined Raed on his daily trip to Nablus and back the following day. Our journey began with a bus from his workplace in Tel Aviv to the city's outskirts, where we had to wait for a bus toward Israel's third largest settlement, Ariel, at a major thoroughfare. Only every second of these buses, which connected Jewish settlements to Israel, was accessible for Raed. As a Palestinian, he was not permitted to enter Jewish settlements and one of the routes to Ariel passed through one such settlement. If he boarded this bus, guards would force him to get off, and he would be stuck outside the gates. After half an hour, we boarded the right bus for Ariel, and it drove into the West Bank on Israeli settlement roads inaccessible to most Palestinians living in the towns along it.

Toward the end of the journey, Raed was not allowed to enter Ariel like all other passengers. He had to get off at a road junction outside, where two soldiers shouted at us to hurry into a side street where the taxis to Nablus waited. This diversion was justified on grounds of security because Jewish settlers waited at the bus stop nearby. Although Raed shared an office with Jewish Israelis in Tel Aviv, he was not allowed to walk close to Jewish Israelis in his home area of the West Bank. We eventually reached a taxi and sat down on its back bench beside another Palestinian worker, speeding along the winding roads toward the approaching lights of Nablus with open windows and loud Arabic pop music. On the next morning, we awoke early to make the journey back.

Thanks to the office hours of Tel Aviv's IT sector, Raed left Nablus comparatively late, around 6:00 a.m., while tens of thousands of Palestinian workers left their homes as early as 3:00 a.m. to make it through the checkpoint on time. Raed's journey toward Tel Aviv started with a walk to the taxi station in Nablus, from where he boarded a van to Qalqiliyah, a Palestinian town at the northwestern edge of the West Bank. Midway, Raed fell asleep. "Every minute of sleep counts," he said, with a smile, before slumbering away. At the checkpoint, zigzag-shaped tunnels of iron bars led into the center of the terminal where Israeli officials checked his documents and scanned his body. Above us on metal bridges were men in plain clothes who walked back and forth, pointing their heavy automatic rifles down on some of the waiting Palestinians every once in a while.

After the crossing, Raed got stuck on the other side of the terminal when the last full minivan to Tel Aviv drove away in front of our eyes. It would take a while for another one to fill up. What followed was a mix of waiting, arguing, discussing, and weighing options. At one moment, Raed seemed to have reached an agreement with one of the drivers, immediately provoking the interference of another. After almost an hour, in a sudden turn of events, we boarded a private van that was about to leave empty. The other drivers were outraged and cursed the driver, one of them knocking his fists at the car window as the driver pulled out toward Tel Aviv. I asked Raed if he ever felt too exhausted and decided to stay in bed. "No, never," he said, seemingly surprised, and contemplated for a few seconds before saying: "All these problems disappear and are forgotten when I enter the office in Tel Aviv."

More than two years after this trip, in the spring of 2017, I met Raed once again in Tel Aviv. I was interested in knowing how his career proceeded and whether he was able to create a more reliable and sustainable situation for himself, thanks to the jobs he had done before. After a longer period without work in Tel Aviv, he was now back in the city, working for a British gambling company as a programmer. Although his career had advanced to a new job with frequent travel to the UK, the temporary work permit was still the same, and the commute was equally exhausting. He was still not allowed to stay in Israel overnight, did not get enough sleep, and hardly managed to save up any money due to large fees taken by mediating labor brokers for his work permit. Because Israeli employers would not hire him as a West Bank Palestinian if he just sent in his résumé, he only found work through a subcontracting "agency" that consisted of brokers on both sides of the Separation Barrier. Not only did they connect him to the employer, but they also organized his work permit and charged Raed large sums for it. According to Raed, the brokers took half of his monthly salary.[39]

Raed's journey reveals the confinement of the Israeli labor regime for Palestinians from the West Bank. More importantly, it shows how this restricted mobility results in a degrading and oppressive experience for a talented young Palestinian programmer whose only "crime" is that he would like to work in Tel Aviv. Although he worked in one of Tel Aviv's fancy office towers for an international company, he had no access to sustainable inclusion in Tel Aviv and lived a kind of double life between his work life and his journey home. For the most part, he could not even take part in the city's social life once he was there, because the time limit of the work permit forced him to go back home every evening. In regulating the Palestinian presence in Tel Aviv through an exclusive mobility regime, the Israeli state maintains their invisibility in the city and ensures that their presence remains volatile and short lived.

The situation is even worse for those forty thousand or so Palestinians who worked in Israel without work permits, many among them in or around Tel Aviv. The town of Yatta, where I conducted field research in 2017, is known to have the largest share of workers who enter Israel without permits from the West Bank. Close to the West Bank's rocky and hilly southern border, it has become a major hub for Palestinians from elsewhere, too.

It would be hard to believe what their journeys toward Tel Aviv and other Israeli cities entail, without actually seeing them. When I was there in 2017, I observed how these journeys unfold. Driving near the concrete barrier that separates Israel from the southern West Bank, a car passed a Bedouin settlement, left the main road for a dirt one, and veered into a field. It stopped next to a gap in the wall. Three men got out, rushed through the opening, and were picked up on the other side—inside Israel. Farther west, the ground became rocky and hilly. I saw how four-wheel drives brought groups of men to another spot where the wall seemingly ended. As the passengers stepped out, a car motored toward them, kicking up a massive dust cloud. The Palestinian men got in, and the car sped away toward an Israeli town.

All of this repeats itself every few minutes each evening near Yatta, one of the West Bank's largest towns. In 2017, municipality officials told me that only about twenty-four hundred of its residents had jobs locally, meaning that almost everyone was dependent on work in Israel. The sons of a family I stayed with in Yatta all worked in Israel, some of them in car wash stations around Tel Aviv, others in construction. To lower the risk of being caught, they lived in Arab residential areas in the mixed town of Lydda (Lod) nearby.

They might see their own future in their oldest brother's memories. He worked in Israel most of his life, since he was seventeen, but never had a permit. Now running an informal business in Yatta, he thought back, and said: "They caught me three times without a permit in Israel, I went to prison. Each time straight to the [military] court . . . if they catch you again you sit in six months or longer. Then I was not allowed to enter Israel for four years. In total I was in prison five times."

From the uncertain and risky journeys through Yatta to the work permit of the programmer Raed: the legal regime and the routes that bring Palestinians from the West Bank into Tel Aviv and other Israeli cities are designed to render them excluded from Israeli sovereign space, despite their presence in Israel as laborers. Such "jurisdictional politics" is employed to govern Palestinians' rights and their mobility.[40] From the viewpoint of Tel Aviv, the circular mobility of these workers is a form of fluctuating urbanization from which no pathway leads to urban citizenship or sustainable inclusion. By definition, their journeys help produce durable inequality and categorical exclusion through processes of shallow and conditional inclusion. Mobility and inclusion become the key components of a regime that maintains the invisibility of an urban minority and its categorical exclusion from the city.

WHAT IS IN A CITY? BOUNDED MOBILITY AND URBAN INVISIBILITY

Without its connections, what would any city be? Seeing how Palestinians move in and out of Tel Aviv makes clear that their connections with the space of the city are fraught with tension and restriction. These *bounded mobilities* are part of the colonial double process of inclusion and exclusion through which Israel controls Palestinian territory, space, corporeality, and identity.[41] Palestinian labor commuters from the West Bank are subjected to a highly restricted mobility regime, which includes legal restrictions to their presence in the city and the space available to them for participating in it. Palestinian citizens of Israel face a number of systematic obstacles, too. Their journeys show how unequal mobility produces their invisibility and undermines their access to sustainable residence and a sense of urban belonging. This highly differentiated mobility regime determines Palestinians' geographic, economic, and social mobility, while controlling, ordering, and bordering the Palestinians in relation to this Israeli city.[42]

At the same time, their journeys suggest that a city's population is much more than the mass of its settled residents and that this very differentiation between those who belong and those who do not is in itself deeply political. The comings and goings of Palestinians in Tel Aviv enable the survival of a mirage: that this Jewish city is essentially non-"Arab." Who moves into it, and how such movement takes place, tells us something about what a city is and what it is not. Recognizing these mobilities as an extension of the city, rather than something that lies outside it, allows us to see how the settler-colonial strategy of eliminating Palestinian visibility from Tel Aviv extends far beyond the boundaries of urban space.

Looking closely at the immersion of unsettled and mobile populations challenges cities that are closed to certain kind of newcomers, because people's mobility interacts with cities and opens access to some urban resources and even to a sense of urban belonging.[43] Yet, in the current regime, Palestinian journeys mostly fall short of realizing a kind of *citadinité* that would allow them to feel a sense of belonging to a city and its urban society.[44] For sure, many Palestinians are perfectly happy without a sense of belonging to Tel Aviv—it is a temporary destination to most of them, one that is used rather than a place to settle in.

Tel Aviv attracts Palestinians and Palestinian citizens in two seemingly contradictory ways. As the urban core of a settler state, it limits their access to urban citizenship while simultaneously making use of their labor power; and, as an ostensible liberal city, it promises a possible way out from their marginalization in the country's periphery, creating aspirations to access its socioeconomic opportunities. The problem is that Tel Aviv does not offer the Palestinians urban access without reserve. The bounded nature of Palestinian mobility in relation to Tel Aviv is key to our understanding of how exactly an urban regime of inclusion limits the entitlements and citizenship of its subjects, partly through creating confined pathways toward economic opportunities that deepen the urban invisibility of the marginalized.

These insights have provided some answers to important questions about the role of mobility in relation to the inclusion of stigmatized urban minorities, some of which have policy significance and should be relevant to decision makers in Tel Aviv: What role do unequal mobility regimes play in the exclusion of minorities from urban citizenship? Can the city do more to address the specific grievances and problems of stigmatized minorities who commute in and out? Where does urban policy end, at the municipal boundaries or at the commuter's doorstep? To what extent, then, can cities become more inclusive in a context where an ongoing ethnonational conflict, a settler colonial occupation, and deeply rooted inequalities predetermine some people's urban access as restricted?

NOTES

1. Porter and Yiftachel, "Urbanizing Settler-Colonial Studies."
2. Saunders, *Arrival City.*
3. Tawil-Souri, "Uneven Borders, Coloured (Im)mobilities," 155.
4. McFarlane, "City as Assemblage," 667.
5. Hackl, "Mobility Equity in a Globalized World."
6. Leivestad, "Chapter 7—Motility"; Kaufmann, Bergman, and Joye, "Motility."
7. Yiftachel, "Centralized Power and Divided Space."
8. Sikkuy, "Equality Zones," 74.
9. Baker, "Regime."

10. Sikkuy, "Sikkuy Boosts Public Transportation."

11. Yashiv and Katsir, "Labour Market of Israeli Arabs," 3–4; Pappé, *Forgotten Palestinians*; Dan Rabinowitz and Abu-Baker, *Coffins on Our Shoulders*.

12. Blatman-Thomas, "Commuting for Rights."

13. Monterescu, *Jaffa*; Rabinowitz and Monterescu, "Reconfiguring the 'Mixed Town.'"

14. Sa'ar, *Economic Citizenship*, 22.

15. Khattab and Miaari, *Palestinians in the Israeli Labor Market*.

16. Hackl, "Mobility Equity in a Globalized World."

17. Assaad and Arntz, "Constrained Geographical Mobility," 451.

18. Kaufmann, Bergman, and Joye, "Motility," 750; Salazar, "Power of Imagination in Transnational Mobilities."

19. Palm, "Outsourcing, Self-Service and the Telemobility of Work," 3.

20. Malik, Nicholson, and Heeks, "Development Implications of Online Outsourcing."

21. Sassen, *Mobility of Labor and Capital*.

22. Arieli, "Israeli-Palestinian Border Enterprises Revisited."

23. Yiftachel, "Shrinking Space of Citizenship"; Portugali, *Implicate Relations*; Blatman-Thomas, "Commuting for Rights."

24. Amitai Ziv, "Arabs in Israeli High-Tech Soars."

25. Baumer, "Former Top Intel Executive Weighs In."

26. Petryna, "Experimentality"; Iain Gately, *Rush Hour*.

27. Shamir, "Without Borders?"

28. Pasquetti, "Legal Emotions," 469.

29. Lamont and Mizrachi, *Responses to Stigmatization in Comparative Perspective*.

30. Brighenti, *Visibility in Social Theory and Social Research*.

31. Hasisi and Weisburd, "Going beyond Ascribed Identities"; Shamir, "Without Borders?"

32. Torpey, "Coming and Going," 255.

33. Vigh, "Motion Squared," 433; Baker, "Regime."

34. Weizman, *Hollow Land*; Berda, *Living Emergency*.

35. Azoulay and Ophir, *One-State Condition*; Gordon, *Israel's Occupation*.

36. Hanieh, *Lineages of Revolt*, 109.

37. ILO, "Workers of the Occupied Arab Territories" (2018); ILO, "Workers of the Occupied Arab Territories" (2019).

38. Joronen, "Spaces of Waiting"; Peteet, *Space and Mobility in Palestine*.

39. The permit system means that Israeli employers often resell unused work permits to brokers, who then sell them to Palestinians at inflated prices. Individual laborers are also forced to pay large amounts to brokers for transportation. The ILO estimated that Palestinian laborers in total lose between

$66 million and $389 million USD in a "broker tax" each year, and affected workers pay up to $716 a month to brokers for permits. ILO, "Workers of the Occupied Arab Territories" (2017).

40. Kelly, "'Jurisdictional Politics' in the Occupied West Bank."
41. Tawil-Souri, "Where Is the Political in Cultural Studies? 160.
42. Tawil-Souri, "Uneven Borders, Coloured (Im)mobilities," 155.
43. Canepari and Rosa, "Quiet Claim to Citizenship," 670.
44. Naciri, "Regards sur l'évolution de la citadinité au Maroc."

A MIDDLE-CLASS GATEWAY TO TEL AVIV

Palestinian Citizens at Israel's Liberal University

MANY MEMBERS OF THE YOUNG Palestinian middle class in Israel encountered Tel Aviv first through the gateway of its main university. The number of Palestinian citizens who studied at Israeli universities grew significantly between 2000 and 2017, increasing by 78.5 percent, from twenty-six thousand to forty-seven thousand.[1] At the time of my research, about two thousand Arab students were enrolled at Tel Aviv University, which, by 2018, increased to around three thousand or 14.5 percent of the total student population. For these students, the university served as an important gateway into their futures as successful professionals in Israel. Although it was built in the area that once belonged to the Palestinian village of al-Sheikh Muwannis, the university's green campus and its modernist white buildings now symbolize the internationalist modernity associated with Tel Aviv.[2] When the state of Israel was founded, The Hebrew University of Jerusalem was still the only university in the country. Campaigns for a second university, in Tel Aviv, first led to a small science campus in the Abu Kabir area, also named after a former Palestinian village, in southern Tel Aviv. Turning the "dream into reality," the "splendor of the Jerusalem campus" was soon to be matched by the newly founded Tel Aviv University.[3]

The university takes up a central position in the imaginary of Tel Aviv as an essentially Jewish and modernist city, with "shallow roots" and an "ostensible lack of memory."[4] When I chatted with students, I often asked them why they chose to study in Tel Aviv over Jerusalem or Haifa, which had more significant Palestinian populations and a more vibrant Palestinian cultural climate. A frequent answer the students gave was that they preferred "liberal" Tel Aviv over the divided and politically "tense" reality of Jerusalem. Moreover, many of the students had grown up in close proximity to Haifa in Israel's north and liked the fact that Tel Aviv was farther away from the watchful eyes of their families. The university was not only an entry ticket into successful professional careers but also a gateway into a large city.

The students are from very diverse backgrounds and have varying aspirations for Tel Aviv. In most cases, the university campus confronted young Palestinian citizens of Israel with a fairly new social world, and, for some, this confrontation initially involved some kind of politicization. Israeli university campuses have long been a microcosm for emerging future trends in the Palestinian community in Israel.[5] Such political activism has a tense relationship with the gradual sacrifices the young emerging middle class of Palestinians in Israel must make to be successful and to access Tel Aviv. This road to success through higher education has been full of obstacles.

The Palestinian citizens have been systematically marginalized in Israeli higher education, where official use of the Arabic language is close to nonexistent in courses, in services, on signage, and on websites.[6] A survey of thirteen hundred Arab students found that half experienced racism and discrimination while at university, including racist comments from the faculty.[7] This overall marginalization reflects the unequal power relationships that prevail in the wider society, with the deeply rooted cultural hegemony of the Jewish majority.[8] Official initiatives by the government and by civil society actors have tried to tackle some of these problems.[9] At Tel Aviv University and elsewhere, officials sometimes imposed restrictions on political events, and the ensuing controversy repeatedly made the boundaries of official tolerance for a Palestinian community on campus clear. This sense of political marginalization has inspired some to think that only a Palestinian university in Israel could change this but attempts to create such a campus were prevented, reportedly for fear of nationalist activity.[10]

The Palestinian people have been described as resilient learners who place a particularly high value on education, and they are said to be among the best-educated people in the Arab world.[11] But fulfilling this national Palestinian ambition of learning at Tel Aviv University—in a Jewish Israeli city—was an entirely different story. While higher education formally produces a highly educated Palestinian middle class in Israel, the day-to-day experience of such class formation does not escape national, racial, and gendered categorizations.[12] Tel Aviv embodies Israeli liberalism through implicit promises of social upward mobility and equal opportunity, but, for the Palestinian citizens, it does so only under certain conditions. As part of their conditional inclusion in Israel's skilled economy, the students learn that they are expected to moderate their political behavior and meet the demand for "good" and hardworking "Arabs." The ever-present threat of disadvantage and stigmatization inspires some to excel far beyond the average, thus inscribing a racializing logic into the formation of class mobility and professional success.

THE UNIVERSITY AS A CONDITIONAL PASSAGE TO CAREERS

Tel Aviv University is where many young Palestinian citizens first experience the process of *conditional inclusion*: a gradual incorporation into the economy that opens socioeconomic opportunities and selective passages to professional success only under certain built-in conditions. The students are often as young as eighteen when they first arrive on the campus, and it becomes the place from which they negotiate their emerging relationship with the Jewish Israeli city.[13] It poses the first opportunity for young Palestinian citizens to maintain normal daily contact with Jewish Israelis.[14] Their curiosity about the city and its life often goes hand in hand with anxieties about being excluded from its opportunities. Some who delve into the city also fear being criticized by other Palestinians for becoming "Aravivim"—a combination of the Hebrew words for *Arabs* and *Tel Aviv* that suggests an internalization of the Israeli stereotype of Arabs and a loss of authentic identity. The problem is that the two anxieties somewhat contradict each other: to access the city, controversial daily compromises ought to be made, but these compromises, in turn, could make other Palestinians suspicious about their close relationship with the Jewish city. Palestinian students thus face a tremendously complex situation to begin with.

One university official who knows much about these complications is the social worker Fadi. His office is inside the dormitory compounds, from where he supports Palestinian students on behalf of the university. Sipping instant coffee from a plastic cup, Fadi told me that a growing number of students are now deciding to stay in Tel Aviv after their graduation despite its Jewish Israeli character. A decade earlier this was still a rather unusual thing to do, especially for women. Unlike many of their hometowns where professional opportunities are scarce, the Palestinians would find "everything" in Tel Aviv to make a positive difference in their lives, as Fadi put it: "Work, life, and money. You are free!"

The pressing question many of them face is how to access the liberal aspects of the city and its economy despite its illiberal characteristics, namely the almost absolute exclusion of Palestinian Arab culture and identity from its space. Their problem is how to access "work, life, and money" and be "free" despite two partly contradictory pressures: (1) the pressure to adapt to the requirements of higher education, work, and social life in the Jewish city, and (2) the recurring pressure to demonstrate political solidarity and meet the expectations of their families and the wider Palestinian activist community. The problem requires at least two balancing acts: (1) between their professional aspirations and the visibility of their national and political identity, and (2) between participating in urban life and meeting the expectations of Palestinian peers, neighbors, or family members.

Fadi witnessed many of these balancing acts while counseling Palestinian students on behalf of Tel Aviv University. He had served in this role for seven years by the time we first met in his office. Fadi hopes to lower the students' rate of failure and wants to improve their grades, saying: "The Arab students think they already climbed Mount Everest when they arrive here, they have a strong feeling of achievement. After that, their way downward starts quickly." According to Majid Al-Haj, a former vice president of Haifa University, Arab students spend the first two years coping with the basic problem of absorption in a university. This is the result not only of language difficulties and other disadvantages but of "a cultural atmosphere many perceive as foreign."[15] Indeed, according to Fadi, many students struggle with the transition from life in a closely knit Palestinian town into this large Jewish city, where "a feeling of estrangement develops."

The estrangement of the villager in the big city is an old theme that is hardly specific to the Palestinian experience of Tel Aviv. But Fadi is referring to cultural and political estrangement. The political climate that engenders such estrangement became clear to me when I was embedded as a PhD research student at Tel Aviv University. I was based at the Department of Sociology and Anthropology, which holds important expertise on Palestinian citizens of Israel, but only a small minority of students and scholars are Palestinian themselves. In parallel to my involvement at the department, I acquired some firsthand classroom experience through my attendance of the university's Hebrew language classes alongside new Jewish immigrants and a single Palestinian.

One day in this language class, an American-born student held a presentation in praise of the Israeli army unit that stormed the Gaza flotilla in 2010, killing many of the activists on board. While opinions on this matter certainly differ, nationalist and militaristic points of view are consistently encouraged by the teachers. The contents of the lessons are equally straightforward in their partiality. One text we read in Hebrew was titled "The Arab Village in Israel," which proclaimed that Zionism modernized Arabs but neglected to mention how Israel's war for statehood effectively erased hundreds of those villages in Palestine. When I pointed out this distortion of the historical evidence in class, using carefully crafted intermediate-level Hebrew, the teacher responded dismissively, saying, "We don't talk about politics here."

Politics was always used to dismiss critical perspectives on Palestinian issues. Needless to say, most of what we read in class was deeply political, as were many of the teacher's explanations. But it was the sort of politics that lay within the consensus of the dominant majority. Sometimes we would ask the teacher for the meaning of a word, and she would paraphrase it in Hebrew. One example was when we did not understand the Hebrew word for incitement. After a few seconds, she provided a hint, saying in Hebrew, "When Palestinian kids throw stones, they do so because of . . . ?" The answer was, of course, "*incitement!*" Once again, I felt challenged by the climate of affirmation and suggested that Israeli military operations in the West Bank may be incitement enough for teenagers to throw stones. A Russian immigrant in class turned his head toward me and said deprecatingly: "You are a leftie, or what?"

Such language courses play an important role as "civilizing" instruments: as a powerful process of entangled state formation and subject formation that fosters norm-oriented self-restraint.[16] Language classes indirectly seek to establish an understanding both of opinions that are outside the Israeli consensus and of some politics being tolerated while others are not. Although I had a Palestinian classmate, Elias, he focused on the language learning and did not get involved in these discussions. He said that he never really spoke much Hebrew before, while adding: "I have to take Hebrew classes to qualify for this system, they don't. They get higher grades than me."

Qualifying for the Israeli "system" was a particularly difficult struggle for Elias, who started out by commuting daily between Tel Aviv and Jerusalem during his first weeks on campus. For several reasons, he was a rather unusual student at an Israeli university. Although many young Palestinian citizens of Israel do not have strong Hebrew skills when they arrive at the university, most are fluent enough. Elias had Israeli citizenship, but his father was from Bethlehem and not an Israeli citizen, while his mother lived in East Jerusalem. As a devout Christian, Elias frequently traveled to Bethlehem where he painted religious icons in a workshop and put them up for sale to tourists. Having grown up in Jerusalem, he attended the Collège de Frères, a prominent mixed Jewish-Arab school in Palestine founded by a Catholic order in 1876. This is one reason why Elias's French was far better than his Hebrew, which is a problem in Tel Aviv.

Elias ended up in Tel Aviv after he had unsuccessfully applied both to the Hebrew University of Jerusalem and to Haifa University. University admission, or "qualifying for the system," generally depended on students' results in both a matriculation exam, at the end of high school, and a so-called psychometric exam, which covered verbal reasoning, mathematics, and English. On average, Palestinian students in Israel have lower matriculation exam scores and are much more likely to fail the psychometric test than Jewish students. Half of all prospective Arab students are rejected from universities because of their poor score on the exam.[17] Between language difficulties, entry hurdles, and a climate of cultural and political estrangement, the passage into professional life is full of hurdles for Palestinian citizens and demands constant adaptation.

BETWEEN CAMPUS POLITICS AND PRAGMATISM: BALANCING STUDENT ACTIVISM WITH CAREER PROSPECTS

The law student Said from the village of Tur'an close to Nazareth had much balancing to do between his aspired career as a lawyer and his political activism. To begin with, his own family history already made it difficult not to be political. Like the families of so many other Palestinian students at Israeli universities, parts of his family became refugees in 1948. They were since forced to live under Israeli occupation in the West Bank.

"Why can't my cousin come here?" Said asked during breakfast at his Tel Aviv apartment, just outside the university. His paternal family used to live in the former Palestinian village of Hittin close to Tiberias. The Israeli state later destroyed the village, leaving only the mosque in its place. A small number of the displaced residents of Hittin managed to remain within this newly formed state, living as Palestinian citizens of Israel in Tur'an, Nazareth, and other Arab towns.[18] This history of displacement and exile, sometimes apparent but more often silent and private, lives on with Said and other students on Israeli campuses. Their personal implication in this history is one reason why they want to be politically active on campus.

Many young students who come to Tel Aviv University experience some form of political awakening at first, and their exposure to the Jewish city helps trigger this awakening. The activist Rami, who went to a Jewish Israeli school before joining Tel Aviv, told me about his own process of awakening: "In my second year at university there was the Gaza flotilla, and after the Mavi Marmara incident we stood here at the university gate holding up signs against the murder of the Turkish activists. One of the photographs of our protest went big in one of the large media, 'Walla.' [Jewish] Friends began un-liking me on Facebook and many others started discussing with me. My classmates felt that because I grew up with them, I would be pro-Israeli, and not Palestinian.

This was in the second year of university, and I wasn't really politically active at that time."

During his first two years, he had only joined a handful of events on campus and went to some of the parties that Palestinian students organized. But when he took a course at Tel Aviv University on the "Jewish-Arab conflict" during his third year, things began to change: "We were nine Arabs and nine Jews who sat together every week for two hours to work on issues of the conflict. I felt that the Jewish Israelis became a mirror for me to discover who I am, what my identity is, that I am not Israeli, but that I have a different national identity. In these three months of the course my Palestinian identity was built."

At the time of my research, he was running in the campus political leadership elections for the nationalist party Balad. Ironically, their immersion at an Israeli university is what politicized some Palestinian students and deepened an awareness of their distinct national identity. Demonstrations and other political events are not necessarily frequented by the majority of the students, but they are very visible.

During 2013 and 2014, I joined a small crowd of Palestinian students and some Jewish and international supporters who came together in front of the university's main entrance to commemorate the Palestinian national "catastrophe" of 1948, the "Nakba." It was a gathering demanding recognition in a highly volatile context: the so-called Nakba Law granted the finance minister the authority to reduce the budget of state-funded bodies that openly reject Israel as a Jewish state or mark the state's Independence Day as a day of mourning. The mere approval of the ceremony at the university a year earlier had unleashed a storm of discussions and arguments in the Israeli parliament.[19] This context highlighted the marginalized status of the Palestinian position in Israeli cities.

For the participating Palestinian students, the Nakba was as much about external recognition as it was a deeply personal and emotional matter. Surrounded by a metal fence put up by the police, some of the students formed the letters N-A-K-B-A as a human chain at the 2013 event, where Said was an organizer. The police fence that surrounded the protesters was a symbol of spatial confinement that also provided protection from the agitated crowds of Jewish Israeli nationalists that stood on the other side, waving Israeli flags and denouncing the Nakba as a lie. Resilient in the face of disturbing provocations, Palestinian students went on and spoke about their family histories, many of which involved the displacement and expulsion from now destroyed villages or confiscated lands. After all, the university itself stood in an area that once belonged to the Palestinian village of al-Sheikh Muwannis, and the event was aware of this fact.

As the counterprotest intensified and the time permitted for the ceremony ran out, one of the Palestinian activists announced through a megaphone: "If you want to go somewhere, walk into university first and leave the campus from another gate, in order to be secure." Dispersing back into the fenced campus area implied a sense of security, while a visibly collective presence created a sense of vulnerability once the police and the fence were gone. This exemplified the limited possibilities of Palestinians in Tel Aviv for expressing their political opinions and commemorating their history collectively, visibly, and securely.

Despite the politicization of students on campus, as the years went by, another more pragmatic aspiration grew more prominent. At his apartment, where he lived with three Palestinian students, Said explained, while we had breakfast, "I came here to lead my life alone and independently, and of course for my studies." "So, Tel Aviv is the right choice?" I asked, prompting another quite different part of the answer: "Here in Tel Aviv we don't have a community like the Jews. They have celebrations and all kinds of aspects of their life they go through together. We are not part of that community. It's hard to be just human here. You are always either Arab or Jew in this place." Said realized, at both work and university, that students who wanted to be successful and accepted needed to become recognized as a particular kind of "Arab" first, to qualify as a "good Arab" that was docile, hardworking, and not visibly an activist.[20] This balancing act demanded sacrifices and compromises.

Political activists have long criticized such accommodating compromises. For example, during the second intifada in the 2000–2001 academic year, national mobilization heavily politicized campuses. In response, university administrators issued a countrywide ban on demonstrations and other political events. What appeared to frustrate Palestinian student activists even more was the pragmatic attitude of their parents, as one student said: "Our parents have been too busy preaching avoidance of political activity. They say that politics is for those who have spare times after classes, and that our time should be devoted to real work, one that creates income."[21] This comment hints at a long-standing tension between generations among Palestinian citizens of Israel: a tension between focusing on "real work" that will lead to success, on the one hand, and being involved in political activism, on the other.

Although the campus also featured political activism, simultaneously, the liberal university space in Tel Aviv embodied the other end of the trajectory, as the place where hard work can potentially be turned into success despite discrimination and disadvantages. Importantly, these ambivalent aspects of Palestinian life in Israel are not necessarily experienced as contradictory and may form a productive "duplexity," where the requirements of daily routine do not

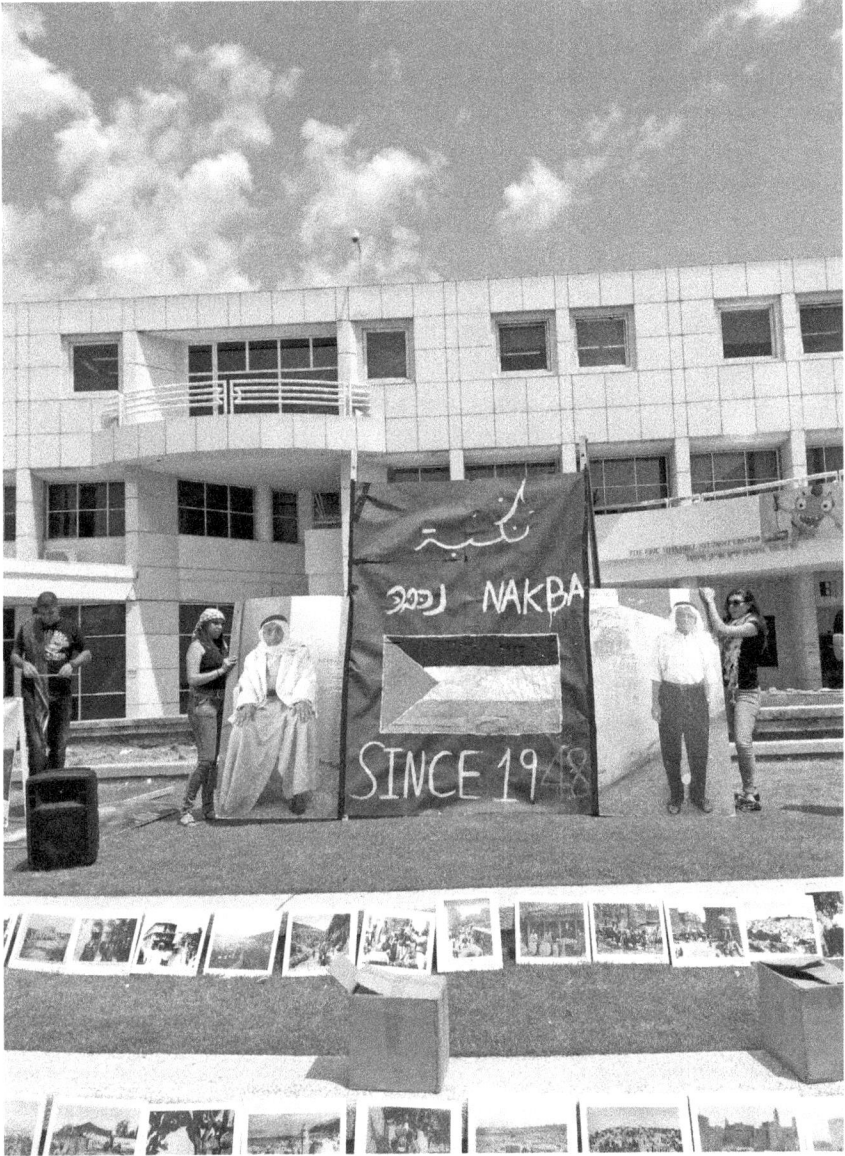

Figure 2.1 Palestinian students at Tel Aviv University commemorate the Nakba of 1948.
Source: Andreas Hackl.

invalidate political activism, and vice versa.[22] Yet, the problem is that they invalidate one another as far as the public visibility of such politics is concerned: For Palestinians in Tel Aviv, becoming visible as nationalist activists can have serious consequences for their access to jobs, housing, and the social and leisure spaces of urban life more generally. The need for a professional career and money, maybe in order to start a family and marry, is often more pressing than the pursuit of larger political goals. As one Palestinian activist and former Tel Aviv resident told me, in relation to fighting injustice: "You can't struggle like this all alone. If I know that the revolution will come in two months, I get into financial problems and struggle. But this revolution is not coming."

During Said's sixth year of studying, his future career as a prospective lawyer in Israel moved closer and the required devotion to "real work" and "creating income" became more urgent. While in his apartment, I asked Said about such compromises. He nodded, stood up from the table, walked into another room, and came back with a kaffiyeh in his hand—the quintessential Palestinian scarf. Said wrapped the scarf around his neck and turned to me: "If I go to university with this kaffiyeh, everybody will look at me and think I am a terrorist. We avoid wearing such symbols. If you want to live normal in this society, you learn to hide politics." Said spearheaded Palestinian political activities on campus, and yet he avoided wearing political symbols for the sake of career opportunities. This also applied to his student job as a waiter in an Israeli restaurant. The university was where middle-class Palestinian citizens learned how to perform the role of a particular kind of person, while making other aspects of identity temporarily invisible. Said had just applied for internship positions at law offices in Tel Aviv and pointed out: "I also avoid posting too much political stuff on Facebook. Some things are difficult for Jews to swallow and employers check Facebook pages."

As they became senior students and soon-to-be professionals, the Palestinians had to carefully manage the visibility of their political activism and their expressions of national solidarity. One of the characteristic features of modern cities has long been "the valuation of individual differences at the expense of what is held in common in social life," sometimes causing tremendous strain for individuals as they negotiate their individual desires and social expectations.[23] The dilemma in the colonial-liberal city of Tel Aviv is that access to "what is common" is as restricted for Palestinians as their ability to have their "different" identity valuated positively. Accessing the economy of Tel Aviv and jobs in Israel, more generally, required tactics of invisibility that could be "trialed" and "tested" during university time.

Similar to Said, the psychology student Ilham felt like she had to compromise on her identification as a Palestinian in certain contexts. On a normal day, she wore a necklace with Arabic letters on it, but, at her first therapy practice during an internship, she had a Jewish patient and decided that she had to get rid of the "elephant in the room," as she called it. "I didn't want to bring it up this way. They know from my accent and name that I am not Jewish anyway." These tactics of immersive invisibility are especially relevant for educated middle-class Palestinians who are professionally ambitious and have the right background to achieve their ambitions in Israel. Making some aspects of identity invisible is one key to strategic destigmatization attempts; yet another is with investments in education and hard work that inspire faith in a liberal meritocratic ideal.[24]

In this self-consciously liberal university space, higher education for Palestinian citizens inspires hopes of excellence, success, and, ultimately, a hope for the positive acknowledgment of their identity by having their acquired qualifications and successes recognized. The neoliberal requirements of self-improvement, professional development, and individualism gain an ethnonational component in a space where access to opportunities is distributed differentially along ethnonational lines. The university space may be a communal ground for meeting friends and peers, both Palestinian and Jewish. But it also serves as a breeding ground of liberal universal values and neoliberal aspirations and hopes: that hard work and educational success help create social mobility and recognition of good citizens and that the mere civility and professional development of individuals translates into equal opportunities in the job market, *despite* being "Arab."

However, the reality I encountered was that Palestinian citizens of Israel needed to be better than others to qualify as equal. The student Amira, who I first met in 2013, expressed her hopes the following way: "I have to work harder on my own in order to keep up with Jewish colleagues. I am working hard so my marks will be higher than theirs and so I will stand out when I am looking for a job." The prospect of discrimination pushed Amira to work harder than the average citizen, driven by the fear of falling behind the imposed stigma and failing. Tel Aviv was the ideal place for Amira's pursuit, and, in her own words, it was "like New York or London, like cities where people won't look at me as an Arab, as if I were stuck in another time or not modern."

These classic liberal qualities of the modern city—as a form of unmarked anonymity among individual urbanites—were meant to transcend differences and create an urban life where being "Arab" mattered less than it did, say, in a divided city such as Jerusalem. Yet, as much as she tried to make this stigma invisible through exceptional performance, she worried about not succeeding after all: "There are still difficulties. Maybe I will be in the same position as my Jewish classmate, even more exceptional, even on a higher scale, of better quality. . . . The fear is that despite all efforts I invest, they will prefer someone who has served in the [Israeli] army."[25]

PRESSURES TO BECOME A "GOOD ARAB"

To borrow wording from Ghassan Hage, Tel Aviv "instills" in middle-class Palestinian citizens the aspiration of universality (such as equality), but it "denies them this aspiration the very moment it encourages them to aspire to it and believe that they are entitled to it"; they have to "endure both the hope and the shattering of hope" as part of this process.[26] The role of the university space for Palestinian citizens in Tel Aviv is crucial for this instillment of aspirations, amid frequent Israeli demands for Palestinians to be "good Arabs."

Since its origins in the early Jewish settlement of Palestine, the category of the "good Arab" has become a powerful and controversial metaphor in Israeli public discourse.[27] It exemplifies the Palestinian dilemma of accessing socioeconomic opportunities in the Jewish Israeli spaces that stigmatize and seek to suppress their ethnonational identity. This stereotypical label refers to "moderates" who do not take nationalist positions and who accord legitimacy to Israel's existence and its actions.[28] While nobody would use this derogatory term as a self-ascription, Jewish Israeli employers, landlords, or colleagues often expect Palestinian citizens to fulfill its underlying criteria.

This became clear when I asked a former Tel Aviv University student and friend to serve as a guarantor for me, as a prospective landlady had asked for an Israeli citizen to cosign the contract for a rental apartment. From a busy road in Tel Aviv, we took a stairway up to a law office, determined to sign the rental contract. We stepped into the office and the landlady greeted us, while my friend, a Palestinian citizen of Israel, introduced herself by saying, "Nice to meet you. I am Lina." Seemingly shocked to hear an Arab name, the landlady coldly replies: "What . . . are you?" (mah . . . at?). After a few seconds of suppressed silence, the owner sank into an armchair and turned to Rima: "So, you are Arab? Do you speak Hebrew? Do you have a job?" As an Israeli citizen, Lina spoke fluent Hebrew and answered that she had a job. Seemingly unimpressed, the owner turned to the lawyer and said, "I ask because we only take *good Arabs*, right?" The lawyer stares evasively into a book on the desk in front of him and nods indifferently: "Only good Arabs, yes."

Although Jewish Israelis are hardly aware of it, the trope of the "good Arab" has its origins in the settler-colonial strategy of pressuring Palestinians into becoming loyal and docile subjects. It is closely related to other colonial contexts, such as the "taming" of Algeria and Algerians through a classic divide-and-rule politics that separated good assimilable subjects from bad subjects, Berbers from Arabs.[29] The ultimate "good Arab" would then be the one who voluntarily serves in the Israeli army, yet "even good Arabs are always potentially bad in a Jewish state."[30] Among Palestinian students at Tel Aviv University, this deeply rooted category became relevant not only in the sense of pressures to keep a low political profile but also in the sense of having to work harder than everyone else in the hope of being recognized as equal: being not only "good" but also "better."

In the case of Amira, the aspiration to gain recognition as a successful and equal professional involved hard work and a good deal of professional self-development. As she told me during one meeting: "Maybe I can volunteer in something humanitarian or anything else that proves strategic thinking, showing that I belong to Israeli society. So, I have to work harder by myself in order to catch up with the level of Jewish colleagues. I am working hard so my marks will be higher than theirs and so I will stand out when I am looking for a job."

She took distance learning courses with US-universities, worked herself up from internships, and earned money from marketing companies as an Arabic-language salesperson, which was a common job for Palestinian students in the city. When I spoke to Amira four years after our first conversation at the university, it became evident that she had a sense of long-term achievement similar to someone who had just completed a long and difficult journey. "Maybe all this success happened because I always had this fear," Amira said, referring to her fear that Jews would always be favored over her in the competitive workplace. She now felt, however, that she was finally in Tel Aviv "because it's a choice, not just a need." She added, "In the past it was a need and a question of access."

Looking back at the years since she started her studies, she said, "My parents always told me to be realistic, that I will go back to the village and that I won't be accepted as an Arab in these firms in Tel Aviv." Many internships, training courses, and jobs later, she felt ready to open her own business in Tel Aviv, saying, "I was so scared that Jewish people will always be better and valued higher than me. But now I am setting the grades myself. This whole journey made me more confident in my career. I did a lot of things I didn't even like. Now I am able to be me."

Some cities require people to do things and be visible as "someone else" for a while until they reach the position, confidence, and aspiration that allows them to be themselves, to be "me." Success, therefore, can entail the requirement of mimicry, or *dissimulation*, which has defined the lives of stigmatized minorities in a variety of contexts, including the practice of taqiya among Shia Muslim minorities.[31] In the colonial context, acts of mimicry reveal the "inherent contradictions embedded in the effort to shape subjects according to political and cultural norms."[32] Colonized people may be pressured to adopt settlers' customs and norms, despite the ultimate inability to fully emulate settler "whiteness."[33] While it is true that mimicry adapts to dominant ideals and identities, it also reflects the flexibility of individual agency to respond to such dominance through adaptation.

Moreover, mimicry is also a tool for colonial space making, a way of "whitening" cities or regions after having cleansed them of indigenous populations.[34] Connecting this spatial mimicry of a settler city to individual tactics of mimicry allows us to see how colonial liberalism seeks to shape colonized liberal subjects as people who are included as inferior outsiders. Amira and many other Palestinian citizens see Tel Aviv as the liberal "white city" the colonists have built, while at the same time aspiring to be recognized as an unmarked and equal part of the city and its ostensible liberalism. Yet, the trope of the "good Arab" shows that even the best "Arabs" remain essentially racialized as outsiders despite their groundbreaking professional achievements.

The experience and fear of stigmatization and discrimination triggered a long uphill struggle in Amira, as she negotiated societal expectations associated with the "good Arab" and even aimed to become far better than others. Yet, it also led to a sense of emancipation and independence, however limited it may have been. By using the socioeconomic opportunities available in the city, in addition to its university, Palestinian citizens make difficult compromises, but they often do so with a clear goal in mind. Their tactics of invisibility and mimicry are strategic in the sense that they have a strong self-awareness of the potential exclusion they are responding to by taking concrete actions to weaken its force. Importantly, the university space is not only a gateway into the Israeli economy but also a space within which the liminality between the city and their hometowns and families plays out, requiring yet another balancing act.

TEL AVIV AS THE FORBIDDEN CITY: THE "DOUBLE LIVES" OF FEMALE STUDENTS

It was meant to be a glorious day for Lina and her family when, after a few extra years of studying for her bachelor's degree at Tel Aviv University, her name was eventually announced by the professor hosting the annual graduation ceremony of her school. Excitement was in the air, and tears in her eyes: an expression of relief and joy but also of uncertainty and regret about the late arrival of this very transition.

In the eyes of many Palestinian parents in Israel, living in Tel Aviv away from home is justifiable as long as their children are studying. Yet, studying can also be a cover for things much less official. Lina started working as an Arabic-speaking service operator, at an IT-company in Tel Aviv, halfway through her university years and moved into her own studio apartment, although her parents were left to believe that she still lived in the dormitories, which were considered more appropriate. In Tel Aviv, studying soon became secondary for Lina, and her time shifted more toward life and work, allowing her to also make new friends. Her income increased, and her lifestyle changed. Simultaneously, all of this delayed her eventual graduation, which was, of course, not entirely unintentional, because graduation would mean going back home, or at least facing the pressure to do so. Eventually, this would lead to questions about marrying and settling down.

Young female students like Lina face the difficult balancing act of how to reconcile their controversial social immersion in Tel Aviv with the competing sense of responsibility toward their families and the wider Palestinian community. As a woman in her early twenties, Lina enjoyed the city's lifestyle but had to manage different roles and lives, one in Tel Aviv, another in her hometown. Her mother acted as a constant reminder of this second world, called "home." Conversations with her sometimes made Lina feel bad for not being home enough, making her feel like an outsider compared to her sisters and youngest brother, who still lived with their parents. At other times, neighbors and family members put pressure on her mother. Once an anonymous caller threatened them over photographs she had seen of their daughters on Facebook. What was especially hard for Lina was that she could not share her life in Tel Aviv with her parents, because she would have to lie about it. Her entire life in Tel Aviv was shrouded in a sense of obligation to keep things more or less covert.

However, although living in the city alienated Lina from life in her hometown, she also became increasingly estranged from Tel Aviv. She began to dislike its Jewish Israeli character, the constant Hebrew speaking, and the leisure consumerism with its high expenses. Some friendships she previously fostered with Jewish colleagues at work seemed increasingly superficial. She was tired of being the "token Arab" in conversations, which often turned political and emotionally troubling. Realizing that she had given up her political ideals for a convenient life in the city, her desire to live in a more Palestinian environment grew stronger the more deeply immersed in the bubble of Tel Aviv she became.

After graduating, she moved back home for a while but eventually took up residence in Haifa, which has a visible and strong Palestinian community of activists and cultural organizers. Haifa was also more acceptable to her family nearby, and it did not have the "immoral" image of Israeli Tel Aviv. What used to be a reason for not living in Haifa became a desirable objective after several years in Jewish Tel Aviv. The university not only fulfills an important function in Palestinian women's balancing acts, because their families recognize studying as a legitimate reason for being in Tel Aviv; it also serves them as a temporary gateway for exploring Tel Aviv's urban and professional life: an exploration that often leads to a feeling of estrangement.

Some of these dynamics are masterfully brought to the surface in Maysaloun Hamoud's film *Bar Bahar* (*In Between*), which follows the fictional lives of three young Palestinian women who end up living together in an apartment in Tel Aviv. The religious computer science student Nour joins Layla and her cousin Salma in their Tel Aviv apartment, because the dormitories are being renovated, initially with the plan of only staying briefly until she finds a new place to stay. At first there is a lot of tension between them, but as each of them faces their own difficult struggles, balancing their individual aspirations with familial and communal pressures to conform, their journeys, ultimately, bring them closer together. The film intentionally pitches extremes against one another, revealing the balancing acts the three women perform between life in Tel Aviv, their romantic relationships, patriarchy, and their families. The final scene first shows them on the dance floor of a house party, from which they eventually all escape to sit on the roof together overlooking the city at night. While Salma and Layla smoke a cigarette, Nour sips from a glass of juice. They sit quietly and seem unhappy, conveying a suppressing silence that underscores the way their constant struggles have scarred them and how their lives in between often end up in dissatisfying double binds. The story of Nour, in particular, emphasizes that many Palestinian citizens see Tel Aviv and its lifestyle as essentially a forbidden city and an immoral place.

Returning from fiction to research, I learned from the social worker Fadi about one female Tel Aviv University student, from the small Palestinian town of Qalansuwa, who had initially approached him for help after being beaten by her father; he had seen a photograph of his daughter in Tel Aviv on Facebook, in which she wore shorts and a short-sleeved shirt while holding an alcoholic drink. Although Fadi admitted this was an extreme case, Palestinian families often viewed Tel Aviv as an immoral and, thus, "forbidden" city. According to Fadi, because of this, female students often ended up living double lives: "They come to Tel Aviv University, where there is no surveillance, where they can do everything they want and are not allowed to do at home; here in Tel Aviv they are person X, and in the village they are person Y. If a girl has a relationship with a guy, she can't just tell her parents. If she goes to clubs, she won't tell. She will dress differently." Female students can do much to resist and go beyond tradition, but the question is whether they are willing to pay the price, said Fadi, adding that "this price includes actual killings; this is also a reality."

The Palestinian female students navigated the possibilities available in this large city parallel to the role expectations of their own communities. Unlike most men, they are often expected to "preserve themselves" in-line with female gender roles and Palestinian-Arab tradition. Indeed, Palestinian women in Israel must maintain a delicate balance between the ideas of egalitarian individualism and their loyalty to their family.[35] In some ways, Israeli cities limit the freedom of Palestinian women, but, in other ways, they have a liberating effect.[36] The same is true for Tel Aviv, but, unlike mixed cities such as Haifa, immersion in this Jewish city is particularly problematic for Palestinian women because many Palestinians see it as, essentially, Jewish Israeli, playful, outgoing, and morally illegitimate.

Some female students at Tel Aviv University nevertheless talk about Tel Aviv as a liberal and anonymous place where they have control over their lives, although defending this control requires difficult negotiations. In her last year of study, the psychology student Ilham shared an apartment with her husband and being married certainly made things easier. Asked whether she would return back home, she once told me: "After living in Tel Aviv for years you can't live in the village anymore. Because you got used to free life; you reach a point where you realize that you will lose it all when you go back home." As discussed earlier, it is common among female students at Tel Aviv University to delay their graduation in order to push back the date on which they are expected to come "back home." Several weeks later, Ilham reflected once again about staying in Tel Aviv: "My parents keep on asking me, 'When are you coming back, when are you settling down?' And then I find myself telling them, 'Next year we will finish studying and then we come back.' But I know deep inside that we will never go back."

Although she is already married, which is one requirement for "settling down," she was still being asked when she would finally settle down. In the eyes of many Palestinian parents, Tel Aviv is hardly a legitimate place to settle down. It is, perhaps, a place to study, and merely one important step in a journey of professional and personal life. Both the village and Tel Aviv have their disadvantages, but, for Ilham, Tel Aviv's exclusive character is, ultimately, less problematic than the restrictions of her home village: "There are traditions I have to obey, occasions I have to attend, holidays, funerals, weddings. Being here [in Tel Aviv] allows me *not* to do all that. Things are under my control [in Tel Aviv]. But when I am [back home] I have no choice.

This is the big thing about living here. To be independent, to control my life and do things the way I want to, being in charge of all the things I hated to do back home, which I did against my own will. I had to hide; I did not feel comfortable doing them."

Although being a student in Tel Aviv allowed Ilham to be "in charge" of everyday life, most female students have a lot of tactical balancing to do between Tel Aviv and their hometowns. Some of them are also political activists and carry the double burden of balancing between politics and pragmatism as well as reconciling their lives in Tel Aviv with their families and their expectations.

The Tel Aviv University student Nour—not to be confused with the fictional character in the film *Bar Bahar*—knew all too well how far these balancing acts could go. She was fifteen when she went to a Jewish boarding school in Jerusalem, although she grew up in an Arab village farther north. Her first encounter with Tel Aviv was after high school, when she joined a Jewish-Arab commune in Jaffa and became involved in activism. "It was so hard for people to understand, and for me to explain, what I was doing in my life," said Nour. She went on to explain her struggle between the village and Tel Aviv: "So I started the big lie. Or maybe it is better to call it double lives, rather than a big lie. Like telling everyone I live with girls and only meet girls. . . . Back in the village, at the age of 19, I was in another world without the freedom I had the years before. Every time I went back to the village, I became a different person. . . . I couldn't go out until after 10 or 11. I couldn't smoke. I had to wear different clothes. Then I applied to university."

She went to live in the dormitories, where she shared a room with two girls from Baqa al-Gharbiyyah, a Palestinian town north of Tel Aviv. One of them wore the headscarf and was quite religious. Nour said they liked her but thought she was "weird." Although she was in Tel Aviv, having to share a room with two Palestinian girls who had different ideas about life was actually "worse than the village": "In the dorms, I was so afraid to be in the headlines. . . . They could say bad things about me, because my lifestyle was different, it didn't fit, like having a boyfriend, going out and coming back late from bars. . . . I felt more comfortable being around Jewish people in the beginning."

The university dormitories mirrored some of the restrictions she had hoped to escape in Tel Aviv, making it even more difficult for her, because now the faraway "village" was present in the form of her very proximate roommates. Male students brought their thoughts with them from the village, too, and tried "to observe and surveil," she explained. At one point, men and other female students called her *sharmuta* (whore). "So, I tried to keep a low profile. I stayed in the dorms for one year and then I moved into an apartment in Ramat Aviv," the mostly Jewish neighborhood around campus, said Nour, "It's like living a whole life in-between." The desire to keep a safe distance from other Palestinians in Tel Aviv only intensifies the feeling of living between two irreconcilable worlds. Moving between them is an important skill for those who make use of the city's social and economic opportunities. The university space becomes not only the ground on which many Palestinians learn how to manage the requirements of inclusion into this Jewish city and its economy but also the space where they learn to balance this controversial inclusion with their visibility as Palestinians vis-à-vis other Palestinians.

It is important to note, however, that many young Palestinian students at Tel Aviv University have neither the flexibility nor the desire to live between two worlds. When I approached the two nursing students Khalida and Fatmeh from Umm el-Fahm, it was immediately clear that their experience of university life had little to do with young women from secular Palestinian middle-class families. We agreed on a time to meet, and the only way they felt comfortable about meeting a male stranger was for me to walk next to them to the bus stop. From there, they took the bus back home every day during this Ramadan season, which Tel Aviv University did not recognize when it time-tabled peak exam time. Khalida wore a traditional Muslim thobe, a *jalabiyah*, and a headscarf. I asked if they would be able to work in Tel Aviv, but Khalida shook her head, saying: "I could work and maybe also wanted to. But any place that would accept me doesn't accept me if I am wearing this, the *jalabiyah*. So I don't work." As we walked through Ramat Aviv, the quiet residential area around the university, I wondered if they enjoyed other places in Tel Aviv and whether it changed their perspective somehow. Faced with these questions, Fatmeh said that they lived together in the dormitories and sometimes went to Cinema City or to a restaurant together, "but only in Ramat Aviv." They had never been to the beach, nor did they walk along the beachside boulevard. Just before we reached their bus stop, where I had to say goodbye, I asked Fatmeh if Tel Aviv was changing her in one way or another.

"Changing me? No! Our customs are how they are. It doesn't matter if I am in Umm el-Fahm or in Tel Aviv. I am not going to change because I am here," she said sternly. "Not even a little bit?" I asked. "No," she insisted. When I added that there were no Arabic books or theaters in Tel Aviv, nor anything else that would cater to Palestinians and their culture, they both nodded, and Fatmeh said: "Yes, it is as if we didn't exist."

The possibilities for Fatmeh and Khalida to immerse themselves in Tel Aviv and explore the many facets of this city were rather limited, not least because they were pulled back to Umm el-Fahm every day during Ramadan and every week outside of the festive season. As their life in the city remained largely restricted to the area around campus, their case serves as a reminder that complex balancing acts of Palestinians in Tel Aviv include diverse trajectories that are highly dependent on individual backgrounds. While Tel Aviv becomes an ambivalent place of careers and fun times for some students, it also features as a forbidden city in the lives of some female students from Muslim Palestinian backgrounds.

MOVING BEYOND DOUBLE LIVES: AN EMERGING PALESTINIAN MIDDLE CLASS IN TEL AVIV

At Tel Aviv University, the liberal and settler-colonial dimensions of this space overlap in myriad ways, and some of this overlap is visibly manifest: what were the land and the orange groves of the Palestinian village of al-Sheikh Muwannis, before the mass displacement and destruction of 1948, is now the home of the main university in Israel's ostensibly most liberal city. The experience of today's Palestinian students shows that this historical restructuring of settler-colonial space as exclusively Jewish Israeli and the contemporary inclusion of individual Palestinians into Tel Aviv are deeply entangled and continue to co-exist in highly ambivalent ways. The university is a key space in the fulfillment of the liberal promise of social mobility and of formal equality among individuals. But, as this promise is always conditional for Palestinians, the university becomes the stage for an attempted "civilizing process."[37] This process offers pathways to conditional inclusion and professional success based on the criteria of "civil" behavior that the dominant ethnonational majority determines. As I show in more detail in the following chapter, Tel Aviv taints class-related achievements for Palestinian citizens because professional success does not translate into a sense of equal citizenship within the city.

The contradictions of this liberal-colonial university manifest themselves among Palestinian students in two parallel balancing acts. In one act, they are required to moderate the visibility of their Palestinian identity to access Tel Aviv and meet certain criteria imposed for economic and professional success. In the other act, they must often minimize the visibility of their lives in Tel Aviv in relation to other Palestinians. They struggle against restrictions imposed by the city and by their families and communities. Both of these balancing acts are made more difficult by the fact that Israeli liberalism foreshadows the prospect of overcoming the exclusion that defines the status of indigenous Palestinians as categorical outsiders. Yet, it ultimately prevents this promise from becoming reality. As an urban space that is simultaneously desired and somehow forbidden, Tel Aviv symbolizes the ambivalent lives of young Palestinian citizens of Israel who must often fight on multiple fronts at the same time.

The university becomes the site for a process of class formation whereby upward mobility and middle-class citizenship are made conditional on the moderation and situational invisibility of national Palestinian identity. While some students learn to hide Palestinian scarfs, Arabic necklaces, or political posts on Facebook, in the hope of increasing their chances of career success and avoiding stigmatization, they may equally choose entirely different paths, while rejecting this framework of conditional inclusion. Crucially, the ones who do the balancing and the ones who are politically active are not two different sets of Palestinian students but, most commonly, the same person who must straddle various fields of activity that become contradictory. Some of these compromises may effectively increase social mobility and help students achieve concrete objectives in the face of recurring discrimination. As one Palestinian film student in Tel Aviv told me, as a way to justify studying at an Israeli university: "I am using their opportunities to be stronger against them."

We see in the next chapter that many of these students will graduate from university to become professionals with offices and workspaces in Tel Aviv and other Israeli cities. This determination to access opportunities against all odds, with the help of immersive tactics of invisibility, will not eliminate the unjust and unequal conditions that define the lives of the young Palestinian middle class in Israel. But it does help them achieve certain pragmatic objectives in response to stigmatization and pressures to conform.

NOTES

1. Zur, "Arabs in Israeli Universities Suffer Racism."
2. Mann, *Place in History*; Levine, *Overthrowing Geography*.
3. TLV University, "Evolution of Tel Aviv University."
4. Mann, *Place in History*, xiv.
5. Rabinowitz and Abu-Baker, *Coffins on Our Shoulders*, 125.
6. Sikkuy, Dirasat, and Van Leer, "Arabic and Arab Culture on Israeli Campuses."
7. Zur, "Arabs in Israeli Universities Suffer Racism."
8. Al-Haj, "Higher Education among the Arabs in Israel," 366.
9. Israeli governments, along with business initiatives and civil society organizations, have developed various plans to counter the marginalization of Arab citizens on Israeli campuses. A multiyear action plan was developed by the Israeli Council for Higher Education in response to policy recommendations by the Organization for Economic Cooperation and Development, for example.

10. See Ali, "Arab Citizens in Institutions of Higher Education," 26. US-based Texas A&M University agreed to open a branch in Nazareth in 2013, planning to replace the existing Nazareth Academic Institute with what was labeled a "Peace University." It should have provided an alternative to Israeli campuses for Arab students. The deal with Texas A&M was struck by Israeli officials, including then president Shimon Peres, and largely excluded Palestinian-Arab officials and academics (Cook, Mondoweiss.net, January 3, 2014). Despite the involved high-level diplomacy, the project was canceled in 2015, reportedly because of legal obstacles to establishing an independent foreign campus in Israel and funding problems, among other issues. Instead, Texas A&M planned to open an ocean observatory; the plan to expand educational opportunities for the Arab population in Nazareth "remains unrealized" (Redden, insidehighered.com, August 27, 2015).

11. Gerner and Schrodt, "Into the New Millenium"; Abu Lughod, "Palestinian Higher Education."

12. Skeggs, *Class, Self, Culture*.

13. Age difference mattered at the university: Jewish Israeli women and men are drafted into the mandatory army service for two and three years, respectively. Palestinian citizens are exempt, meaning that they arrive much younger, less experienced, and with fewer professional networks. Some courses, such as medicine, require students to be at least twenty years old, effectively forcing some Palestinian students to postpone their studies. Some leave and take up higher education abroad, either in Arab countries, such as Jordan, or in Europe and North America.

14. Rabinowitz and Abu-Baker, *Coffins on Our Shoulders*, 117.

15. Shtull-Trauring, "Interview with Haifa Professor Majid Al-Haj."

16. Elias, "Power and Civilisation."

17. Dirasat, "Uphill Climb," 9.

18. Zochrot, "Remembering Hittin."

19. Lis and Nesher, "Israeli Students and MKs Clash."

20. Hackl, "Good Arab."

21. Rabinowitz and Abu-Baker, *Coffins on Our Shoulders*, 121–22.

22. Jean-Klein, "Nationalism and Resistance," 92.

23. White, "Ambivalent Civility," 448.

24. Michèle Lamont et al., *Getting Respect*, 265.

25. The military service is where many young Israelis forge their first professional networks, and job applicants' roles and units in the army are a frequent topic in job interviews. Palestinian citizens are formally exempt from compulsory service and employers may evaluate this negatively, some even use a lack of military service as an indirect knockout tool of candidates.

26. Hage, "Affective Politics of Racial Mis-Interpellation," 121.

27. Hackl, "Good Arab."

28. Cohen, *Good Arabs*, 3.

29. Prochaska, *Making Algeria French*, 2, 234.

30. Kanaaneh, *Surrounded*, 67.

31. Sözer, *Managing Invisibility*; Virani, "Taqiyya and Identity in a South Asian Community."

32. Ram, "White but Not Quite," 736.

33. Babha, *Location of Culture.*

34. Ram, "White but Not Quite."

35. Sa'ar, "Lonely in Your Firm Grip," 734.

36. Herzog, "Choice as Everyday Politics," 10.

37. Elias, "Power and Civilisation"; Davetian, *Civility.*

THREE

—⟆—

WORKING IN THE CITY

Palestinian Middle-Class Citizens and Labor Commuters between Anonymity and Forced Invisibility

ON A SQUARE BELOW HIGH-RISE towers in Tel Aviv, white-collar workers rushed from their offices to the nearby train station in the Diamond Exchange District, one of the city's major commercial areas. I was here to meet the young engineer and recent university graduate Suha, a Palestinian citizen of Israel who worked for a technology start-up. She was dressed in smart office attire, and, at first glance, nothing distinguished her from the passing crowds. Then I saw the golden necklace she was wearing, which spelled out in shiny Arabic letters, *filistin* (Palestine). I asked her, "How do your Jewish Israeli colleagues react to this statement?" Touching it for a second, as if surprised to rediscover it, she said, "I take it off when I enter the office, and when I leave the office, I put it on again. At work, politics doesn't exist."

Palestinian citizens are often the sole "Arabs" in the offices of Tel Aviv, which makes them vulnerable to discrimination and stigmatization. In order to make successful use of Tel Aviv's jobs and universities they must adapt in particular ways. "Politics," as Suha put it, better stay outside of the workplace. This serves as shorthand for moderating controversial opinions and aspects of Palestinian identity in exchange for an unproblematic access to the city's economy and urban life. The various tactics include hiding Arabic language items and political symbols, avoiding certain topics in conversations with colleagues, and closing the office door when making phone calls in Arabic. Whatever the tactic, such situational concealment responds to the constant possibility of being disadvantaged and singled out on the basis of their Palestinian-Arab identity.

What begins at university for most middle-class citizens reaches deep into the offices and workspaces of the city, highlighting a continuity of the settler-colonial elimination of Palestinian visibility in Tel Aviv between education and the sphere of work. Individual tactics of immersive invisibility help middle-class Palestinians negotiate their access to jobs, careers, and urban life, more generally. At the same time, their immersion in the city offers a sense of anonymity and privacy in relation to other Palestinians who might deem their activities or presence illegitimate. The Palestinian middle class of Tel Aviv is, therefore, invisible in plain sight: they are "anonymous together," as the marketing expert Farah told me.

Farah had studied and worked in the city for thirteen years when we first met at a restaurant one late morning. As we sat down and started to chat, a waiter took our order. I asked for a coffee, and she ordered a glass of sparkling wine, saying that she never orders soft drinks in bars and restaurants. She had long become used to Tel Aviv's leisurely lifestyle. Importantly, for her, the city provided some distance and anonymity from other Palestinians whom she would not want to meet by coincidence in the wrong situation. "I think a lot of Arabs in Tel Aviv just like being anonymous in the city," Farah explained.

This anonymity works in two ways: it allows Palestinians the ability to remain unmarked as a Palestinian in the eyes of Jewish Israelis, and to be simultaneously undisturbed by other Palestinians. It is the kind of invisibility one chooses, which is only accessible to a minority of privileged urbanites. This includes forms of withdrawal and civility that ease social interactions between citizens who are both strangers and different.[1] Not to be seen as "different" carries political meanings for Palestinian citizens in a Jewish Israeli city. As visible Palestinians, they were outsiders who could not really enjoy the city's impersonal qualities in the same way as the Jewish residents could.

This became evident in Farah's personal life, which shows us that Jewish residents often relate to Palestinian citizens as strangers underneath the shiny surface of the city's life. When Farah went out drinking with friends, Jewish men sometimes approached her without realizing she was "Arab." They would sometimes ask about her background and her "accent": "Then, they often ask, 'Where are you from?' And when I say I am Arab, they say, 'Really?!'" According to Farah, this moment usually led to an abrupt end of these conversations. It hinted at the dilemma of being either misrecognized as a non-Palestinian immigrant or recognized, then stigmatized, as an "Arab." This experience recalls Frantz Fanon's description of "Negroes" in France who found nothing more exasperating than being asked, "How long have you been in France? You speak French so well."[2] As Fanon's important critique of racial passing highlights, striving for success and tactics of invisibility do not escape racialization: no matter how successful a black person may become, they may still be met with suspicion or perceived as inferior.

The ambivalent experience of Palestinian immersion in Tel Aviv has consequences for how we make sense of Palestinians' middle-class status within this urban space. Liberal ideology often frames upward mobility in terms of race-neutral universalism in a seemingly color-blind meritocracy, where class-related achievements can transcend racism.[3] However, the question of class development in Israel/Palestine has long been deeply bifurcated along ethnonational lines.[4] Palestinian citizens of Israel are generally considered "second-class citizens" due to the systematic discrimination and inequality that locks them into disadvantaged positions. Although they are considered to be "wealthier, healthier, and more numerous than ever before . . . they still lag behind their Jewish counterparts."[5] It is true that educational and professional attainments are associated with middle-class status among Arabs and Jews alike. But the diverging experiences and meanings of such class status are always influenced by the underlying inequalities and differences in political power. Indeed, ethnic and racial discrimination are often chronic and inescapable problems for young indigenous people in settler states, as their lived realities are riddled with exclusion, isolation, and marginality despite class-related achievements.[6]

A settler city such as Tel Aviv makes this very clear. The prospect of social upward mobility through its offices and universities appeals to both Jewish and Palestinian citizens, but the Palestinians will always experience *success* as racialized and as conditional on political moderation and forms of invisibility. This makes it difficult for them to develop a deeper sense of urban belonging and citizenship. The Palestinian experience of being middle class or upper middle class in Tel Aviv is, therefore, different from that in other cities and towns, such as the mixed city of Haifa. Here, a strong Palestinian middle class has contested state suppression of Palestinian nationality and established independent Palestinian cultural institutions.[7] While "middle class" signifies a communal achievement in addition to an individual one in Haifa, Tel Aviv decollectivizes the Palestinian middle class into islands of disconnected individual immersion. This difficult reality explains why many Palestinian citizens who come to Tel Aviv as students and employees from the towns and villages of the North move back up to Haifa at one point or another. As Nadeem Karkabi states, "Tel Aviv-Jaffa is deemed unsuitable to develop a Palestinian cultural life led by a strong urban Middle Class," because Jaffa is too embattled and fragmented, while being "overshadowed by the neighboring metropolis of Tel Aviv."[8]

Even outside of the compromises that Tel Aviv demands from them, the active promotion of a new Palestinian "middle class" has been associated with an upwardly mobile and essentially *moderate* kind of Palestinian persona.

In this stereotypical framing of middle class as apolitical, individuals are seen as prioritizing meritocratic ideals over the "collective Palestinian struggle."[9] Since early Jewish settlement, Zionism has indeed sought to inscribe a contradiction between individual Palestinian success and political activism, as Jewish authorities and the Israeli state used access to status, power, land, or wealth as a bargaining chip in recruiting supporters and collaborators who were then labeled "good Arabs."[10] One kind of Palestinian middle-class status is, therefore, associated with an accommodationist approach to Israel. At the same time, Palestinian elites and an educated young middle class have long been the most outspoken critics of the Jewish Israeli colonial regime and some of the most determined Palestinian nationalists within Israel and in the occupied territories.[11] We will see that Tel Aviv actively responds to this dual notion of Palestinian middle class as both political and apolitical in specific ways, pressuring them to prioritize the one over the other in their daily balancing acts.

ANONYMOUS TOGETHER: THE ISOLATED IMMERSION OF MIDDLE-CLASS PROFESSIONALS

Status and class are important enablers when it comes to Palestinians' immersion in Tel Aviv, as long as they are not too visible as Palestinians. The ambivalence of this relationship became clear when I met members of a social group of highly skilled professionals—all Palestinian citizens—who worked or lived in Tel Aviv. It was a group of highly educated and successful individuals, such as the marketing expert Farah, introduced above. They held regular dinners in restaurants where they socialized and listened to invited guest speakers. Many were the only Palestinian citizens in both their respective companies and the buildings in which they lived, that is, if they lived in Tel Aviv at all. According to one active member, the group started because they all developed a sense of apolitical disconnection as Palestinian professionals in the city. Different members approached the group differently. While it was just a casual dinner for some, others saw it as a more serious attempt to contribute something positive to the Palestinian community in Israel. Tellingly, Farah said she felt very little incentive to join the group when she first heard about it: "I was a bit scared of suddenly meeting all these other Arabs. Here in Tel Aviv, we Arabs don't know each other. [We] see that there are a lot of other Arabs, but they ignore it. They don't really want to have a community within a community in this city. It is not what they come for. . . . We are anonymous together."

The group had about thirty-five affiliates at one point and usually met for dinner in a restaurant, which created a sense of hypervisibility and discomfort for Farah: "Once, we met in a restaurant and invited [the politician] Ahmed Tibi as a guest. The waiters and the other guests stared at us, although we were in a separate back room. When the men walked down with Tibi at the end of the meeting, chatting loudly in Arabic, walking between the tables, they attracted a lot of attention. People at this place saw 30 Arabs and probably thought, where did they come from?"

The city's residents may have been used to encountering "Arab" individuals and isolated employees, but Tel Aviv certainly was not used to their collective appearance. Such collective visibility represented "politics" and controversy in and of itself.

In a way this was intentional because the communal meetings were meant to offer a break from the isolated routines of their Tel Aviv lives. "[In these meetings] we don't talk about business, but we talk about community issues and politics," explained Munib, one of the group's initiators, adding, "But outside these meetings, in Tel Aviv, there is no sense of community." The city imposed a contradiction between professional success and urban life, on the one hand, and inner-Palestinian connections, on the other. These pressures of decollectivization continued a history of settler-colonial elimination, as an ongoing process of erasure, through forms of conditional inclusion.

At the workplaces of highly skilled Palestinian citizens in Tel Aviv, interactions with other Palestinians were often tense and complicated and raised questions about visibility and recognition. The medical doctor Tamer from Nazareth, who had lived and worked in Tel Aviv for several years, talked about such "strange interactions" in the hospital. He was the only Arab doctor among thirty staff in his section, but it also included an Arab nurse and two Arab nursing interns:

> Once I stood there surrounded by Jewish doctors. It was the first time I
> met one of the new Arab nursing students. There was tension between us.
> We didn't speak Arabic but I spoke Hebrew; there was this communication
> failure on the first day. I asked myself, why? Maybe because she has a
> headscarf and it confused me, because I am not used to this background.
> It's not natural for me. But maybe it was the setting at the hospital. I am an
> Arab and I am in charge. And she is an Arab nursing student, it wasn't easy. I
> should have talked Arabic to her from the beginning, not Hebrew. But I didn't
> because I thought maybe she didn't want to speak Arabic in this context
> surrounded by Jewish staff, so I didn't. If we would have talked Arabic from
> the beginning, it would have worked out better.

Whether it is a group of Palestinians having dinner in a Tel Aviv restaurant or two colleagues at work: being collectively and visibly Palestinian in front of

Jewish Israelis sometimes causes ambivalent feelings about the kind of public recognition they aspired to achieve. The very act of "connecting" around their shared identity and language appeared to violate the implicit conditionality of their inclusion at the workplace, threatening their fragile status as an unmarked colleague. When Tamer was still a junior doctor, as he remembered in our meeting, he was often careful "not to work more than others," saying that he built "a wall" around himself by not trusting anyone when they asked him to fulfill certain tasks, suspecting that they would demand more work from him simply because he was Arab. The experiences of Palestinian professionals of middle- and upper-class status in Tel Aviv are revealing about how ethnonational identity and class interact with "the subtle forms of power that saturate everyday life" in workspaces.[12]

"HELPING BEHIND THE CURTAINS": A PALESTINIAN COLLECTIVE OF SUCCESSFUL INDIVIDUALS

Being a Palestinian employee in Tel Aviv is often a rather lonely business or a "lone pursuit," akin to the "defensive individualism" among poor, work-seeking black Americans.[13] Such defensive individualism prioritizes self-reliance and hard work in the face of difficulties, paralleled by an absence of networks and a climate of distrust, noncooperation, and stigmatization. A sense of "abandonment" is key, therefore, to contemporary capitalism, because self-creation is often the only thing left in workers' lives when they are thrust back on their own strategic and emotional resources.[14] A globalized neoliberal economy of Tel Aviv combines with the settler-colonial estrangement of Palestinians to produce a particular kind of isolation, tied to a contradictory relationship between class formation and the stigmatization of their identity. As the political and collective invisibility of an urban minority is associated with access to the city's skilled economy, this conditional inclusion inscribes the historic process of settler-colonial elimination of the Palestinian identity into class formation within "liberal" Tel Aviv.

Israeli liberalism has long been an ambivalent experience for Palestinian citizens. It promised formal equality but only within the limits of deeply rooted inequality and discrimination between Jewish and Arab citizens. As Dan Rabinowitz suggests about the Palestinian citizens he studied in the Jewish development town of Upper Nazareth: they were subordinates within the Israeli system that discriminated against their identity, but they also subscribed to liberal core values and norms in the hope of overcoming this discriminating stigma. Some hoped to become "champions of meritocracy, professionalism, hard work, universalistic pluralism, [and] freedom of individual choice."[15] In doing so, they distanced themselves from collective political concerns because Israeli liberalism tends to reduce these big issues to personal and pragmatic choices.

The dinner group of Palestinian professionals in Tel Aviv were all involved in forms of meritocratic immersion in Tel Aviv, but their shared experience of this noncommunal and apolitical existence also triggered a desire to reconnect and forge a covert community that talked about "big issues." Once they did, many realized that they shared a common experience in Tel Aviv. Many of these professionals knew that they had to work harder than their Jewish colleagues to get equal opportunities. In order to be equal, they had to be better than others. Some successful professionals often emphasize the power of individual choices, speaking from a position of privilege.

When I met with Munib in his Tel Aviv office, he criticized what he saw as a common assumption: "This assumption is that it is harder to be accepted, harder to succeed for Arabs in Israel. If you accept this assumption, you will surely not break through the barrier. But if you want to go beyond this assumption, you will have to work twice as hard as others and be twice as good as the regular employee."

Munib was an executive at a law firm in Tel Aviv who had been living in the city for four years at the time of our first meeting. "I wanted a place where the sky is the limit," he explained. Munib also enjoyed the lifestyle of the city and said that he regularly attended wine workshops and wine tastings after work. It was one of his hobbies. Despite the pleasures of Tel Aviv, he spent most weekends with family and friends back in Haifa, explaining to me that Tel Aviv is to him a rather "lonely city," because it lacked a sense of Palestinian community. At the same time, he admitted that he often "chose to be a stranger" in Tel Aviv. This is a kind of anonymity by choice that builds on the privileges of middle- and upper-class status.

The negative side of this estrangement is why Munib and a few others formed their group of about thirty-five Muslim and Christian Palestinian citizens of Israel in the first place. They all either lived or worked in Tel Aviv, and their shared middle- or upper-class status was a defining element from the beginning.

"The idea was to organise a group of [Arab-Palestinian] professionals who have arrived at a certain standing in the Israeli business arena and in Tel Aviv," Munib said over a coffee outside his office, adding that the aim of the meetings was to have a productive exchange over how to advocate for change for the benefit of "our community." Invited guest speakers included government ministers, members of parliament, civil society organizers, and representatives of international organizations. Featuring some very well-known and successful people, the group operated on a shared basis of success, class, and status.

Seven years after our initial meeting, Munib told me about how the group had evolved, into the year 2020, as an effective network of influential Palestinian citizens that "help behind the curtains." Explaining how the group matured from a networking dinner meeting of friends to a source of influence, he said: "Not many concrete things happen, because it's not formal. But it's a lot of well-connected people from the Arab community, and each one is serving in one or two or three Boards and as directors in other organizations.... If I serve in the Board of Directors in one organization and I need help for something, I can use the connections from the group. It's a circle of connections and power. Sometimes it's also connected to money; we are businesspeople, we have money."

In 2020, the group had already been collaborating with a very influential binational advocacy group of leading Palestinian and Israeli businesspeople for two years and took their meetings from restaurants in Tel Aviv-Jaffa into the houses of leading businesspeople all over the country. Munib said: "It is concrete: we are helping behind the curtains, organising donations from individuals, advancing education, civil rights . . . we are using the connections to support causes." Giving another example, he explained that one of the organizations they supported had a mentoring program that helped Palestinian citizens in need get into the labor market. Other challenges they have addressed with concrete networking and support were violence within the Palestinian community and the challenges of education.

INDEPENDENT YET DIFFERENT: SWIMMING AGAINST THE STREAM

Wanting to remain anonymous was one reason the marketing expert Farah was reluctant to join this group in the first place. But she also said that, as professionals in their thirties and forties, they all shared the legacy of a certain generation of Palestinians in Israel: one generation before today's students at Tel Aviv University, and two after her grandparents, "who lived through the Nakba and were sure about their identity," said Farah. She said that her parents were born "into the reality of Israel, scared of surveillance" during the early years of the state and its two-decade military rule over the Palestinian minority. They were public employees: the mother a teacher, the father in agriculture. Theirs was a particular political trajectory led by some traditional leaders and the establishment, some of whom had no choice but to accept Israel's sovereignty as a necessary evil and hope for more rights.[16] Farah's father still tells her "not to talk about this on the phone" when she talks about politics. As teenagers and young adults, she and her siblings were told not to attend political events and not to sympathize with any movement.

"My father said: when you will be older you would have black stains on you; we were neutralised and my parents were afraid to lose their house and their life, that's why they shut up," said Farah, adding that this was why she and her siblings learned to focus on opportunities, not politics: her brother worked for Ernst and Young, other siblings lived in Germany and run businesses there, while she worked in advertising. "We grab the opportunities; we are independent and different at the same time." The problem was that in Tel Aviv, to be independent she sometimes had to downplay the difference. She knew well that accessing opportunities in Tel Aviv demanded sacrifices.

As a university student, Farah felt that some of her Palestinian peers viewed her as a "traitor" because she never participated in political activities. Tel Aviv only seemed to further this tendency. Working for ten to twelve hours a day in a Hebrew-language environment also affected her Arabic language skills. "If you are an Israeli abroad and you meet Israelis, you speak Hebrew and you will be happy. Here, we don't always do that," she said, suggesting that she usually avoided contact with Palestinians she did not know in Tel Aviv. The anonymity and formal equality that is seemingly granted by citizenship and a liberal city ends where visible Palestinian identity and collectivity begins. Certain forms of invisibility, therefore, become a core component of the production of Palestinian status and class in Tel Aviv. At the same time, highly skilled individuals can turn part of their "difference" into benefits.

The lawyer Nazmi was another member of the group. He worked in a Tel Aviv downtown building called "Zion tower." One day we met for lunch and when we sat down, Nazmi answered a phone call, speaking Arabic at first, and then a little bit of Hebrew, until he eventually switched back to Arabic. This switching between the two languages and English was common among Palestinians in the professional context of Tel Aviv.

Nazmi was born and raised in the town of Taybeh in central Israel but went to a private high school in Haifa. His professional trajectory was somewhat unique because he was one of very few Israeli citizens who received a scholarship to study in Jordan right after the Jordan-Israel Peace Treaty was signed in 1994. He studied there for five years and, after graduation, decided to submit applications to law offices in Tel Aviv, focusing on those offices that dealt with commercial law and business cases. Although he thought that his chances "were practically zero," he was eventually hired, for one main reason, as he argued: "I was swimming against the stream like a salmon."

Nazmi's experience of studying in Jordan proved to be beneficial to the employer. "They thought it was interesting. It made a good impression." He had been working in that company for thirteen years at the time we met. Since proving himself as a successful lawyer, his relationship with Tel Aviv became "more natural." While the aspiring students at Tel Aviv University had to make difficult sacrifices when it came to the visibility of their identity, Nazmi's success and status gave him a certain freedom and confidence: "I emphasize my identity, I never sneak it beneath, I never make an effort to leave it behind. The opposite, I always emphasize it. I am not someone who understands integration as giving up one's identity. . . . You can be on the radar or under the radar. When political conflicts happen, I don't mind being under the radar. But I am not afraid to be on the radar."

I asked Nazmi whether he thought that such confidence was possible because of his status and his rather privileged position. "Yes, it's true," he admitted, "I am successful and this is one reason why it's easier to say these things. When I was younger, I was trying to hide under the radar." When he joined the law office in Tel Aviv for the first time, back in the year 2000, the second intifada had just broken out. "It was terrible. I felt what's happening is wrong, and the attitude of the people was terrible," he said, referring to Jewish Israeli colleagues in Tel Aviv. Then he took a dive "deep into the ocean" and tried his best to keep it together and continue to work.

Recurring feelings of estrangement as "Arabs" in the quintessential Jewish city are one aspect of the lives of successful Palestinian citizens, despite their status, in addition to what some called feelings of "loneliness." Nazmi spoke of feeling "some kind of loneliness in this bubble," where he has been "in no-man's land for so long." His wife and family lived up north away from Tel Aviv. Being in Tel Aviv, "as an Arab, was hard for me and for others," said Nazmi, adding: "You go on the streets and you hardly meet someone from your own society. . . . Working in Tel Aviv is like moving away from your society." Although he admitted to having Jewish friends in Tel Aviv, he felt that it was "not the same; not the social field you would like to have."

While some of these highly skilled professionals lived in Tel Aviv, others only worked there and commuted on a daily basis. In both cases, there was a concern with Tel Aviv as a social bubble that simultaneously incorporated them and excluded part of who they were; a city offering opportunities and an urban lifestyle, but at the cost of a particular type of loneliness as isolated individuals who were expected to remain invisible as a Palestinian minority.

The Christian Palestinian Ayman was another member of the dinner group, and he lived in Tel Aviv permanently. Meeting him in a café in one of the city's most expensive residential areas, I asked about his relationship with Tel Aviv and how the city related to him as an Arab. "I have many identities on many different levels," he told me, adding that these many identities do not have to contradict each other: "They work together. I like to say I am a Palestinian *Tel Avivi*. Identities are like Facebook pages for me. You can like any page you want ... and you can live with it in peace."

Originally from a Christian family in Haifa, Ayman came to Tel Aviv straight from the Technion, Haifa's prestigious university for science and technology. When me met, he had already been living in Tel Aviv for twenty years and said, "There used to be an Arab here and there, but today there are many more Arabs in the city; you hear a lot of Arabic in all kinds of places." It may have been very unusual to live in Tel Aviv as a Palestinian twenty years ago, but, according to him, now things were "more open, more diverse." "It used to be literally a white city, and now it's a diverse city."

The way Ayman placed himself within a liberal interpretation of diversity in the city sits uncomfortably with the recurring stigmatization of political Palestinian identity that so many of his brethren experienced. The idea of freely choosing his identity like "Facebook pages" springs from a rather privileged position that is also rooted in the particularity of the Christian Palestinians in Israel. Dan Rabinowitz found similar patterns among Palestinian Christians who lived in the Jewish development town Natzerat Illit, who—as a minority twice over—were "natural candidates for an unconditional embrace of liberalism."[17] Largely urban and better situated economically, Christian Palestinian citizens of Israel have long been represented as elites. Being part of a stigmatized national minority within the Israeli state, while being an elite minority within their own nation, has created an ambivalent combination of powerlessness and empowerment.[18]

Perhaps partly influenced by this Christian legacy, the advantages of professional success and the promises of urban individualism resonate strongly with Ayman's perspective. At the same time, members of marginalized minorities who are offered the chance to develop individually must often realize that their participation requires them to adhere to norms and values of the very system that denies their people collective rights.[19] As their class and status allow access to the city's socioeconomic opportunities, most of these successful individuals are not inclined to struggle for collective recognition as a Palestinian minority within Tel Aviv. As a former Tel Aviv University student and young entrepreneur put it, "I am not coming here to claim the rights of my land and so on. This will take place elsewhere."

However, as Ayman's work in advertising and communications was highly successful, he also worked on communication strategies with the Palestinian

National Authority (PNA) in Ramallah. His experience only underlined the contradictory relationship between Palestinian politics and Palestinian life in Tel Aviv. Reflecting on his attendance of the Davos World Economic Forum with the PNA's delegation, he said: "I should say I am from Tel Aviv but can't say it. A few times I had to shut up there." Combining different senses of "identity" that are deemed contradictory is not without dilemmas and friction, even for the educated upper-middle class. When the former president of Israel, Shimon Peres, spoke at the forum, Ayman wanted to talk to him as an Israeli, although he was officially there as a Palestinian. And when the Palestinian chief negotiator Saeb Erekat spoke, he wanted to say something from an Israeli perspective, but as a member of the PNA delegation, he could not talk to Erekat as an Israeli.

Overall, the partial adoption of a depoliticized liberalism beyond identity politics appears to determine parts of Palestinian middle- and upper-class formation within Tel Aviv. With the position of being in Tel Aviv also came a certain disinclination to promote collective senses of Palestinian national identity because so much of what is beneficial about Tel Aviv depends on being politically unmarked. Ayman appeared to have little time for the politics of nationalism and liberation. He criticized the Palestinian people for "lingering in the past." During the dinner meeting of the group, which had the Palestinian politician Ahmed Tibi as the invited guest speaker, Ayman could not help but confront him by saying that "foreign workers integrate better in Israel than Arabs." When I asked him about the discrimination and inequality that Palestinians in Israel face, and about the enduring effects of the mass displacement of 1948, Ayman only said: "How much time passed since then? 70 years? It's time to move on."

In many ways, Tel Aviv represents a particular way of "moving on" for parts of the successful Palestinian middle and upper class in Israel. It offers jobs with competitive salaries and globally connected companies. It has wine bars, restaurants, and beaches. It allows them to advance, to a certain extent, as professionals and immerse themselves anonymously in urban leisure spaces. This approach of moving on demands a certain degree of forgetting: the implicit acceptance of the city's liberal present at the expense of claims for collective recognition that would be rooted in Palestinians' history as a colonized people on this land. In this sense, to have a future as professionals in Tel Aviv, Palestinians may feel inclined to ignore the past, which would challenge the city's self-definition as a modern, forward-looking metropolis with multicultural diversity. Where steps are taken for the advancement of collective issues in the Palestinian community, this happens through networking and investments "behind the curtains."

While middle- and upper-class status entails certain privileges, it also turns situational invisibility and anonymity into a choice and an individual resource. This story is an entirely different one for the working class of Palestinians and Palestinian citizens of Israel who toil in the kitchens and construction sites of Tel Aviv. To them, the positive liberal qualities of the city are often out of reach and overshadowed by the harsh reality of hard work and racism. Rather than being strangers by choice, the city and their labor render them invisible and push them to the margins of urban life.

"THE CITY THAT NEVER STOPS": LABOR AND INVISIBILITY AMONG PALESTINIAN WORKING-CLASS CITIZENS

Invisibility has very different qualities for middle- or upper-class people and marginalized working-class urbanites.[20] The Palestinians who toil in an invisible underground of the city's economy tend to have jobs rather than a highly skilled career. One of Tel Aviv's many nicknames, "the city that never stops," has a different quality for them than for those who party by night and work in offices by day. The Palestinian laborers toil for long hours and often have several jobs. Many are living in overcrowded apartments or even sleep on mats in construction sites.

Palestinian citizens of Israel often remain "stuck" in a poverty trap due to their relatively low education levels, limited geographic distribution, and inadequate resource allocation as well as discrimination and stigmatization.[21] In 2010, upon joining the Organization for Economic Cooperation and Development, Israel pledged to reduce the economic disparity between Jewish and Arab citizens, but Israel's equality legislation is not readily enforced and discrimination exists in many sectors, accentuated by examples like the courier UPS not employing Arab drivers because they do not get security clearance to enter the airport.[22] The various initiatives that call for a deeper integration of the "Arab" labor force build on the assumption that more economic inclusion leads to better integration overall. The problem for many working-class Palestinians in Tel Aviv is not only a lack of economic inclusion but also the restrictive conditions under which such inclusion takes place.

The stereotypical working "Arab" in Tel Aviv has built the city's skyline, cooked its restaurant meals, cleaned its apartments, and sold its vegetables; another example are the many Palestinian cleaners employed at Tel Aviv University. When I met Hasan, who worked as a cleaner, during his lunch break, he and a colleague were eating their sandwiches in a common room. Hasan lived in Jisr az-Zarqa, the last remaining Palestinian town on the Mediterranean coast in Israel. After lunch, we sat down on the university lawns in the shade of a tree. With headphones dangling from his neck, he wore a black T-shirt and a golden bracelet on one of his arms.

As we chatted about his work and his life, he told me that he was only sixteen years old, which was why he was officially not allowed to work for more than eight hours in a row. In fact, he worked eleven hours a day. "Jisr is a small town without work," he said in justification of his presence in Tel Aviv. It is simply where all the jobs are, "but I don't do anything here except work." Indeed, Hasan never experienced Tel Aviv in the way its Jewish Israeli residents did. He also had little chance of entering any of the highly skilled career pathways Palestinian students at Tel Aviv University were preparing themselves for. His immersion in the city and his ability to access its famed "liberal" life and bustling economy were very limited. He made use of the city's jobs, being physically present, and yet he lived the life of an urban underdog.

This was certainly true for the workers of a falafel eatery close to where I lived in Tel Aviv. It was a well-known place that served delicious Middle Eastern food. Owned by a Jewish Israeli, most of its employees were Palestinian citizens of Israel and some were Palestinians from the West Bank. They prepared sandwiches, cooked in the kitchen, and served hungry customers at the tables. I often saw them walking down the tree-lined Dizengoff Street in their white uniforms. At night I could see them strolling back up after a long and exhausting shift. It was strikingly difficult for them to find any spare time to meet for a longer conversation. They simply worked most of the time, and, if they were not working, they slept or rushed back home to spend a day with their families. Moreover, their unglamorous work life in Tel Aviv was not exactly something they were proud of and wanted to share. Doing hard labor for Jewish superiors, in their case under harsh and degrading conditions, was an exhausting reality and a somewhat debasing necessity to them.

One night I met up with eighteen-year-old Ahmad after his evening shift. Ahmad, who was an Israeli citizen, walked toward me with a paper cup of coffee and a welcoming smile. We sat down on a roadside bench that was surrounded by the humming flow of the city's traffic and its many pedestrians. Ahmad was one of the youngest employees and usually cleared and wiped the tables as the one who held the lowest rank in the employee hierarchy. But why, I asked him, did he come to Tel Aviv in the first place?

"Why I came to Tel Aviv? This is where the money is. A lot of Arabs come here in order to make money. Afterwards, many try to open a place in their hometown," he said matter-of-factly. He came to make use of the city's jobs, and he did it for a clear purpose. Ahmad never really had it easy: his father died when he was young and pressures to earn money brought him to Tel Aviv for the first time at the age of fourteen. He then worked as a cleaner in residential buildings and shopping malls, cleared the tables of Tel Aviv beach restaurants, and worked in a factory in Umm el-Fahm for some time in between. Of the 8,000 shekels (around $2,000 USD at the time) he now earned each month, 3,000 shekels went straight to his mother, who lived in the West Bank and did not hold Israeli citizenship. For Ahmad, the Israeli saying that Tel Aviv is the "city that never stops" (*Ir le-lo hafsakah*) lacks the glamour it symbolizes for many. He works up to fourteen hours a day for six days a week, rushing back home only during Sabbath, when the falafel eatery closes its doors and its kitchen is allowed to rest. At the same time, Ahmad complained, his employer ignored the main Muslim holidays.

Despite the hardship Ahmad felt incredibly privileged compared to Palestinians in the West Bank, who lived under the regime of the Israeli military occupation. And yet he felt humiliated as a second-class citizen within Israel, saying: "If I tell a Jew that I live with nine others in one apartment in Tel Aviv, they would laugh out loud. We are occupied people here. We cannot move in any direction, not here and not there, without them giving us the permission." He did not want to move around Tel Aviv too much anyway, because much of what he would see was a politically adverse and even forbidden place to him. "As a Muslim, life here is *haram*. The way they dress . . . ," he said, pointing toward a group of lightly dressed young women walking past us, "like that!"

Haram means that something is forbidden, or taboo, and Ahmad frequently used it to describe Tel Aviv and its lifestyle: "We, as Muslims, don't like alcohol and a lot of other things happening here. If you offered me sex with a girl here, I would say no, haram! I don't pray, but I am a Muslim and I fast." Already anticipating a negative answer, I asked him if he could imagine living in Tel Aviv and raising his children there one day. "In Tel Aviv? Of course I can't raise my kids here," he protested. "It would be in Umm el-Fahm. I don't like getting close to people here in Tel Aviv. They all drink, they are playing around with girls; I don't like that and if I sense it, I just turn away."

His dissociation from the city also had other reasons. The bench we were sitting on was just beside the memorial of the Dizengoff Center suicide bombing, which killed thirteen Israelis in 1996. "Do you know what happened here?" Ahmad asked me, pointing at the memorial, saying it was a suicide attack. "That's how they see us. Of course, it's wrong to do that, but what I am saying is that there are people in this city who don't even talk to us Arabs. 'You are Arab? Leave!' they say. They don't have any respect, they have it all, and we are below their feet," said Ahmad, raising his legs and touching the sole of his shoes to illustrate his point.

Playing devil's advocate, I said that if I were Israeli, I might say: "Why do you complain if you are making a good salary in Tel Aviv?" Ahmad smirked, answering: "I would tell you, 'I work at your place and you give me money.' The people in Tel Aviv say, 'Arabs, come work with us.' And yes, I am working from morning to evening at your place, so give me money." Working in Tel Aviv for an economic purpose was fine but attempting to live in it was haram. Tel Aviv was a place to be used while being used, no more than that. There was an unwritten contract Ahmad signed with his conscience that excluded the possibility of any deeper urban immersion. This hints at the fact that Tel Aviv is generally viewed as haram in the Palestinian-Arab imaginary, and, in the Middle East, more generally: a morally polluted and politically adverse place.

After several cigarettes and a lot of people watching, Ahmad told me about his ideas for the future. He wanted to start his own business and thought about learning a proper profession sometime soon. He mentioned Mohamed, one of his colleagues at the falafel eatery, who was a learned chef and earned more than him. But even he toiled in Tel Aviv because his own business in Umm el-Fahm failed. In order to get his own chance at becoming a business owner, Ahmad needed "every Shekel to survive" until then.

Ahmad disliked Tel Aviv but also praised it. It was taboo but also a curiosity. Indeed, he called it one of the most developed cities in the world with a lot of progress. "You can see a 90-year-old riding a bicycle, others are jogging, people here live 24 hours," he said, seemingly amazed and excited. But, then again, he added, "the hard thing about Tel Aviv is that everything is nice *but also haram.*" He meant this in cultural and political terms because he saw Tel Aviv as "an occupied place," saying that Israelis managed to always stay on the top of things, like a drop of olive oil in water (*zayy nuktat az-zeit*). But, at the same time, he said that Palestinians were everywhere in Tel Aviv: "If there were no Arabs in Tel Aviv, the city would close down. The buildings, who will build them? The restaurants, the shops, the malls—every second worker is Arab!"

At the end of our conversation, Ahmad turned to his smartphone to browse through videos about Umm el-Fahm, explaining that he was a supporter of the Northern Islamic Movement, which was led by the charismatic hard-liner Sheikh Raed Salah and would later be outlawed. Ahmad leaned over and showed me a video of Palestinian youths confronting Israeli police forces with stones in his hometown, then another video of a march by the Northern Islamic Movement, and a documentary film titled *Here Is Palestine: Umm el-Fahm*. It started with an interactive map of "Palestine" and then zoomed into Umm el-Fahm. "You have to watch this if you want to understand what's going on here in Tel Aviv," he said. As the film proceeded, Ahmad chipped in every now and then: "This is our roundabout, this is a famous lawyer, this is a demonstration," and so forth. Even if Ahmad tried harder, he would not have enough time to delve into Tel Aviv. He simply could not imagine living in it. It was truly a foreign place to him, and the degrading character of his work contributed to this estrangement. The city did not give him a chance to belong, so why should he?

During the course of my time in Tel Aviv, I encountered hundreds of Palestinian workers, whether they were bus drivers, waiters, salespeople, or builders. The city's hospitals and pharmacies are also staffed with Palestinian citizens, as are its cafés and restaurants. Although there is no absolute difference between working-class and middle-class Palestinians when it comes to their immersion in Tel Aviv, my regular encounters with Ahmad and his colleagues made more than clear that they had little choice or freedom to feel as *Tel Avivians* and enjoy the city's famed leisurely qualities. For Ahmad, sipping coffee from a plastic cup while smoking a cigarette on the roadside was all the glamour he got from Tel Aviv. For these workers, invisibility was not only due to tactics of stigma-evading concealment but also the result of the restrictive and exploitative conditions of their labor. Confined to workspaces and overcrowded apartments, and with the aim of saving as much as possible of their earnings, taking part in Tel Aviv's consumerist urban life was not only difficult but also undesirable. In the following section, we explore another kind of marginalizing invisibility affecting the urban lives of those Palestinians who commute between Tel Aviv and the occupied West Bank under a restrictive permit regime and difficult conditions.

PALESTINIAN LABOR COMMUTERS IN TEL AVIV'S INVISIBLE UNDERBELLY

Most Palestinian labor commuters from the West Bank cannot really take part in the city's life without Israeli citizenship. They can only use the city in the most pragmatic way, usually earning more than twice as much as they would in the occupied West Bank. Once on their way into Tel Aviv, a restrictive labor regime governs their urban presence through a mix of space, race, and documents—through spatial closure, exclusion from citizenship, and a racial hierarchy based on separate legal orders for Jews and Palestinians.[23] Some 130,000 Palestinians from the West Bank worked in Israel by the end of the second decade of the twenty-first century (ILO 2019). Although there are no official numbers, it appears likely that thousands, if not tens of thousands, work in the Greater Tel Aviv area. For most of those with regular work permits, staying overnight is forbidden, even if they are regularly employed in the city. This limits their ability to use the city and forces them to either circulate in and out of Israel or risk it and hide underground. They are largely invisible urbanites simply because their presence is restricted to construction sites and workspaces. Tens of thousands of Palestinian labor commuters in Israel do not even hold work permits, which Israeli authorities often deny them on questionable security grounds.[24] To them, staying invisible as Palestinians in public is a matter of survival and not really a choice. One of those who worked in Tel Aviv without a permit was Ibrahim.

Agreeing on a place to meet him was a challenge in itself, and I had a difficult time finding him at the bottom of the city's busy Carmel Market. Ibrahim was from the city of Nablus and had already been working in Tel Aviv for several years without a permit. His wife and children had to stay behind while he hoped to make good use of the available jobs in Tel Aviv to earn a living and pay for his children's education. Away from the crowds of the market, we sat down on a shaded bench in a park adjacent to the old Hassan Bek Mosque that survived in Tel Aviv. We had a common friend, and so Ibrahim trusted me and shared his experience. Yet, he seemed nervous and was constantly on the watch like a fugitive or "smuggler," as he would later describe his situation. As an "illegal" Palestinian in Tel Aviv, urban space was a minefield for him. From the bench we sat on, the mosque was clearly visible, and I learned that its cool stone-walled interiors served Ibrahim and other Palestinians as a sanctuary away from the city's exposed public spaces.

Ibrahim had worked in Tel Aviv for about seven years. "They caught me a few times," he said, adding that his third jail time lasted seventeen days, and another lasted nine. "I am here without a permit. Why I don't get it? They say because of security reasons. But I don't know why exactly." He usually worked as a painter for subcontractors who tell him where to go and what to do. Every three weeks or so, he went back to Nablus to bring cash home to his wife and six children. In his own words, he came to Tel Aviv "for the money despite the dangers," and, above all, to support his family and to pay for his daughters' university fees.

Unlike Palestinian citizens, and, especially, unlike the educated middle and upper class, Ibrahim could not take part in the city's life and did not manage to transform the benefits of working into any form of sustainable upward mobility. Forced to remain invisible, urban inclusion and a sense of citizenship were an impossibility for him. At the same time, the absence of opportunities back home had made him dependent on this city's economy. Instead of immersive invisibility, he had to cope with a structural form of forced invisibility and economic dependence.

On days without work, he often spent hours inside the mosque. At night, he slept in the construction site of an unfinished building with nothing else but a water boiler and a mat on the floor. He said that the kettle was his only belonging he did not carry in his pockets. "I sleep on the floor on a mattress. I have no place to wash myself. I plug in my kettle and charge my phone there, that's all," said Ibrahim. An informal arrangement with the people who run the building site made this lodging possible. His part of the deal was to take care of the construction site at night, thereby acting as an informal security guard. Some site managers charged him money for sleeping there, others did not. On a very good day of work, Ibrahim made about 300–400 shekels in Tel Aviv (around $80–110 USD at the time). On a bad day, he just waited for the next phone call.

When I asked Ibrahim if he would prefer to be a *citizen* of Israel in Tel Aviv, he said: "They have money and the borders are open for them. They are closed for me. I can't go to work in a bank, or in a hotel. I am like a smuggler here." As we continued to talk, his glance frequently scanned the area around us. Tel Aviv was a restricted and dangerous area for him. "I can't walk wherever I want. I won't go to the beach, it's too risky," he said, pointing down to the shoreline. "If I don't have work, I stay inside the mosque, where I feel safe." Similar to unauthorized migrants who must make themselves absent from the spaces they occupy, Palestinian workers in Tel Aviv exist in a "hidden dimension" of urban reality, one that is widely known but invisible.[25] The ambiguity between being hidden yet physically present is what makes these workers such a valuable resource in the informal economy. Just like they are able to make use of the city, the city uses (and abuses) them as a cheap labor force.[26] This pattern of inclusion is both a result of and a contributor to ongoing settler-colonial elimination: Israel's enduring colonization of the Palestinian territory has destroyed the Palestinians' basis for a viable economy that can support the labor force,[27] while the precarious and invisible incorporation of laborers from these territories into Israel ensures their presence as working bodies only, not as people with an indigenous identity, rights, and a legitimate claim to the land.

Like many other Palestinians of his generation, Ibrahim used to work in Dubai and in Jordan when he was younger. "Now I am 56 years old," he said, adding, "I am asking myself how much longer I can do this kind of work? All over the world, if you stay in a country for ten, twenty years, don't they give you an opportunity to stay and work normally after a while?" From the viewpoint of low-skilled Palestinian workers' experiences, Tel Aviv mirrored the exclusive aspects of the Israeli state and its citizenship regime rather than being a liberal or inclusive "city for all." Ibrahim and the Palestinian citizen Ahmad are not part of the usual narration of Tel Aviv's story of economic success and diversity, but they are undeniably present and essential to the functioning of its political economy. They are the hidden pulse of "the city that never stops."

INVISIBLE SUCCESSES: HARD WORK AND
URBAN ACCESS WITHOUT RECOGNITION

Looking at the experiences of Palestinian middle- and upper-class citizens and the working-class side by side shows that Tel Aviv requires both of these groups to employ diverse tactics of invisibility. At the same time, differences in class and legal status entail diverging capacities to access the city's economy and its urban life. Middle- and upper-class Palestinian citizens can manage the visibility of different aspects of their identity to circumvent stigmatization situationally and immerse themselves into the city's economy and its social life. Sometimes they must be conscious of retaining anonymity in relation to other Palestinians, too. The story is very different for Palestinian citizens who toil on construction sites and work long shifts in restaurants, and different again for Palestinians from the West Bank who are caught up in a limiting labor regime. While differences between citizenship and noncitizenship formally divide working-class Palestinian citizens in Israel from commuters who live in the West Bank, they share the experiences of being stigmatized as Palestinians or Arabs and work in similar semiskilled jobs under conditions of urban invisibility. Their work brings home important cash, but the conditions of their urban inclusion marginalize them in an unrecognized underbelly of the city.

Despite their relative privileges, middle- and upper-class Palestinian citizens who seek out professional success and urban life within Tel Aviv are caught up in a whirl of contradictory currents. One requires them to carefully manage their visibility as Palestinians in Tel Aviv, and the other constantly threatens to push their "Arab" identity to the surface. Pragmatic needs lead many to prioritize social mobility and urban access over claims for recognition and equality within the city, but, at the same time, this pragmatic bargain imposes glass ceilings on how far they can advance as outsiders in a Jewish Israeli metropolis. Inas Said, a Palestinian entrepreneur in Israel, put it the following way when I asked him about the difficulties of Palestinian citizens in Tel Aviv: "It is a catch-22. Their only chance to find a job is to be individualistic. . . . As an Arab activist, of course I want them to have more rights. But on the other hand, I don't want to be the person causing them to lose the last opportunity they have." In this sense, Palestinian citizens in Tel Aviv face an implicit contradiction between professional success and claiming "more rights" and between individual class mobility and claims for equality and recognition.

Immersive invisibility certainly opens up situational access to professional achievements and to some of the ostensibly "liberal" qualities of the city's urban life.[28] The city's economy racializes the experience of the Palestinian middle-class and undermines its ability to establish a visible collective. By pursuing access to the "neoliberal city under the illiberal state,"[29] the hope of the Palestinian middle-class is to gain access to the distinctively *urban* dimension underneath an exclusively *ethnonational* dimension. This response, as a specific urban strategy, can thus be seen as a form of temporary destigmatization. Instead of gaining *recognition* and *cultural membership*, to cite the dominant form of destigmatization,[30] immersive invisibility prioritizes the hope for socioeconomic access over that of political recognition. Ultimately, these tactics of immersive invisibility do not empower people to straddle the gap between identity politics, for which justice requires recognition, and class politics, for which justice requires economic redistribution.[31] Tel Aviv has transformed these two aspirations into mutually exclusive aspects of Palestinian inclusion, because economic access is granted only on the condition of minimal visibility as Palestinians. This became evident in the group of influential Palestinian businesspeople who networked for the benefit of their community but did so consciously "behind the curtain." Their redistributional efforts lacked a sense of collective recognition within Tel Aviv.

Within a settler-colonial city such as Tel Aviv, the liberal urban economy is already predetermined as ethnonational and exclusive. Tactical compromises merely allow Palestinians to react to shifting contexts and insinuate themselves into the "other's place" fragmentarily, "without taking it over."[32] They do not reclaim a city but face a daily struggle for *the right to use the city*.

What the long-term outcome of the hard work and professional careers of Palestinians in Tel Aviv will be is difficult to ascertain. Their achievements may become a stepping-stone for future successes that have collective significance, because some vulnerable urbanites can make gains only through quiet "structural encroachments."[33] These encroachments, nevertheless, produce outcomes and changes, even if not directly or openly. A case in point are the female Palestinian citizens who leave their hometowns and immerse themselves in mixed Arab-Jewish cities like Haifa, thereby achieving small-scale "micropolitical changes" with cumulative effects.[34] However, Tel Aviv is not Haifa, the mixed city where a Palestinian cultural space has thrived.

Tel Aviv is an often hostile place for Palestinian citizens, but it can, nevertheless, trigger small-scale changes for a new generation of successful middle-class citizens. If we come back to the former Tel Aviv University students Said and Amira, this becomes evident. The law student Said, who censored his own political visibility to get internships in Tel Aviv law offices, benefited from this temporary immersion in the long run: another internship and about two years later, he cofounded his own law firm in Nazareth, the largest Palestinian town in Israel. It self-consciously advertised in Arabic language on Facebook and catered to Palestinian clients, capitalizing on the skills and networks Said had acquired in Tel Aviv. Meanwhile, Amira's fearful "journey" through Tel Aviv's discriminatory employment market eventually led to her greater self-confidence, and, as she put it four years after I first met her, it allowed her to develop herself and arrive at a "new me" while transforming the gained experience into her own business start-up.

However, I am cautious about seeing these isolated achievements as a form of transformative "alter-politics," of creating alternatives outside the dominant political imaginary.[35] Tel Aviv does not offer the space for a Palestinian anti-politics against colonialism, capitalism, and Jewish Israeli domination. Rather than facilitating the transformation of oppositional concerns into a search for real alternatives, *immersive invisibility* abolishes oppositional concerns in exchange for a meritocratic, individualistic, and ostensibly liberal alternative that nevertheless continues to racialize those who aspire to it.

NOTES

1. Sennett, *Fall of Public Man*.
2. Fanon, *Black Skin, White Masks*, 35.
3. Meghji and Saini, "Rationalising Racial Inequality."
4. Locker-Biletzki, "Rethinking Settler Colonialism."
5. Ghanem, "Israel's Second-Class Citizens," 37.
6. Bailey, "Indigenous Students."
7. Karkabi, "'Palestinian Cultural Capital' in Israel," 1171.
8. Karkabi, "'Palestinian Cultural Capital' in Israel," 1180.
9. Grandinetti, "Palestinian Middle Class in Rawabi," 62–64.
10. Cohen, *Good Arabs*.
11. Rabinowitz and Abu-Baker, *Coffins on Our Shoulders*.
12. Ortner, *Anthropology and Social Theory*, 128.
13. S. Smith, *Lone Pursuit*.
14. Sennett, "Culture of Work," 133.
15. Rabinowitz, *Overlooking Nazareth*, 184.
16. Cohen, *Good Arabs*, 232.
17. Rabinowitz, *Overlooking Nazareth*, 185.
18. Sa'ar, "Carefully on the Margins," 216.
19. Rabinowitz, *Overlooking Nazareth*, 185; Collier, Maurer, and Suarez-Navaz, "Sanctioned Identities, 8.
20. Harms, "The Boss"; Wacquant, *Urban Outcasts*.
21. Yashiv and Katsir, "Labour Market of Israeli Arabs," 4.

22. *The Economist*, "Israel's Arab Labour Force—Out of Work."

23. Yael Berda, *Living Emergency*, 36.

24. ILO, "Workers of the Occupied Arab Territories" (2017).

25. Coutin, "Being en Route," 196.

26. Farsakh, *Palestinian Labour Migration to Israel*.

27. World Bank, "Area C and the Palestinian Economy."

28. Hackl, "Immersive Invisibility in the Settler-Colonial City."

29. Bayat, "Politics in the City-Inside-Out," 110.

30. Lamont, "Addressing Recognition Gaps," 423.

31. Sylvain, "Essentialism and the Indigenous Politics of Recognition," 253;
Fraser, "Social Justice in the Age of Identity Politics.

32. DeCerteau, *Practice of Everyday Life*, xix.

33. Bayat, *Life as Politics*, 18.

34. Herzog, "Choice as Everyday Politics," 7.

35. Hage, *Alter-Politics*.

FOUR

PLAYING IN TEL AVIV

Leisure and Fun in the Palestinian Underground

"HAIFA WORKS, JERUSALEM PRAYS, AND Tel Aviv plays." Often recited by Israelis to underscore the differences in the urban cultures of the three cities, this saying attaches a straightforward attribute to Tel Aviv: this city of leisure and fun has an outgoing lifestyle and plenty of bars, beaches, and parks. Tel Aviv's playing has been controversial for the Palestinians ever since the city's founding days. When Tel Aviv celebrated its twentieth anniversary in 1929 with a commercial fair, Mayor Meir Dizengoff emphasized the city's role in the "resurrection of the Jewish Nation"; after calling for a boycott of the celebrations, Arab political activists declared that "a free Arab will not betray his people" and compared Palestinians who visited the fair to those who frequented the city's nightclubs in pursuit of "foul objectives."[1] Little has changed on this front since then. Immersion in Tel Aviv beyond the mere practicalities of work or study is still seen as a loss of identity and political solidarity among many Palestinians. The young and unmarried Palestinian citizens in Tel Aviv, especially, continue to face pressures from family members, who warn them about having too much fun in this Jewish city. Few of them are entirely deterred. From the city's beaches and bars to the underground parties of a vibrant lesbian, gay, bisexual, and transgender (LGBT) scene, many Palestinians and Palestinian citizens have fun and spend their leisure time in Tel Aviv.

The problem is that they can do so only by carefully calibrating the visibility of their social lives and leisure time in the city, so that Palestinians' free time in Tel Aviv often ends up being not so free after all. While their participation in the nightlife and events of the Jewish Israeli mainstream is fraught with tension, only a few alternative spaces exist where the Palestinian citizens are free to gather to have fun collectively. Despite its ostensible liberalism and openness,

93

Tel Aviv forecloses the possibility of free expression for Palestinians, who must carefully calibrate their visibility in relation both to Jewish Israelis and to other Palestinians. Invisibility is, therefore, both a tool for realizing individual desires and a product of systematic urban marginalization.

To have fun, to feel pleasure, and to spend leisure time are different in meaning but all of these can push the boundaries of societal and political norms. *Fun* is somewhat antithetical to discipline and hierarchy and often happens collectively, making it an important part of people's agency and identity.[2] *Pleasure* is traditionally defined as a sensual and bodily experience of individuals.[3] More recently, though, it has been redefined as a publicly experienced affect that is akin to fun: "Pleasure as a 'public feeling' generated in moments of convivial encounter" that "exceeds the individual's psychic or corporeal enjoyments, and translates into the kind of enjoyment that arises from collective practices."[4] Because of their often convivial and collective character, the spheres of fun and pleasure are affected by the eliminative tendencies of this settler-colonial city: Palestinians can have fun in Tel Aviv only if they do so invisibly and by concealing aspects of their Palestinianness. Yet, even then, they remain potentially "problematic" suspects and can easily be denied access, as seen by the frequent rejection of Palestinians at the city's nightclubs.

Urban *leisure* may appear less political at first sight, because it is deeply entangled with consumerism. Spending time in cafés or restaurants involves consumption and often publicly marks people's class status, first, through the consumption itself, and, second, in the public display of leisure.[5] As a highly class-differentiated category, leisure is, therefore, always experienced in relation to power and discipline.[6] At the same time, claiming the time and space for leisure offers people an alternative to the world of work and the more tiring aspects of capitalism; it also allows individuals to temporarily break free from the disciplined constraints of family, community, and society.[7] People's experiments with new ways of experiencing a city through leisure sites can reshape dominant ideas about "morality," while challenging what is legitimate and appropriate.[8] These ideas include discourses of honor and modesty that determine the freedom of people with different gender identities to make choices about their lives.[9] By having leisure time and fun, people claim space and sometimes push the boundaries of dominant notions of civil behavior and cultural norms.

These boundary-pushing characteristics of leisure, fun, and pleasure have important implications for an indigenous urban minority that is not only stigmatized by the settler majority but also criticized by members of their own community for delving into a settler city that is deemed immoral. We will see that having fun in Tel Aviv is especially contentious among unmarried Palestinian women and members of the LGBT community, because they are often subject to gendered ways of controlling their freedoms and their visibility. As they challenge what is considered legitimate and appropriate, they must employ situational tactics that calibrate the visibility of different aspects of identity across differently marked places.

PRIVACY AND THE VISIBILITY OF LEISURE

Managing one's visibility is a key tool for Palestinian balancing acts between participation in a settler city and concerns about individual privacy. It is necessary for maintaining access to the liberal qualities of large cities, which can allow young women and men to increase their control over the course of their everyday lives.[10] Some urban leisure spaces are also known to offer a sense of privacy that cannot be had elsewhere. In Cairo, western-style coffee shops have become a site where middle-class women balance their place within the transnational cosmopolitan community with their more traditional Egyptian identities.[11] The difference about Tel Aviv is that "Western-style" places are rarely neutral in this sense because they are perceived to be Israeli places. Yet, waiters and chefs at restaurants and cafés are often Palestinian. The need to control both privacy and visibility during leisure time in Tel Aviv, therefore, requires looking in two directions at once: to manage their visibility as Palestinians within Jewish Israeli spaces, and to be careful about the other Palestinians they might encounter as they immerse themselves in Tel Aviv.

One summer evening, I walked around the city with Lina, a former Tel Aviv University student, when she suddenly recognized Palestinian friends on the other side of the street. As if breaking out of an invisible cage, they all greeted and hugged each other enthusiastically. Alongside Lina's friend Salma were three Palestinian men. Standing on the sidewalk, they all began speaking Arabic. Realizing how unusual this was, Lina said, "Wow! We are five Arabs here standing in the heart of Tel Aviv." Then Salma ran into the middle of the street, jokingly screaming "Allahu akbar!" (God is great), toward the shopping mall on the other side. "It's like we are having a demonstration here," one of the others said, and they all laughed with exaggerated joy that spread from this incidental gathering. Tellingly, merely meeting other Palestinian friends and speaking Arabic on the streets of Tel Aviv already felt like staging a political demonstration. It unleashed joyful feelings similar to those of the lone traveler who spots a familiar face in a foreign land. Yet, as with some travelers, the stigmatized minority urbanite does not always seek contact with the familiar.

The initial joy quickly turned to feelings of discomfort for one of the men, who was gay and worked as a fitness trainer in Tel Aviv. He looked familiar to my friend, and, although they would later recognize each other as coming from the same town, they did not bring it up. "I didn't want to scare him by saying 'I know you from somewhere,'" Lina told me later. To protect his anonymity, he went by a fake name that could be either Arabic or Hebrew. Meeting the wrong person at the wrong moment can be risky for Palestinians in Tel Aviv, especially for those young men and women whose urban immersion challenges dominant societal norms or familial expectations, either because of their gender identity or their lifestyle.

On another day, Lina and I ate something in central Tel Aviv, and, this time, *she* made use of tactical concealment. Sitting down at an outdoor food court, we ordered two bottles of beer when Lina suddenly turned to me in shock: one of the waiters, she said, was from her hometown! The convenient anonymity Tel Aviv provided immediately faded and was replaced by unsettling exposure. She asked me to change her order from beer to water, saying to the waiter that it was a mistake. As I would later learn, they both knew exactly who each other's families were but pretended not to know.

The young man took our order in Hebrew, and, after a few minutes, Lina decided to break the ice. "Don't we know each other from somewhere?" she asked the waiter, who smirked for an instant and then answered in Arabic, "Yes, we are from the same town." Their small talk continued for about a minute, at the end of which she asked for his name. "My name is Adam," he said rather hurriedly. After a few seconds of silence, he added that his real name was Ahmed. "But here I am Adam," he continued, just before his manager told him to stop speaking Arabic during work.

This scene shows how Israeli pressures on Palestinians to be invisible by changing their names and not speaking Arabic can unfold in the same situation that requires gendered tactics of invisibility to safeguard privacy among Palestinian woman during leisure activities. There was much at stake for the Palestinian woman who ordered beer in Tel Aviv, which risked provoking undesirable gossip spreading in her religiously conservative hometown.

Because leisure and fun are often public, they demand particular care from Palestinians in Tel Aviv. Immersing themselves in distinctively Jewish Israeli bars, restaurants, or public spaces is not the only option, however. Some have managed to create their own alternative spaces of Palestinian conviviality and fun within the city, which are often hidden or at the margins of urban space. Such alternative spaces include underground parties, hidden bars with Arabic DJ-nights, and the private space of apartments.

DANCING IN THE SHADOWS: A PALESTINIAN
LGBT PARTY IN TEL AVIV

The parties of "al-Qaws," a Palestinian LGBT organization, took place in a south Tel Aviv club hidden away in a side street. The organization promoted gender and sexual diversity in Palestinian society, supporting a community of "individuals that are able to live and celebrate all layers of their identity," while opposing the idea that Tel Aviv offers "freedom" through assimilation.[12] I joined one of their parties with a female Palestinian friend, walking into an unlit side street of South Tel Aviv past a couple of parked cars. Small groups of young men were just getting ready for the night, changing some of their clothes and putting on makeup to the tune of dance music played from a car radio. Here, it seemed, no one would catch them off guard too easily. Many of them have come from distant villages and towns, some from East Jerusalem, and some from the occupied West Bank if they were permitted to cross the checkpoint into Israel.

A little later inside the club, a handful of young Palestinian men stood around chatting in the large dark hall. Two of them began dancing to Arabic music, dressed in skirts and glittering outfits. Soon the club filled up with more guests of all ages and genders. Some ordered drinks from the bar, glancing toward the dance floor, which slowly began to fill up. Drag queens were among the party guests, too. Dressed glamorously, they attracted much attention on the dance floor. At some point during the party, one of the drag queens danced above the others on an elevated podium, after having stripped down to very little clothing. Some of the Palestinian men at her feet tried to touch her until one of them lifted her down and pulled her against his body as her legs wrapped around him. He slapped her backside and, eventually, set her back on the ground. She walked off with a smile and got back up onto the elevated dance floor.

It was an intense and highly sexualized party, unusually so for Palestinian events and even for the outgoing standards of Tel Aviv. Almost everyone there spoke Arabic, and, although this was still in the midst of Jewish Tel Aviv, it was a different kind of "Tel Aviv" that became meaningfully implicated within the Palestinian identity—an underground formed in the shade of the city's lights. This shade offered temporary relief from the tense exposure felt elsewhere. It was the one night of the month in which they could be both Palestinian Arabs *and* LGBT, instead of compromising the visibility of the one for the benefit of the other.

To be sure, not everyone at the party was Palestinian. The Jewish boyfriend of one of my friends told me, matter-of-factly, that he did not really like the Arabic music, maybe because, as with most Jewish Israelis, he did not speak any

Arabic. He said he mainly joined the party to do his boyfriend a favor. It must have been strange for him to be one of the few Jewish Israelis at a large party in a Tel Aviv nightclub, in the quintessential modern Jewish city, surrounded by Palestinians. It was the feeling usually reserved for the Palestinians who tried to blend into the city's Jewish clubs. The al-Qaws party was a temporary inversion of the norm, becoming a majority-minority gathering of Palestinians and Jewish citizens within the city, and it reconciled otherwise contradictory forms of visible being.

Members of ethnic minority groups often experience urban nightlife in spaces of the majority with feelings of estrangement and ambivalence, trying to belong but not quite belonging.[13] The parties organized by al-Qaws offered an alternative experience and an escape from the rigidity of this urban outsider position. For the young Palestinian Mahmoud, who often joined the party, this space was the only nightlife experience he could freely attend as the person he felt he really was. As one of three hundred thousand Palestinians in East Jerusalem, he held an Israeli-issued "blue ID" that granted him permanent resident status without citizenship. He could move around Israel freely and access jobs or education in ways that Palestinians living in the West Bank could not. As someone who still lived with his parents in a dense Palestinian neighborhood of Jerusalem, he had to carefully manage his visibility between his hometown and Tel Aviv. When we met up in Tel Aviv several weeks after the party, he told me: "The first thing I change when I move from Jerusalem to Tel Aviv is my clothes. I can't wear everything in Jerusalem, so I change my clothes in the car. If you look into my baggage, you will find all kinds of things there. My shoes, T-shirts, pants, jackets, makeup."

Although not cross-dressing, at our meeting, he wore a white jumper, a long silver necklace, and skintight trousers. Having a car enabled him to change his appearance between the two places and effectively manage different kinds of visibility and invisibility. Wanting neither to be recognized as gay in his East Jerusalem neighborhood nor as Palestinian on the streets of Tel Aviv, he used tactics of invisibility to balance these two worlds and the associated desires for external recognition. Estrangement and racism were common in Tel Aviv's nightlife because nightclub bouncers often turned back Palestinians, which made spaces like the al-Qaws party all the more important. Indeed, the same techniques that soldiers employ at military checkpoints between the West Bank and Israel are employed in bars, as queer Palestinians are often denied entry when their papers reveal their Palestinianness.[14] Nightlife then becomes a frontier of settler-colonial control over colonized gendered bodies and their mobility.

A deeply rooted sense of attempted domination by the settler majority over queer Palestinians becomes evident in their often tense and terrible experiences. Queer Palestinians face regular abuse, degradation, and threats of violence when using online dating apps and in cruising spaces. These experiences trigger situational acts of concealment of their Palestinianness, such as avoiding speaking Arabic. Such acts of muting and concealment are as much a strategic and pragmatic response to a potentially hostile environment as they are a means of accessing forms of pleasure.[15] Tactics of invisibility have both a disabling and an enabling component, allowing for the evasion of stigmatization, immobilization, and threats, while also providing access to spaces and experiences that would otherwise be inaccessible.

The party of al-Qaws usually ended relatively early so that everyone could go home unproblematically, as boundaries and checkpoints had to be crossed and outfits needed to be changed. Mahmoud preferred to drive back home later at night, so that "people don't see me," since he tended to "forget" himself in Tel Aviv. "Then I see I am already late, my parents are calling. Then I have to change my clothes, have to take off my makeup. . . . It's always hard to go back," he said. Mahmoud's dilemma was that he could not be fully visible and positively validated with both his national identity *and* his gender identity, neither in Tel Aviv, nor in Jerusalem. The parties aimed to reconcile this dilemma at least temporarily, merging the recognition of Palestinian identity with a dedicated gay space. "Imagine you are stressed all the time, you are hiding yourself, are not free. And when they do this party, you can do everything there. You can share your emotions," Mahmoud explained.

The event was intentionally invisible for both worlds it sought to reconcile. Hidden underground in south Tel Aviv, it was removed from the city's mainstream nightlife and from its mainstream gay life. Organized in ways that allowed Palestinians to join it covertly and get back home without raising suspicion, it was equally removed from the wider Palestinian sphere. This phenomenon challenges the idea that visibility is the main strategy in queer activism.[16] In a similar vein, the Palestinian alternative music scene in Israel insists on making its ethnonational particularity visible.[17] Within Tel Aviv, however, spaces of Palestinian nightlife and queer activism were often intentionally underground and invisible for reasons of privacy and protection.

This invisibility was also a product of their outsider status from the viewpoint of the city's "settler homonationalism," whereby certain queer bodies are reconstituted as worthy of recognition and protection by nation-states while others are not.[18] In the settler-colonial context, homonationalism includes attempts at sexual colonization of indigenous peoples and expresses a "normative constitution of modern settler queer projects."[19] But, as homonationalism has become a kind of master narrative that pretends to explain all things in all places, it suffers from a limited capacity to shed light on the complex everyday experiences of queer Palestinians, who are constrained by overlapping structures and practices of power in their mobility.[20] This becomes clear when we consider that many Palestinians deemed immersion into the nightlife of Tel Aviv as controversial in and of itself. Alternative Palestinian activists, especially, often dissociated themselves from Israeli culture at large.[21] This made the visible presence of "fun-loving" Palestinians in Tel Aviv highly problematic, not only in relation to Jewish Israelis but also in relation to other Palestinians.

The official "pinkwashing" did not help. Tel Aviv's vibrant gay scene, and its function as a leisure space for Palestinians, is used to brand Israel as a liberal democracy that respects civil rights and saves victims from their own society. Israel has thus attempted to co-opt the Palestinian LGBT community under the name of liberalism and respect for minorities, hoping to distract from its own human rights abuses and its ongoing colonization of the Palestinian people. Partly in response to pinkwashing, many queer Palestinians emphasize that they engage not only in a struggle against homophobia within their own culture but equally so against Israel's policies of colonization and occupation.[22] Sometimes it is the initial experience of becoming immersed in Tel Aviv that triggers such a critical awakening.

COMING OUT OF TWO CLOSETS: "I ERASED MY IDENTITY. I WAS NO LONGER MYSELF"

Amid the difficulty of securing protected Palestinian spaces of fun and leisure within Tel Aviv, the temptation to simply blend into the Jewish scene can be strong for young Palestinians in search of urban life. Salma, who was part of the enthusiastic meeting between friends described earlier, worked as a nurse in a Tel Aviv hospital. She grew up in a "difficult and violent" home and leaving it was, therefore, one of her dreams. She moved to Tel Aviv as soon as she had finished her studies in Jerusalem. Blending into the city of Tel Aviv turned out to be challenging, and she tried not to connect with "other Arabs" during her first years. However, Salma soon felt increasingly estranged when she went out to party with members of the Jewish LGBT community, saying: "I realized later on that in fact I erased my identity, I was no longer myself."

What followed was a decisive turning point when she and her Jewish girlfriend broke up after a two-year relationship. In search of familiarity and support, Salma went to see an old Palestinian friend. They sat together and talked, listening to Umm Kulthum, the famous Egyptian singer. "That day I realized what I was missing all this time: I didn't speak Arabic," Salma remembered. And yet it was much more than her native language she had neglected: "Part of being accepted to this circle of going out in Tel Aviv, of going to bars, was to constantly hide myself and my identity." For Salma, blending into the Jewish Israeli LGBT scene involved a process of co-optation and an attempt at identity erasure. She participated, at first, but eventually broke away from it: she came "out of the closet" in cultural and political terms by rejecting these assimilatory pressures.

This process of awakening involved several key moments during her life in Tel Aviv that indicated something is not quite right. The mother of Salma's former girlfriend once expressed a fear that, one night, Salma would wake up and strangle her daughter. This was said against the backdrop of the violent events during the second intifada, when a climate of suspicion, fear, and hatred dominated Jewish-Arab interactions in Israel. Later on, Salma and others formed a new movement from the ground up. Under the name of "Black Laundry," they moved beyond the assimilationist politics of the LGBT community in Israel, linking queer and feminist issues with the struggle against the occupation.[23] Black Laundry also sought to go beyond the depoliticized category under which queer Palestinians and their "party-lifestyle" had become subsumed.

Much earlier still, Salma would repeatedly ask herself the same question: "Which part of yourself do you hide in the closet? Once the Arab, once the lesbian." Only through Black Laundry was she able to reconcile the two parts of her identity. "All parts of my identity were accepted," she said, while adding that Tel Aviv also helped her explore herself and her identity away from the pressures of her family and develop it in direct confrontation with Jewish Israeli society. After a long journey, Salma said, "Tel Aviv is mine." The confidence to go out and enjoy the city as a lesbian Palestinian built on a challenging struggle.

Salma seemed to be an especially strong-willed person. One morning we sat in a Tel Aviv café as the waitress brought over the bill. We got used to speaking English, but, when the waitress put the tray with the bill down on the table, Salma switched from English back into Arabic, telling me that she liked doing this on purpose to make a statement in Tel Aviv. "The cliché is that Arabs serve Jews, but I enjoy being served by them."

Not everyone is as outspoken as Salma, and some Palestinians in Tel Aviv feel estranged from al-Qaws and other movements that try to combine a national struggle with their gender-based struggle. The gay Palestinian Saleh "came to Tel Aviv to escape the village," where his family was scared about what others might think about their son. Saying he never felt any sense of belonging to the Palestinian community, Saleh felt closely connected to the Jewish LGBT community in Tel Aviv, most of whom he considered to be "leftist." His main concern was the "cultural difference" he felt toward other Palestinians, saying, "I have always been pro-Israel." Saleh did not deny that anti-Arab racism existed or that blending into Tel Aviv was difficult. He used his individual struggle to criticize everything that imposed collective belonging on individuals, emphasizing the responsibility of each individual instead. "I don't have to defend Arabs only because I am part of them. I am an individual," he said. Much later, I met up with Saleh ahead of Tel Aviv's Pride Parade. Holding a large rainbow flag and dressed rather casually, he seemed excited about this event of collective fun, which others disliked as an Israeli pinkwashing event. Saleh seemed completely incorporated into the framework of LGBT liberalism that promises to go beyond the stigmatization of difference while ultimately failing to live up to its promise. This flawed framework dictates that to be a free individual, one must ignore or even reject one's Palestinian identity.

Indeed, simply living in Tel Aviv and trying to enjoy its many public spaces and leisure activities is hardly ever without tension and racism for Palestinian LGBTs. Abdallah, who also went to the al-Qaws party, explained: "There is discrimination here [in Tel Aviv], sometimes just when I am in the bus, or when I go to the gym, or want to order something. In the beginning I didn't want to say my name out loud when ordering something."

Instead of his real name, he would say something that sounded more Hebrew. Blending in and trying to be invisible was a tiring experience. Abdallah's boyfriend was Jewish. "His parents don't know about me, simply because I am Arab. I am gay and Arab, and my parents don't know I am gay," Abdallah said, adding that it would be a shock for his parents to see him having fun on the streets in Tel Aviv. He was careful and would not go to any clubs or gay parties in Haifa, which was too close to his hometown and provided less privacy.

Over time, Abdallah grew more confident. Now he wanted people to know he is Arab, saying, "When you hide your identity, your environment can see that you are weak." Abdallah participated in the Purim festivities in Tel Aviv, when some Palestinian LGBTs enjoy the anonymity of masquerade and dressing up in Tel Aviv's nightlife. Meeting him over a coffee, he walked in with his boyfriend's dog, which was decorated in a pink ballet tutu to fit the occasion. The ability to show such gendered visibility made Tel Aviv the right place to live for him and many others, who felt that they could not fully be themselves. As a large city that provided a sense of anonymity, Tel Aviv's Jewish character also meant it was far away from the watchful eyes of most other Palestinians. He said that Purim was an especially well-frequented party, because "all the Palestinian gays are coming to Tel Aviv. It's a day of enjoyment, that's all."

Despite the merits of living a life in Tel Aviv and enjoying the city, Abdallah had a longing for a life abroad. While several Palestinian citizens I knew from Tel Aviv left for work or studies in places such as Germany, the United Kingdom, or Australia, the topic of Palestinian emigration has been highly controversial due to political pressures to hold onto the land. This is one reason why numbers of permanent Palestinian emigrants from Israel have traditionally been low, although a little higher among Christian Palestinian citizens. Yet, one can see the growing phenomenon of internal migration from Palestinian towns into mixed and Israeli cities, where, ultimately, they feel estranged, as a "first step in their migration abroad."[24] For Abdallah, it seemed that no matter where he was—in his hometown or in Tel Aviv—one part of his identity had to be suppressed or hidden. He said that the freedom to live his sexual identity in Tel Aviv outweighed the disadvantages of living invisibly as a Palestinian within Jewish Israeli society. Yet, it was tremendously difficult to feel at home and at ease there.

IN SEARCH OF PRIVACY AND CONTROL: PALESTINIAN WOMEN BETWEEN URBAN ANONYMITY AND CULTURAL FAMILIARITY

Considering the amount of concealing and hiding required from Palestinians in Tel Aviv, one can be forgiven for simply staying at home. In a climate of stigmatization and tension around visibility, the private home fulfills an important function as an enclave within urban space. One such enclave was the apartment of three sisters who had moved to Tel Aviv from their hometown Ramleh, after serious problems within their family. These included the sudden death of their mother, the subsequent bankruptcy of their father's business, and domestic violence. They had lived in what they called "a palace," but without electricity and heating for months, after their father had lost all of his money in a shady business deal.

The apartment the sisters shared with a friend was just off a busy main road that runs through the area of Ramat Gan, east of central Tel Aviv. Here, the early Israeli state developed a modern Jewish urban system in areas of former Palestinian villages, which were depopulated in 1948.[25] Today's Ramat Gan marks the eastern extension of Tel Aviv's urban sprawl. Slightly cheaper than the center, it was popular among new urban arrivals. For the three sisters, the area offered control and anonymity away from controlling family members in their hometown, but their apartment was also a necessary refuge from the pressures of Tel Aviv. At home, they made up their own rules and supported each other.

One evening, I was invited to join them for dinner at the apartment. A private home in this city was especially difficult and important for Palestinians, first because they often found it difficult to be accepted by Jewish landlords who are suspicious of "Arabs"; and second because of an increased need for personal, cultural, and political privacy in this foreign urban space. "Tel Aviv wants to tell you that you are free, that here you can do whatever you want and you have free choice. But at the bottom line, this is not true," said Khuloud, the oldest sister, while sitting on their sofa in the living room. Soon food was served, and Sahar, the sisters' roommate and friend, began preparing the charcoal and tobacco for the narghile. This ritual accompanied an evening of enjoyment for the young Palestinians, who could speak Arabic freely, away from the buzz of Hebrew-speaking Tel Aviv. However, smoking the pipe would be unusual for young local women back in Ramleh: being in Tel Aviv enabled some forms of being and disabled others.

Sahar stood on their balcony, incinerating the blazing charcoal by spinning it around the air in circular movements. When the narghile was set up, we joined her to sit outside. Sitting around in a circle on pillows, we played cards, and, at one point, Khuloud jumped up, saying that they needed to put on the Egyptian singer Umm Kulthum whenever they played cards, "as a tradition." It seemed like they consciously enacted a cliché-like Arab atmosphere as a way to counter-balance the near-total absence of Palestinian-Arab culture within Jewish Tel Aviv.

While playing cards with Khuloud, the two other sisters, and their roommate, we began talking about Tel Aviv and their free time in the city. Would they try to meet other Palestinians in the city when they went out, I asked. "We always hide things from our community," said Ruwaydah, Khuloud's sister. "It's more intense for girls. And this is not only about drinking. When other girls hear that we live here in Ramat Gan together, they are often shocked." People from their hometown found their lifestyle in this Israeli city as unmarried girls rather strange, to put it mildly. The image of Tel Aviv as a playful party city only caused this suspicion to grow. Relatives thought Tel Aviv was all about celebrating. Sahar, who worked in a supermarket, said that many of her friends feel like Tel Aviv is "abroad." Her sister always says it is too far away for her to visit. "We have a lot of privacy here," she added with a smile, indicating that the absence of family visits was not necessarily a bad thing.

Indeed, daily interactions with other Palestinians in the city often troubled them. When grocery customers spotted Sahar's name tag, or saw her wearing a T-shirt with Arabic writing on it, they always seemed surprised: "They ask with a negative tone, 'What are you doing here? Do you study?' They always need a reason. If I say I just live here and work, they are confused." Whenever other Palestinians realized she was Palestinian, too, they immediately asked her all the questions she generally hoped to avoid. These included where she was from, which school she went to, her father's name, and so forth. As Sahar explained all this, Khuloud chipped in: "They go underneath your skin these people. Here in Tel Aviv, I don't really want to meet other Arabs." She felt more comfortable in the secure space of their own apartment, keeping things between close family and friends. Moreover, working hard and having some debts to pay, they did not go out much in Tel Aviv, because it was very expensive.

Months after this evening of cards and narghile, their landlord sold the apartment, so Khuloud and her sisters had to find a new home. They eventually found one in Jaffa's Ajami neighborhood, an area with a significant Palestinian population just south of Tel Aviv. A few months into their new lease, we met in a newly opened café on Jaffa's clock tower square. One of the main benefits of their new location seemed to be that it was "a more Palestinian place," as Khuloud put it enthusiastically, indicating a change of heart since we last met in Ramat Gan. She began working at Café Salmah in Jaffa, which had just reopened and promised to create a truly Palestinian space. From their private enclave in Ramat Gan, they moved into an "exclave"—a private life that was very close to, but still disconnected from, the local Palestinian population.

A few weeks later Khuloud already regretted some of her choices, complaining that she was not paid enough and saying that she felt humiliated by the owner's lack of respect for her work, which involved serving, cleaning, and cooking. Khuloud described her tipping point the following way: "Now he brought a second waitress, she is Jewish and 17 years old. Now I have to speak Hebrew all the time? She will serve the tables and tell me at the bar, '*tneele shtei beerot*' [give me two beers] No, enough! Why do they have to enter every single space we try to build for ourselves, why is he bringing a Jewish waitress? And one that is 17, of course she will work for the salary he proposes."

Although they seemed happy about having left Ramat Gan behind them, Khuloud's idealistic hopes for a Palestinian environment were quickly shattered. "Palestine is just a memory, not more," she would later say bitterly. Their new residence also created tension between their freedom to do whatever they wanted, as they had in Ramat Gan, and the proximity of the Palestinian community of Jaffa. The people who "go underneath your skin," as Khuloud put it earlier, now lived around them.

One day after Khuloud finished her shift, we met up with the others and walked to their apartment together. On the way, we stopped at the Abu al-'Afia sandwich shop. Maysa, the youngest of the sisters, was kind enough to wait with me at the eatery while the others went ahead to the apartment. When she received a text message from her older sisters, she suddenly turned to me, saying with a smile: "Can you go into this shop and buy [cigarette] papers for us?" Because they now lived in a Palestinian area, they had to be careful about what they did and what others knew of them doing. Gossip about the sisters from Ramleh buying papers to roll cigarettes—or joints—was not exactly what they wanted their Palestinian neighbors to hear or think about. However, these things did not matter when they lived in Ramat Gan. Maysa explained:

> In Ramat Gan, we were surrounded by Jewish society and no one asked us about what we do, we could do what we wanted. In Jaffa, we have to take much more care about what we do. We lower our voices on the street. Here we live in the middle of the Arab community. They are probably all wondering how these girls can live alone in an apartment. . . . of course, the atmosphere around Jaffa is nice. But being within the Arab community also means that they always look at you from one perspective, not looking at you based on who you are, but based on how you should be.

There is a sad irony to this, because it reflects the dilemma of having to hide something wherever you go: as Palestinians in a Jewish area, and as young women in a Palestinian area. Wherever they lived, they had to manage the visibility of one part of their life or another. They had to "lower their voices" on each of the two streets they lived on: in one place, because the people around them actually understand their language; in the other, because merely speaking the Arabic language between four young women attracted attention in Tel Aviv.

Another day, we all met on the beach for a picnic, again with narghile and a deck of cards. They sometimes enjoyed their weekends this way, and the beach seemed to offer a less marked space than other places in the city. It was cheaper, too. Unlike Beirut, where the "pleasures of the beach" are mostly privatized,[26] Tel Aviv's beaches are almost entirely public. Different stretches of the beach are known to be frequented by different kinds of people, including ultraorthodox Jews, LGBTs, tourists, Palestinian families from Jaffa, and people with dogs. Although in this sense, some of it is highly differentiated space, it also provides an open and unregulated escape from the city for those in search of leisure and fun. At the time, a new extension of the beachside boulevard, the *Tayelet*, had just been completed. It now stretched all the way from Jaffa to north Tel Aviv and allowed people at both ends to walk up or down as far as they wanted.

Once, I noticed two young Palestinian women from Jaffa sitting on the stairs of the promenade, chatting in Arabic and drinking Bacardi Breezers in the sun. On another day, I saw two other Palestinian women from Jaffa stretching and jogging along it, one of them wearing a T-shirt saying *Palestinian* in Arabic letters. Often one would see families from Jaffa strolling up north and back. Promenading originally emerged as a bourgeois sociability, but it is a "non-transgressive form of leisure" accessible to almost everyone.[27]

For the youngest of the three sisters, Maysa, not even the beach provided relief from the challenges of her life in between Ramleh and Tel Aviv. At the beach, she received repeated phone calls from a young man from her home-town, who knew her and cursed her insultingly. At one point, Khuloud took the phone from her and screamed at whoever was listening on the other end of the line. Later, she explained: "The guys in Ramleh know she lives in Tel Aviv and think she is a whore because of that. They call her, insult her, and think she will have sex with them." Tel Aviv's immoral image rubbed off on the young women and influenced the way other Palestinians judged their presence in the city, as if it polluted their honor and their authentic Palestinian identity.

For Maysa, enjoying Tel Aviv was complicated by her relatively close rela-tionship to her hometown, Ramleh. During most of the week, she commuted to Ramleh for work, and, as the youngest child, she was still more closely con-nected to the family. When their mother died in a car accident, Maysa was only sixteen. Her father and others in the family put the older sisters under a lot of pressure after that, but she was spared much of the trouble as the youngest one. Now she had to straddle the two worlds at once.

One day I accompanied Maysa to Ramleh, where we had a few hours before her work began. After a stroll through town, we sat down in a local restaurant for lunch and talked. It was here in Ramleh where they lived in their old man-sion for two months without electricity and heating after their father lost ev-erything in a business deal. Maysa's position between Tel Aviv and Ramleh was complicated. The day before our trip, one of her cousins drove by her at the bus station in a taxi, saying that he wanted to talk to her. They sat in the taxi, and he asked why she left the house, saying that he wanted to "help her come back home, to reconcile with her father." She told me: "I said I can only reconcile alone. He said that I followed my sisters who left home and they affected me in a bad way. 'You should come back to your home, people talk badly about you,' he said. 'And if they talk badly about you, that's bad for your family, bad for finding a husband.' He said the community is watching me."

The underlying connotations are that Tel Aviv is sinful, involving transgressions and a liberal lifestyle locally associated with secular Jewish Israelis. Maysa was torn between multiple injunctions and desires. "I can't decide where I want to be, I am drifting between here and there," she said. The movement between Tel Aviv and Ramleh caused much dissonance. Initially, Maysa had stayed when her sisters left the family home, but once she finished school she wanted to follow them to Tel Aviv. Now she wondered: "How could I have left without being seen the same as my sisters, without society talking about me the same way they talked about them?" The image of Tel Aviv as a playful city did not help. "They have this idea that the one who is going to Tel Aviv moves from club to club, goes to parties and drinks alcohol 24 hours," she said.

The circumstances of their family crisis made it difficult for Maysa to even imagine a life in Ramleh. At the same time, she was conflicted whenever her sisters drank alcohol or smoked. She tried to distance herself from these things. It seemed that neither way made sense, and, thus, Maysa was trapped in limbo: unable to enjoy Tel Aviv and let herself go and unable to reintegrate into Ramleh. "I see people in Tel Aviv and see their good life and I want this kind of life for everyone, also for me. But at the same time, I can't live this life. I am not part of this community."

ALTERNATIVE JAFFA:
ESCAPING MAINSTREAM TEL AVIV

Palestinians who live, study, or work in Tel Aviv often spend some of their leisure time farther south in Jaffa, which has a handful of alternative cultural spaces and dedicated Arab neighborhoods, amid deepening gentrification and luxury real estate developments for Jewish Israelis.[28] Other Palestinians deliberately choose to live in Jaffa, although they work or study farther north in Tel Aviv. Historically, it has been Tel Aviv's Jewish population that Orientalizes Jaffa and "occupies" it on holidays and weekends for leisure and shopping.[29] Increasingly, though, Palestinians together with left-wing Jewish Israelis have used their marginal position in creative ways, creating nested spaces of Palestinian leisure and fun within Israeli-gentrified Jaffa.

One of the leading actors in this movement was Muhammad Jabali, a DJ and cultural activist who worked as a computer specialist for online firms. When I discussed the invisibility of Palestinians in Tel Aviv with him, he said that "some things should stay underground. We are not ready for visibility yet." The regular party he hosted as a DJ in Jaffa was, indeed, somewhat invisible and intentionally marginal.

Jabali hosted the Middle Eastern dance music nights in the Anna Loulou Bar, where he became a local icon. The entrance to Anna Loulou is on a side street in the lower part of old Jaffa; it is almost impossible to spot without knowing about it beforehand. Sometimes a bouncer greeted patrons outside and at other times one had to ring the bell before entering. The doors were covered in thick anti-noise foam pads, and, once indoors, dull lights and rough stone walls led into a cave-like retreat in the very back. The bar's Jewish owners confessed that the bar never had any underlying political agenda.[30]

When I lived in Tel Aviv, Jabali's nights featured a regular crowd of Palestinian Tel Aviv University students, many of whom lived in Jaffa. At one point, the place was also promoted as a hotspot for the alternative gay scene. At the same time, it attracted some local Palestinian men of an older age and a hip female Palestinian middle-class crowd. In short, it was a place of contrasts. Alongside hip-hop, dance, and alternative Arabic music, the DJ set occasionally released music that inspired the crowd to dance *dabkeh*, the Levantine circle folk dance. The atmosphere intensified into the late hours with the help of beer and plenty of *araq*, the local anis spirit. In many ways, the place was both hideout and retreat—it was dark, hidden, and alcohol infused, played Arabic music, and welcomed the mixing both of Jews and Arabs and of Palestinian men and women.

The place allowed those who lived in Tel Aviv to have fun as "Palestinians," without having to immerse themselves into predominantly Jewish bars with Hebrew music and mainstream Israelis. But, at the same time, not every Palestinian fit into this crowd. "The place tried to be as inclusive as possible," said Jabali about Anna Loulou. It was a complicated mix, however. Part of it was an occasional clash of generations and intentions. Among them were obtrusive middle-aged men whose imaginations were stirred by alcohol and the presence of young women on a dance floor. Although local Jaffans were there, too, many of the Palestinians there came to study or work in the Tel Aviv area from towns in the Galilee and Triangle regions in Israel's north. Jaffa Palestinians, on the other hand, sometimes wondered about the sinful young middle-class crowd who used their hometown as a playground alongside Jewish Israelis from Tel Aviv. This diversity of age, gender, and origin was at once the essence and the difficulty of this place.

According to an article in the Israeli paper *Haaretz*, Anna Loulou was a place where "Israelis and Palestinians, straights and gays, Mizrahis and Ashkenazis" could all be "comfortable in their identities," where "the absence of compromise was the embodiment of acceptance."[31] When the Israeli couple who originally established the place got tired of running it, in 2016, some of its clients and employees banded together and purchased it, to oversee it and ensure its continuing existence. Anna Loulou offered the Palestinians in Tel Aviv and Jaffa a hideout from Tel Aviv and a sense of temporary ownership and recognition within an alternative mixed space. The DJ night of Muhammad Jabali offered a regular event that provided a secure and predictable communal experience for otherwise dispersed Palestinians in Tel Aviv and Jaffa, mixed with like-minded left-wing Jews and the occasional international visitors.

Having fun helps people temporarily break free from the disciplined constraints of daily life and from normative obligations.[32] Palestinian alternative fun in Jaffa both contested and mirrored their marginal position within Tel Aviv, symbolized by invisibility as both a protective shield and an indicator of their urban marginalization. In search for similar venues in Israeli cities and mixed towns, the Palestinian citizens have long tried to reclaim and appropriate spaces for music and art, with the mixed city of Haifa being an important alternative cultural center.[33] This search was more precarious in Tel Aviv and Jaffa. The fact that Anna Loulou, one of the only nightlife spaces that catered to Palestinians in Tel Aviv, was founded and owned by Jewish Israelis emphasizes their vulnerable position. Any attempt at establishing Palestinian authenticity in this city appeared to lead to a number of political compromises.

THE SEARCH FOR AUTHENTIC FUN: CULTURAL ESTRANGEMENT AND POLITICAL COMPROMISE IN TEL AVIV-JAFFA

One bar in Jaffa that has flourished during the time of my research was Café Salmah, which some Palestinian Tel Aviv University students used as a regular hangout. The place had Arabic signs and sold Palestinian beer and T-shirts with Arabic print on them. According to the regular customer Hussam, who lived in Jaffa and worked in Tel Aviv's high-tech sector, this political and cultural visibility also had a downside: "The last owner of Salmah was too extremist. Her business failed. She made it all Palestine. So, I told the new owner that if he wants to make money, Jews have to feel comfortable to come. But, of course, we should keep our culture and language."

It was the same dilemma that haunted individual decision-making in Tel Aviv, as a choice between blending into Jewish Israeli spaces or expressing Palestinian assertiveness. Now deeply gentrified, Jaffa offers plenty of bars and cafés with an "Oriental" Arabic atmosphere, but few of them are run by Palestinians and even fewer have a clear political agenda. Salmah did so in terms of the music it played and the language it used. Its Facebook page was in Arabic, and its Arabic-language logo had an English translation, rather than a Hebrew one. In the heavily marked space of highly differentiated Jaffa, such characteristics send specific signals and construct clear boundaries. But, in Jewish Israeli areas of Tel Aviv outside of Jaffa, few alternatives exist to Jewish institutions and the overall dominance of Israeli culture.

In addition to Salmah and Anna Loulou in Jaffa, Tel Aviv University students organized parties in a club in South Tel Aviv and in other locations. One student party, in 2015, was titled "Neon Sensation Party," in which party guests could make themselves glow in the dark while dancing to house music in a central Tel Aviv location. With ticket sales in Jerusalem, Haifa, and Tel Aviv, this party had more than five hundred, mostly Palestinian, attendees on its Facebook page. However, its advertising had no specific reference to anything Palestinian, and the description was in English. Being careful with Arabic signage was also a result of past experience. Organizers of the student parties told me that Israeli venue owners are careful not to hold any event that is openly hosted by Palestinians, which could be interpreted as nationalist or political.

Even the most prominent politicized Palestinian musicians, the hip-hop group DAM, had to adapt when they wanted to give a concert in Tel Aviv. These Palestinian rappers started off with English rap and turned to Arabic in reaction to the impact of conflict, occupation, and violence on identity and nationalism.[34] One night I joined an album release concert by DAM, held in a club in South Tel Aviv. It is perhaps the most famous Palestinian hip-hop group and its three rappers grew up in a neglected neighborhood of the nearby city of Lydda (Lod). Very much like the DJ nights of Muhammad Jabali, their concerts attracted a following of both Palestinian and Jewish Israeli fans as well as foreigners who were living in the country or visiting.

At the album release, there were many Palestinian citizens of Israel but at least half of the crowd seemed to consist of Jewish Israelis and internationals. Staging quintessential Palestinian music in front of a mixed crowd in the heart of Tel Aviv complicated the question of who the "insiders" actually were. To begin with, the rappers of DAM seemed unsure about which language to use when talking to the crowd: Hebrew, English, or Arabic? After asking the crowd who were Palestinians, who were foreigners, and who were Jewish Israeli, in the manner of bands as they try to rouse an audience, they ended up using a combination of the three languages between the songs. What may be interpreted as an expression of positive cosmopolitanism left a somewhat bitter aftertaste for some of the Palestinians who had hoped for the rare authentic Palestinian experience in Tel Aviv.

During a DAM concert in their hometown Lydda (Lod), in 2005, a similar mix once triggered rapper Tamer Nafar to call out to the local Palestinians at the concert, "Yo' Arabs! Where are all the Arabs?" (*Ya Arab! Sha'b al-Arabi wayn?*). Until that moment, the Jewish Israelis in the crowd were participating more visibly and actively, being more familiar with the style and dance of this cosmopolitan music. But when the call to "Arabs" was followed by a famous anthem from the times of the Palestinian intifada, the Palestinian crowd suddenly sprang to life and chanted along. This moment activated their sense of belonging and ownership over the space, and, until this point, "the Palestinians in attendance [had] looked and acted as though they were the outsiders."[35] This shift signaled to the Jewish crowd in attendance that they were, in fact, the outsiders.

If this mix were already a challenge in Lydd, a mixed Jewish-Arab town and the place where DAM grew up, a private venue in Tel Aviv further complicated things. The concert took place under an Israeli roof in an Israeli city that officially does not even recognize the existence of the Palestinian community within. Palestinian organizers in Tel Aviv often depend on Israeli host spaces and are sometimes torn between the difficulty of generating an authentic Palestinian communal feeling and the need for a compromise when holding events in such Jewish-owned spaces.

This constant need for compromising also defined the Al-Saraya Theater in Jaffa, which hosted concerts and events for the Palestinians in Jaffa and Tel Aviv. According to Muhammad Jabali, who served on the theater's board, "It's the only Arab cultural institution in the city, but it's not independent." Al-Saraya existed precariously within the so-called Arab-Hebrew Theatre. Dependence on Israeli funding was a problem, according to Jabali: "You can make an Arab theatre, be radical in your content, but then you have no support. You are at the peak of your community, politically and in terms of identity, but all this is exactly what you can't say when you sit in the ministry [to request funding]. Wherever you walk in this country as a Palestinian institution, you will step into Israeli mud. Whatever you start, you will need Israeli institutions." Certainly, maintaining islands of distinctive Palestinian culture and fun in the midst of a Jewish Israeli city demanded a lot of compromising.

When I met Jabali another time, he had just announced his "retirement" from the weekly DJ sessions at the Anna Loulou bar. After three years of playing there, he had had enough and wanted to move on. "It was exciting for me. But now I need to do something for my home, I want to be in financial security," he said, adding: "You can't struggle like this all alone. If I know that the revolution will come in two months, I get into financial problems and struggle. But this revolution is not coming. And now we are losing Jaffa to Tel Aviv."

Even the most dedicated activists experience a breaking point at which they focus on the pragmatic side of life in the absence of a "revolution" in waiting. The alternatives for having fun in Tel Aviv were rather sobering to most Palestinians, some of whom simply considered it politically inappropriate to join in. Talking about the so-called Tel Aviv "White Night," a night of live music and celebration with cultural venues remaining open until late, the Tel Aviv University student Said told me, "If I was in any other country, I would have participated, even without feeling a sense of belonging to the country. But I never felt any belonging to these Israeli festivities." These events offered opportunities to blend in and become immersed, anonymously, in a large event, but such inconspicuous immersion was far from easy to bear as an observant urban outsider.

I realized this when joining the Purim night celebrations, which involved a big Israeli masquerade, with a Palestinian friend. With us was another friend who worked as a foreign journalist for a European newspaper. Committed to "just enjoy it," and not in the mood for conversations about politics, the three of us walked along the mundane Rothschild Boulevard. To our surprise, a group of young Arabic-speaking men with masks passed us, laughing and chatting euphorically. These celebrations were rather well frequented by young Palestinians and especially the LGTB community, who could become immersed in Tel Aviv with masks without the risk of being discovered by the wrong people.

On the other hand, we noticed Jewish Israelis who dressed up as soldiers and other military-related personas. One was dressed as what seemed like a particularly tasteless Israeli interpretation of an "Arab"—a kaffiyeh on the head and a target plate hanging down from both sides of his body, connected via a string that rested on his shoulders. Others were dressed as Saudi-style sheikhs. To be immersed anonymously in the crowd amid these less than subtle provocations was simply too difficult to abide. My friends and I sat down in a restaurant with the plan to have dinner but felt increasingly frustrated and numbed by the whole experience. My Palestinian friend had never been out on Purim before, despite having lived in Tel Aviv for many years. She had pushed herself to give it a try but ended up feeling disenchanted and tense. The desire to simply have fun was suffocated by the feeling that there was something utterly wrong about it. This exemplified the unresolved tension many Palestinians in Tel Aviv felt between a curiosity about urban life and a desire to take part in it, on the one hand, and a sense of political responsibility and the frequent experience of political estrangement, on the other hand. To have fun in Tel Aviv not only demanded the invisibility of Palestinian identity, but also required the silent acceptance of a hegemonic Israeli culture of fun, which, for the Palestinians, is always heavily politicized.

URBAN CITIZENSHIP AND THE
FREEDOM TO HAVE FUN

While having fun can be simply an escape from normative obligations and organized power, it can also undermine hegemony and the regime of power on which certain strands of moral and political authority rest.[36] The often covert and ambivalent practices of leisure and fun among Palestinians in Tel Aviv escape norms and cross boundaries in myriad ways, but they also remain confined within marginalized urban islands of suppressed joy. Fun and leisure in the city of Tel Aviv reveals a key dilemma of urban immersion for the Palestinians as members of a stigmatized minority: it inspires a hope for urban freedoms but immediately restricts these potential freedoms. As a result, the spaces of collective Palestinian fun remain marginalized, while the city estranges individual Palestinians who immerse themselves in its Jewish Israeli spaces. In this contradictory and ambivalent space, invisibility becomes both an individual desire and a product of systematic urban marginalization.

Although rarely discussed as such, the freedom to have fun and enjoy leisure visibly and collectively is a key indicator of urban minority citizenship. Indeed, "when you are having fun you're free and only if you're free can you have fun."[37] The lack of freedom for the Palestinians is evident in the need for safeguarding their invisibility and privacy, as a result of overlapping domains of power and control from the Jewish Israeli and the Palestinian communities. This need for invisibility is also due to fun being a potentially transgressive phenomenon and "a deviation from the norm" that is always gendered, while the marginalization of certain identities pushes its expressions into hidden subcultures.[38] Against this background, Tel Aviv restricts the space for Palestinian fun and leisure in at least two ways: (1) the freedom to have fun collectively as members of a stigmatized minority and (2) the freedom to have fun as an unmarked individual.

This restricted freedom is further complicated by the continuing rejection of Palestinian immersion in Tel Aviv as a legitimate and accepted thing to do among the wider Palestinian community. The dual illegitimacy of their leisurely urban immersion requires dual tactics of invisibility. Because fun and leisure are often public and transgressive, random encounters between strangers occur frequently and often in unexpected ways. The pressure to protect their anonymity is highest for Palestinian women and members of the LGBT community, as they become frequent targets for the external projection of societal

norms and their boundaries.[39] Tactics of invisibility and situational concealment become relevant tools for navigating the intersection of the struggle for
gender-based liberation and the struggle against racism and discrimination.

These individual tactics of invisibility are in a symbiotic relationship with
the systematic invisibility that is imposed on the Palestinian minority within
Tel Aviv. As the city's Palestinian public culture is dispersed and restricted
to marginalized hidden spaces, some individual concerns about visibility are
satisfied more easily, too. This means that the categorical marginalization of
a minority in this settler city and the individual need to protect one's own
privacy in relation to other members of that minority coproduce the experience of invisibility and uncertainty that defines the dual illegitimacy of being
Palestinian in Tel Aviv.

As per the saying, "Haifa works, Jerusalem prays, and Tel Aviv plays," this
play ultimately involves a number of acrobatic balancing acts for the Palestinians. Through forms of leisure and fun that demand tactics of invisibility, marginalized urbanites quietly make claims for access to an urban leisure space,
finding niches and appropriating public and private spaces for times of joy and
conviviality. However marginal these spaces may be, they allow for individuals
and small collectives to use the city despite the dual illegitimacy of Palestinian fun and leisure in Tel Aviv. Although Palestinians continue to follow their
desires and do what they want to do, without giving up who they are, they often
realize that the one comes at the expense of the other: doing what you want
to do as a Palestinian in Tel Aviv always requires you to carefully manage the
visibility of "who you are."

NOTES

1. Azaryahu, *Tel Aviv*, 47.
2. Jonsson, "Serious Fun."
3. Freud, "Beyond the Pleasure Principle"; Jacques Lacan, *Four Fundamental Concepts of Psychoanalysis*.
4. Khalili, "Politics of Pleasure," 585.
5. Deeb and Harb, *Leisurely Islam*, 14.
6. Coleman and Kohn, *Discipline of Leisure*, 1.
7. Khalili, "Politics of Pleasure."
8. Deeb and Harb, *Leisurely Islam*, 10.
9. L. Abu-Lughod, *Veiled Sentiments*.
10. Herzog, "Choice as Everyday Politics."
11. Koning, *Global Dreams*.

12. al-Qaws, "About Us."

13. Koefoed and Simonsen, "(Re)scaling Identities."

14. Ritchie, "Pinkwashing, Homonationalism, and Israel–Palestine."

15. Ritchie, "Pinkwashing, Homonationalism, and Israel–Palestine."

16. Ritchie, "How Do You Say 'Come Out of the Closet' in Arabic?"

17. Karkabi, "Staging Particular Difference," 326.

18. Puar, "Rethinking Homonationalism."

19. Jackman and Upadhyay, "Pinkwatching Israel, Whitewashing Canada," 200.

20. Ritchie, "Pinkwashing, Homonationalism, and Israel–Palestine."

21. Karkabi, "Staging Particular Difference," 317.

22. Elia, "Gay Rights with a Side of Apartheid," 58.

23. Ziv, "Performative Politics in Israeli Activism."

24. Ibrahim, "Emigration Patterns among Palestinian Women," 210.

25. Golan, "Jewish Settlement of Former Arab Towns," 146–47.

26. Khalili, "Politics of Pleasure."

27. Khalili, Politics of Pleasure, 8.

28. Monterescu, *Jaffa*, 273.

29. Monterescu and Schickler, "Creative Marginality."

30. Monterescu, *Jaffa*, 274.

31. "Jaffa Bar Takes a Leap beyond Coexistence," Haaretz.com, February 8, 2016.

32. Bayat, *Life as Politics*, 130–31.

33. Karkabi, "Staging Particular Difference," 319.

34. Eqeiq, "Louder Than the Blue ID."

35. McDonald, *My Voice Is My Weapon*, 235–39.

36. Bayat, *Life as Politics*, 130–31.

37. De Grazia, *Of Time, Work and Leisure*, 423.

38. Fincham, *Sociology of Fun*, 41–43.

39. Sa'ar, "Lonely in Your Firm Grip"; Ritchie, "How Do You Say 'Come Out of the Closet' in Arabic?"

FIVE

—᙭—

A CULTURAL EXILE

Palestinian Artists in Tel Aviv between Individual Liberation and Political Co-optation

WHENEVER ANISA ASHKAR WAKES UP in the morning, she contemplates for a while until a meaningful word or phrase comes to her mind. Then she paints it on her face in black Arabic calligraphy. Sitting on a sofa inside her Tel Aviv studio, she says: "I started doing it 14 years ago because I am Arab. They always thought I am French, or from somewhere else. In Tel Aviv, people don't get that I am Arab. 'Are you Brazilian?' they ask. I wanted to underline that I am Arab. I wanted to have ownership over my body."

The routine began when she started studying art at Beit Berl, a large college north of Tel Aviv. One day she appeared at school with the calligraphy added to her usual makeup. It was a primarily Jewish Israeli college where people in her immediate environment did not speak or read Arabic. Turning her face into a space for expressing her Arab identity came as a shock to many of her peers, relatives, and friends. Some fourteen years later, she worked as an artist and lived between her hometown Acre and Tel Aviv-Jaffa, where her studio was located. In this Jewish Israeli space, the regular performance gained renewed relevance to her: it was a visible refusal to accept being misrecognized as a Brazilian. She also used the artistic routine to remind herself of something: "It's to remind myself that I am Arab, because I am constantly in Jewish or foreign space."

The city of Tel Aviv poses particular challenges and contradictions for Palestinian citizens whose work lies in the creative arts. Unlike the mixed Jewish-Arab city of Haifa, which has long featured a vibrant Palestinian culture scene, Tel Aviv offers a limiting environment for Palestinian artists, and their work creatively engages with the ambivalence of immersing as Palestinian citizens in a Jewish Israeli city. Art often becomes a space for expressing people's marginalized realities and identities, and, therefore, it represents a performative aspect of politics in divided societies.[1] This performative aspect is highly ambivalent in the work of Palestinian artists who lived in Tel Aviv, because the city's settler-colonial emergence has largely erased Palestinian identity and the Arabic language from within its space. This predicament poses some difficult questions: Who can produce what kind of art in what language, and for what audience, within this space? What balancing acts become necessary for Palestinian minority artists who immerse themselves in the city of the political Other, while simultaneously representing aspects of identity this urban space actively suppresses?

Palestinian citizens who live as artists, musicians, and writers in Tel Aviv will answer these questions differently, based on the respective audiences they speak to and the art they produce. This will become evident in the following portraits of three Palestinian citizens of Israel who have all lived and worked in Tel Aviv as artists: the performance artist Anisa Ashkar, the queer writer Raji Bathish, and the musician and actor Mira Awad. Each of these artists in their own way creatively engages with the ambivalence of being a Palestinian in the midst of a Jewish Israeli city. Ashkar uses her facial calligraphy as a direct response to being misrecognized, Bathish faces the limits of writing for an Arabic-speaking audience while living in a city where most people do not speak the language, and Awad had to reconcile her desire to use Tel Aviv as an independent woman while collaborating with Jewish artists, as public expectations were put on her as a Palestinian celebrity in Israel. Their artistic expressions can become a vehicle for representing and communicating alternative visions about the relationship between identity, place, and citizenship. At the same time, artists' ambivalent experiences are an indicator of the impossibility of reconciling the contradictions between who they are and where they are. Much like leisure and fun, art is a highly visible and often contentious domain of life that lays bare how the settler-colonial strategy of eliminating Palestinian identity and power takes on various "liberal" and ostensibly inclusive forms in Tel Aviv. Such art both challenges and represents the ongoing marginality of its producers.

Some art forms have historically been more closely associated with marginality than others, such as street art, performances, or word art. Those who are marginalized in a particular city may use artistic expressions and performances in an effort to gain recognition for their identity as one that is no longer marginal but integral to a city or nation.[2] In this sense, art often includes claims for recognition, equality, or integration. Indigenous minorities, in particular, have used forms of vocal or artistic expression to bring their own definitions of indigenous identities and social issues to the attention of nonindigenous publics.[3] None of the artists featured in this chapter employed indigeneity as a key feature of their art. But as Palestinian citizens of Israel, they all struggled with the contradictions of immersing themselves and working in the art scene of a settler city.

Settler art has long played an important role as a medium for the erasure of Palestinian culture and history: Zionist settlers used art to create a myth of "natural occupancy" and "nativeness" for immigrating Jews, while eliminating the indigenous Palestinian Arab presence.[4] This refers both to the particular images Zionist art created and to specific settler-colonial spaces that came to occupy formerly Palestinian houses or areas, such as the Ein Hod "artists' colony" that occupies the former Palestinian village of 'Ayn Hawd.[5] Much like colonial settlements, settler art "seizes land by making claims" about nativeness and belonging, while mobilizing settler-colonial representations of the nation.[6]

Today, art galleries in Israel continue to police the degree to which Palestinian art can be radical. Likewise, leading Israeli cultural organizations have long ignored and undermined Arabic music and banished it from mainstream broadcasting.[7] Moreover, hardly any bookstores in Jewish Israeli cities stock Arabic works despite Palestinian citizens making up some 21 percent of the Israeli population. With the exception of one or two bookstores in Jaffa, it is far easier to find literature in any major European language than in Arabic across the city of Tel Aviv. This absence is a direct result of the setter-colonial elimination of Palestinian culture and the definition of the city as a European-style, international Jewish metropolis.

What survives of Palestinian-driven art within Jewish Israeli Tel Aviv partly remains dependent on this historical restructuring of the relationship between space and identity. Although art can generate new possibilities for formulating indigenous resistance in some contexts,[8] the liberalism of the Israeli art scene has actively undermined any such radical challenge. Art, therefore, expresses both the possibilities and the limitations of Palestinian inclusion and signifies the wider predicament of Palestinian citizenship in Israel. This involves a condition of dual exile: the dilemma of not fitting into the Israeli art scene, on the basis of being a Palestinian citizen, while also not being welcomed into the Palestinian art scene elsewhere, as graduates of Israeli art colleges or recipients of Israeli funding.[9]

In this politically adverse space, art offers an alternative form of expression that is not necessarily overtly "political" but nevertheless manipulates boundaries and makes invisible aspects of identity and personhood visible. Citizens who are disenchanted by mass demonstrations and civil society initiatives have used art as a new "technology of the self," expressing a strengthened notion of individual sovereignty in neoliberal cities.[10] This individual struggle for sovereignty and its gendered and political dimensions lie at the heart of the three Palestinian artists portrayed here. For Ashkar, facial calligraphy is an attempt to regain control over one's identity and its public visibility. She searched for individual sovereignty—as a way to control her body and identity—in the midst of recurring classification and misrecognition: through pushing marginalized subjectivity to the surface of the recognizable, this art responds to the external "categorization" and misrecognition of her identity.[11] Although Palestinian citizen artists sometimes contest the hegemonic character of this Israeli city, ultimately, they cannot escape its limiting effects and the recurring misrecognition of their work.

REFUSING INVISIBILITY: EMBODIED ART AND THE MISRECOGNITION OF PALESTINIAN IDENTITY

As noted earlier, Ashkar, who painted Arabic calligraphy onto her face, grew up in a neglected neighborhood on the outskirts of Acre. Born in 1979, she was one of eleven children in her family. She told me that she made first contact with the world of art during a calligraphy course organized by her aunt, which inspired her to learn and study in Israeli institutions. Speaking in her Tel Aviv studio, she explained how she grew beyond these classic teachings: "I crossed the Arab border. When I started to write calligraphy on my face, others began commenting on it, not accepting it as art."

She picked Tel Aviv as the place to live and work mainly because the city was just where "stuff was happening," she said. Being located in this city as opposed to Haifa, for example, which has a stronger Palestinian culture scene, makes sense for artists who seek to exhibit in Jewish Israeli galleries and direct their art at Israeli and international audiences. Moreover, "all artists want a little bit of art happening, go to theatres and museums, and this is in Tel Aviv," she added, as we were sitting on a sofa in her spacious studio just off one of Tel Aviv's main roads. Next to us on the floor lay a freshly painted canvas spread out to dry. Throughout the studio, other pieces of artwork were on display, some of them featuring Arabic calligraphy. Looking at the script that framed her eyes on that day, I managed to recognize the phrase 'allamoune, "they taught me." I asked her why she chose this phrase. She said it was simply what came to her mind that morning, "'they taught me,' because this morning I felt something that reminded me that I studied."

As we spoke, Ashkar mixed some Hebrew words into her Arabic, which was not unusual among Palestinian citizens in Tel Aviv. It seemed as if her facial art served as an internal reminder of her Palestinian identity and the Arabic

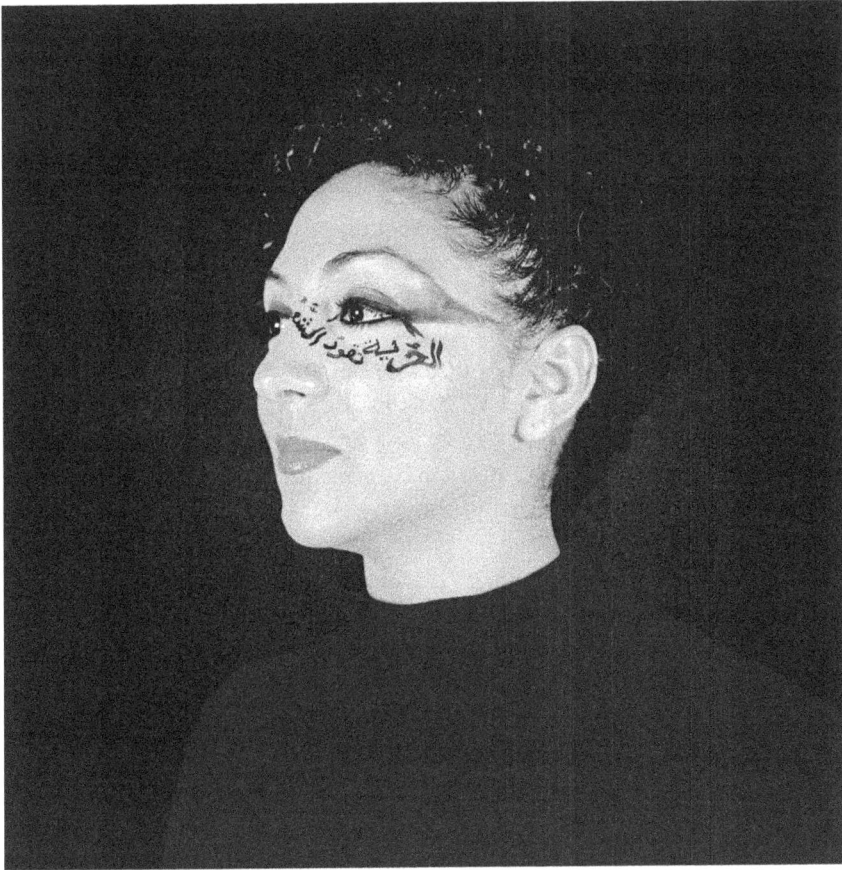

Figure 5.1 The artist Anisa Ashkar with facial calligraphy that proclaims: "Freedom leads the people."

Source: Anisa Ashkar.

language in a space where Hebrew dominated most aspects of daily life. Externally, too, it served as a reminder for others in the cafés and streets of Tel Aviv, where her art provoked a variety of reactions. "There is always discussion about it. People ask: 'Is it art? What kind of art is that?'" she explained, adding: "The normal person asks: 'what's that?'" Her usual answer to "why?" was something along the lines of the answer she gave me: "It's about my identity I have inside. I don't want to be Jewish, and I don't want to be a foreigner."

Her performance offered her a public platform to openly declare her Palestinian-Arab identity instead of being misrecognized as a foreigner.

This was useful in unexpected ways, she said, with a smirk. On one hand, "It's good that people see it and then go on distance from me. They ask me and I say I am Arab, and then they say, 'really, ahm . . . ok,' and go away." On the other hand, the facial calligraphy brought up interesting conversations, too, as it "leads to a special relationship" with people and the space she is in. But most people simply got confused when they saw it, and this included other Palestinians, too, as Ashkar explained: "They don't understand it. They ask me, 'what is your opinion? Where does your opinion lie? With who are you?' They can't define me. The Jews tell me often, 'no, you are not Palestinian.' The Palestinian says, 'I don't understand.'"

This lack of understanding may be partly because most of her art is abstract and not straightforwardly political. To Palestinian activists, her performances may fall short of qualifying as a radical intervention that challenges dominant Israeli conceptions. Although having one's face covered in Arabic calligraphy is a rather straightforward expression, Ashkar sees it as a symbol for the balance between two poles that make up her identity. "I have two parts in my personality and identity. I am Palestinian, if I like it or not: I know my identity. And on the other side, I have the Israeli ID, I live here and work here in Israel." In this interpretation, the facial art embodies a bridge between public space and the Palestinian identity that is suppressed in a place like Tel Aviv. Her art involves a claim to be seen in space and to use this space, like a bird breaking out of an invisible cage, she says, "Look at me, I am Arab!"

Despite this upfront performance, Ashkar did not see herself as an activist. Nor did she attend political protests and demonstrations, saying that "to survive and breathe here is political. To be an Arab artist in Israel is political. You talk about protests? My face is a demonstration." To be "political" is not necessarily the key aim of her art, but, in a place like Tel Aviv, Palestinian art may well be considered political for its very existence.[12] This interpretation of art mirrors the idea that any Palestinian art is implicitly also an act of defiance or resistance in the face of colonization and erasure, including "the desire to be visible, to be heard, and to be documented"; it allows for the expression of a Palestinian identity that has been denied, subjugated, and silenced.[13] Ashkar's art is the main locus for the possibility of transformation to her. It's "a type of warfare,"—"quiet, yet diligent and penetrating," according to the Israeli curator Naomi Aviv, who commented on Ashkar's work.[14] This act of "penetrating" the Israeli public with a declaration of Arab identity mirrors a famous piece of work of the Palestinian poet Mahmoud Darwish, who had just returned from exile to a life under the military regime in Israel, when he famously declared in a 1964 poem titled "ID card": "Write Down: I am an Arab."[15]

Painting your Palestinian identity onto your face was not the safest way to go about one's daily life in Israel at a time of widespread anti-Palestinian racism and an ongoing political conflict. When Ashkar was about twenty-one years old, her father saw the face painting for the first time and urged her to take it off. "He asked me, 'you think that looks nice?' He also said that they [the Jews] will kill me if I walk around like this and they know I am Arab." It was the time of Palestinian suicide bombings in Israel during the second intifada, when the public spirit of Jewish-Arab relations in Israel was very polarized. Some fifteen years later, Ashkar sometimes still felt vulnerable as a visible "Arab" in Tel Aviv in the midst of recurring violent conflict, polarized nationalism, and Jewish Israeli extremism.

The period of our meeting was at a time of adversity. It was only one day after the abduction of Mohammed Abu Khdeir, a sixteen-year-old Palestinian from East Jerusalem, on July 2, 2014. He was burned to death by Israeli extremists in a revenge attack for the kidnapping and killing of three young Jewish Israelis in the occupied West Bank. Only a week later, the Gaza conflict escalated. It was not an easy time to wear Arabic calligraphy in an Israeli city. "Something is changing now," said Ashkar. "People take the things in their own hand and attack people . . . this is the atmosphere. To feel safe in this place seems like an impossible word right now. When I walk on the streets here in Tel Aviv, I feel a lot of anger, yes."

The art of Ashkar is not just the calligraphy she wears. Performance art was a natural extension of her line of creativity and some of these performances implicitly addressed the predicament of Palestinian citizens of Israel. In one installation, Ashkar used a dichotomy between white and black in a series of tar paintings of abstract shapes with Arabic phrases written into them: the black color as blackness and otherness, like her; and the white as a representation of the landlord, the neighbor across the street, the "White City" of Tel Aviv. Another theme in her installations is cotton, which goes back to the place where she grew up. The Barbur neighborhood of Acre had long been refused access to electricity and suffered from sewage problems. Its houses featured roofs that had to be held together by disused car tires so they would not be blown away by the wind from the sea. Nearby, the white cotton fields of the kibbutz Ein Hamifratz marked the boundaries of her childhood space, the end of the Arab world and the beginning of the Jewish world, although she frequently played in the fields.[16]

Between Acre and Tel Aviv-Jaffa, her artwork was often a reaction to what goes on in her day-to-day life, as a Palestinian Arab woman with feminist ambitions who worked in the Israeli city of Tel Aviv. As a performance artist, she absorbs and manipulates elements from this life and simultaneously makes people confront a reality she generates. Her work is a way of confronting foreignness and its relationship with her Palestinian history. As one scholar suggests about Ashkar's work: "Exile is a state that still lives in the world of the artist . . . in her daily life on the streets of the Israeli city of Tel Aviv. . . . Sometimes she chooses to walk through Jaffa in a desperate attempt to ease the sense of foreignness and the weight of distance."[17] This role of Jaffa to her was one reason why Ashkar insisted that Tel Aviv always be mentioned in conjunction with its historical Palestinian neighbor Jaffa, hyphenated as Tel Aviv-Jaffa.

The occasional walk through Jaffa is something many Palestinians in Tel Aviv referred to, whether they were artists or not. It symbolizes the state of living in exile on your homeland. Indulging in romanticized memories and history played an important role in satisfying the occasional longings for an alternative urban feel. Every Palestinian in Tel Aviv, then, has a story about their history and identity. But while many keep these stories underneath the surface of daily interactions in the Jewish Israeli city, Ashkar openly carries one part of her story around. Crucially, "she goes out with her story *without asking for permission*."[18] In doing so, she counters the invisibility of Palestinian identity within Tel Aviv. However, she does so on a personal level by tagging herself visibly as "Arab" but without any further radical statement that could pose a challenge to Israeli policies or actions.

The "political" in this case does not go beyond the "personal" level of seeking individual sovereignty, as opposed to making claims for collective sovereignty. Through this performance, she embodies Palestinian identity rooted in her own experience: the invisibility of Arabic she confronted in Tel Aviv, her family's land being taken away by a kibbutz, the stories of the transformation of Acre into an Israeli city and of the white cotton fields she walked in but did not own. Although this art is rooted in the senses of Palestinian and feminist identity, its abstract and personalized nature also limit its radical transformative potential.

Part of these limits are prefigured by the logic of conditional inclusion, which forces Palestinian artists to operate within a framework of "acceptable" art if they want to exhibit in Israeli museums. The individual freedom to express an alternative identity does not necessarily apply to museums and art spaces in Tel Aviv, few of which were willing to break political taboos. The focus on art as a bodily and abstract expression of personal and individual sovereignty, therefore, reflects the absence of Palestinian sovereignty on a collective and institutional level, which includes restrictions on the kind of art that is tolerated and exhibited within Tel Aviv.

As a consequence of its marginalization by Israeli institutions, the Palestinian art scene in Israel has long been fragmented. The rare exhibition opportunities often come as group shows with Jewish Israeli artists and have a distinctly "political tone to them," with the Palestinian artist often included as a token representative, or "pet Arab," as a demonstration of Israel's democratic and inclusive character.[19] Palestinian art is often co-opted by the Jewish Israeli art scene, as long as its content does not pose a radical challenge to what is acceptable and tolerable.

The 2013 exhibition *Effervescence* may have been one rare exception, as it put the spotlight on a new generation of Palestinians in Israel's binational Jewish-Arab cities. According to a commentary by its Jewish Israeli curator Rona Sela, "As Israeli institutional exclusion, segregation and erasure from public space intensifies, so too does the struggle for change."[20] Some considered the exhibition an achievement precisely because it was hosted in a mainstream institution in Tel Aviv, the Nachum Gutman Museum. Gutman is acknowledged as the most important painter of early Tel Aviv, "the painter of Zionism."[21] Yet, others considered it to be a political sellout and an act of normalizing Tel Aviv as an ostensibly inclusive city that welcomes political diversity.

Part of the exhibition's content certainly went beyond what is deemed acceptable in the Israeli mainstream, including a portrayal of the violent transformation of Palestinian towns into Israeli cities.[22] Tellingly, the Jewish public perceived it as highly political and controversial, with news coverage calling it "an intifada substitute in the heart of Tel Aviv."[23] Although this exceptional project made a perspective visible that is otherwise absent from the urban space of Tel Aviv, the possibilities of radical Palestinian art in this city are severely limited by the dependency both on Israeli institutions and on the Jewish Israeli public being their main audience. How inescapable the constraints of Tel Aviv are for Palestinian artists who use the Arabic language as their medium for communication becomes particularly clear in the story of the writer Bathish.

IN LITERARY EXILE: WRITING ARABIC IN THE HEBREW CITY

Ashkar used Arabic calligraphy to communicate an otherwise misrecognized or suppressed aspect of her identity to the public of Tel Aviv, although most people in Tel Aviv would not be able to read it. Much of her art, as it was exhibited in Israeli museums and gets consumed by the Israeli art scene, was not directly aimed at a Palestinian-Arab public. This was different for the Palestinian writer Bathish, a poet, novelist, screenplay writer, and cultural activist who was born in Nazareth, the largest Palestinian town in Israel. He experienced the difficulties of being a Palestinian writer in Tel Aviv during seven years of living in the city, until he moved to Haifa because he could no longer bear the absence of the Arabic language and the lack of a Palestinian culture sphere.

Bathish initially moved to Tel Aviv as a content writer for a marketing company, saying that this decision was somewhat controversial at the time. Tel Aviv, after all, was the city that symbolized the Jewish Israeli Other, as he explained when we met in Fattoush, a well-known Palestinian café in Haifa, a year after he had left Tel Aviv. His experience of living there had influenced much of his writing at the time; indeed, one of his books is titled "A Room in Tel Aviv" (*ghurfah fe tel-abeb*). "A lot of Palestinians live in Tel Aviv," he told me, "But when a Palestinian chooses to write about Tel Aviv, it's a shock. The response tends to be: 'Why do you write about the capital of the enemy?'"

Sitting in the busy café in Haifa, he explained that part of his work on Tel Aviv was intended to reveal a very basic fact: "that Palestinians there actually existed." Also, writing queer literature in Arabic challenged taboos and stereotypical images both in Israel and in the Arab world. According to him, writing about a Palestinian in Tel Aviv with fluid gender identity functions as a shock in two ways. As a Palestinian writing about Tel Aviv in Arabic, he revealed an insider literary perspective on a largely invisible and unrecognized part of Tel Aviv. In writing as a gay Palestinian *from* Tel Aviv, he highlighted the unrecognized status of Tel Aviv as a city where Palestinians still existed. Some of his writing is provocative and explicit, involving sexualized narratives of Palestinians and their Jewish lovers, and of individual pleasures, passions, and fears. This is, in part, how Bathish experienced Tel Aviv, as a place both of tension and of pleasure.

His original intention was to become a Palestinian political writer based in Tel Aviv, but, eventually, he was unable to surmount the obstacles and contradictions this precarious and ambivalent existence entailed. In his daily life in the city, he said, "there is a filter that makes you not speak Arabic and makes you afraid of speaking Arabic. If you walk into a shopping center, something almost physical stops you from speaking out loud."

Sitting at a table in a quiet and dark room inside the café in Haifa, occasionally taking a sip of coffee, he added: "Tel Aviv is a city that hates the Arabic language. It's a city that sees itself as secular, western and white. The Palestinians coming to Tel Aviv from the North, they want to work, study, or they want the openness and the lifestyle. But if you want to speak loud in Arabic in this city you already have a problem."

Being visibly Palestinian, then, is, in and of itself, a social and political "problem" there. W. E. B. Du Bois famously invoked a question posed to black

Americans that underscores their predicament: "How does it feel to be a prob-lem?" And this question prompted him to ask, "Why did God make me an outcast and a stranger in mine own house?"[24] In response, affected individuals often developed a double consciousness, in the sense of always looking at one's self through the eyes of others and adapting their actions and public visibility accordingly, in the hope of avoiding being stigmatized. Arab minority citizens in the United States today are constantly made aware that their identity is perceived as such a problem.[25] As Bathish delved more deeply into Tel Aviv's social life, he too became increasingly aware that invisible immersion can be enjoyable for some time but that, ultimately, it offers no safe haven from being stigmatized as a "problem."

This was different in the early stages of his urban immersion. Soon after his initial arrival, he began to love his own "disappearance" in this urban space, as he put it, speaking of Tel Aviv as a place that offered the "anonymity of liv-ing like on an island." Life in the bubble clearly had its advantages for a queer Palestinian artist, but this came at a cost. Sometimes he found himself in awk-ward situations that he described as a "strange" form of "self-Orientalization." As Bathish put it, self-Orientalization is like "going to Jaffa and hearing [the Egyptian singer] Umm Kulthum somewhere, thinking that you just love it." Estrangement does strange things to people. Similar to Du Bois's double con-sciousness, the concept of self-Orientalization usually refers to how the targets of Orientalism—often immigrants from Asia living in the "West"—internalize Orientalist images as a form of self-adjustment to external pressures to con-form to white versions of stereotypical ethnoracial identity.[26] Palestinians in Tel Aviv use the term in a slightly different way, to mock their own occasional longing for the traditional and somewhat stereotypical aspects of Palestinian-Arab culture while being in this foreign space.

Ultimately, it was the impossibility of his professional and artistic life in the city that pushed Bathish out: "It is as if Arabic is forbidden in Tel Aviv. I couldn't be part of a cultural and literary space there because it was in Hebrew. I am part of the Palestinian writing scene. But I also need to live it day by day. But in Tel Aviv I felt exiled in my own country. Even though there are a lot of Palestinians in Tel Aviv, they are swallowed up in the urban space. They become invisible."

At the heart of this dilemma was that Palestinians' immersion in Tel Aviv "swallowed" them up in highly individualistic and collectively invisible ways. The idea of an active literary community is very different from that reality. Living as a writer in exile on your homeland was worse in that respect than, say, living in proximate exile in Beirut, where Palestinian art long flourished in a politicized "free-for-all atmosphere."[27] Haifa, as the Palestinian cultural capital in Israel, was very different from Tel Aviv and offered a collective sense of community, which is why he eventually moved back there. The settler city of Tel Aviv, on the other hand, has historically erased Palestinian identity and the Arabic language from its space. The result is an unresolvable tension between the need for visibility and recognition of being a Palestinian writer and the forced invisibility of Palestinians as a submerged urban reality.

When I asked Bathish why it was so difficult to connect with other Arabic-speaking artists in the city, he put some of the blame on the lack of political and cultural organizing among Palestinians in Tel Aviv. Another major problem was his difficult position in relation to the city's mostly Jewish Israeli art scene, which always welcomed "Arab" artists under the condition that they were not too radical and spoke Hebrew.

The Israeli liberal left, some of whom welcomed him to literary readings, parties, and events, turned him into what he called "an Arab representative brought along for a showcase." In practice, this included experiences of public encounters that made him feel like an outsider. Visibly upset by the mere memory of it, Bathish said in a rather emotional tone: "A few times I read in Arabic in Tel Aviv, and there was *translation*. It was a joke! I am speaking the ancient language of Arabic, read it, in the Middle East, where the Arabic language is the main language, but no one speaks it. This is absurd."

As a settler-colonial city, Tel Aviv implanted itself into a region in ways that opposed the cultural and political character of its surroundings, as a Hebrew-speaking city. Early Zionist settlers needed to speak some Arabic if they wanted to communicate with indigenous Arabs, but the Jewish study of Arabic has primarily been encouraged for security reasons until today. This means that, even if there were Jewish Israelis in Tel Aviv who could read and understand Bathish's writing, they would be able to do so for the wrong reasons. Unless they were Arabic-speaking Jewish immigrants with roots in the Middle East, they would have likely learned it at school or in the Israeli army to serve the state's political agenda. This Israeli type of Arabic did not bring its learners closer to those who speak the language, rather it was "intended to help the learner comprehend 'the Arabs' in an impersonal and sterile way, or to decode 'what the Arabs want' without regard for the Arabs as their neighbours—not to mention as citizens of the same state."[28] Instead of building bridges, Arabic studies in Israel came to symbolize barriers and express a political desire for control.

Ashkar turned the foreignness of Arabic within Tel Aviv into the heart piece of her own daily performance, which was mainly directed at Jewish Israelis. A similar sense of foreignness involved a bitter feeling of being out of place for

Bathish, whose work was addressed to an Arabic language audience. His work incorporated fascinating accounts of Palestinian life in Tel Aviv and thereby critically intervened into the mainstream narratives that did not recognize a Palestinian Tel Aviv at all. Yet, his Arabic prose could not be consumed by many of those he was writing about. The conditions of inclusion into the literary space of Tel Aviv, including the consumption, distribution, and recognition of the work, undermined the visibility of the Arabic language and the formation of a Palestinian cultural space.

At the same time, the city's urban life inspired aspects of life and art that had yet to be recognized as realities grounded in a Palestinian subjectivity that is positioned within Tel Aviv. Some of these realities, in turn, inspire artistic production from a position of *creative marginality* that challenges nationalistic hegemony over individual subjects.[29] Although responding to and challenging aspects of urban exclusion, artistic and creative marginality risks to replace collective struggle with "utopia": artistic expression is powerful in the way it organizes visibly in space, but it is "disempowered when it comes to organizing *over* space."[30] In this sense, Bathish was unable to counter the exclusion of the Arabic language from this particular urban space because his participation in the Israeli art scene only worked under the conditions of being co-opted and translated. This process of translation implies much more than merely linguistic conversion. The historical processes of settler colonialism that shaped this city in opposition to Palestine and the Arabic-speaking Middle East could not simply be undone through critical writing.

Out of place and in between seemingly contradictory worlds, the position of the Palestinian writer in Tel Aviv is one of linguistic and political "exile at home."[31] Ultimately, Bathish ended his chosen exile because he did not want to be the "token Arab" writer for Tel Aviv's literary scene any longer. He argued that future generations of Palestinians can nevertheless enjoy the city, if "you have the will to pay the price for it." Between 2005 and 2012, he invested much energy into what he called "survival in cultural terms," in addition to the main issue that troubled his urban immersion: the language, the tongue, the estrangement. As he summarized the problem: "It's very hard to live in a place that is afraid of the language you think in."

WALKING ON A THIN STRING: A PALESTINIAN CELEBRITY BETWEEN LIBERATION AND CO-OPTATION

Awad has been viewed as a controversial celebrity in the Israeli and Palestinian public spheres, not least because she was the first Palestinian citizen to represent Israel in the Eurovision Song Contest. She performed the song, "There Must Be Another Way" alongside the Jewish Israeli singer Achinoam Nini. When their participation was officially announced, the disastrous 2009 Gaza conflict had just started. The mission Operation Cast Lead of Israel's military killed some 1,391 Palestinians, among them an estimated 759 civilians.[32] As Israeli bombs dropped on Palestinians in the besieged Gaza Strip, many began to wonder how she, as a Palestinian, could represent Israel abroad. Recalling that period, Awad told me in an interview in Tel Aviv: "We had to cope with a lot of criticism. A song about peace but there is no peace. But our song included a lot of pain, but with some hope for the future in our song. The [Boycott Divestment and Sanctions] BDS movement called on me to step down. Naturally, I was already thinking that when the war started. I was already thinking, 'What? Am I going, why? Should I be going to a pop contest now representing Israel that is bombing the hell out of Gaza?'"

Awad had already been a celebrity on Israeli TV by then, due to her role in the TV series *Arab Labor*. It focused on the life of Amjad, a Palestinian citizen of Israel who has a love-hate relationship with his Arab identity but also does everything to integrate into Israeli society—the quintessential "good Arab." In the series, the lawyer played by Awad has a Jewish boyfriend. In real life, she was married to a Jewish Israeli and lived in Tel Aviv.

Born to a Christian Arab-Israeli father from the Ramah village in the Galilee and a Bulgarian mother, she grew up with multiple senses of identity and language. Her early life and upbringing may have influenced her later life and musical career: she spent several years within the Israeli Hebrew-speaking secular education system, while the majority of Palestinian citizens of Israel attended Arabic-speaking schools within their communities. While her father worked as a physician in Karmiel, a Jewish town, she studied at an Israeli music school and went on to live in Tel Aviv, "the hub of Jewish-Israeli cultural production."[33]

Especially because of her Eurovision performance, some Palestinians see Awad as a real-life example of the stereotypical "good Arab." Since its origins as a term used by early Jewish settlers and Israeli state agents to label collaborating Arabs,[34] it has become a powerful and controversial metaphor in Israeli public discourse. The "good Arab" exemplifies the Palestinian dilemma that in order to be included and accepted within Israeli liberalism, Palestinian citizens are required to qualify as loyal and trustworthy in ways that are defined by the Jewish-settler majority.[35] The fictional character Amjad of the TV series *Arab Labor*, for example, does everything to be accepted by Jewish Israelis in the hope of attaining their privileges. The problem is that these privileges are always conditional.

When Norman Issa, the actor behind the fictional character Amjad, refused to perform in a theater show in an illegal Israeli settlement in 2015, Israel's culture minister quickly threatened to withdraw support for Issa's own theater. Only when Issa offered a replacement show did ministers take back their threats, with the culture minister saying, "I gave him a ladder to climb down, and he used it." The whole episode led Gideon Levy to proclaim that Israel has no more room for "good Arabs" "who are not total collaborators."[36] In the course of her Eurovision participation, Awad was accused by a collective of Palestinian artists and intellectuals alongside left-leaning Jewish Israeli artists and peace activists of "collaborating with the killing machine," namely Israel and its military operation in Gaza.[37]

As a metaphor, the "good Arab" designates an ambivalent space of conditional inclusion that is especially relevant for Palestinian public celebrities and artists in Israel, who often collaborate with Israeli institutions, can be dependent on Israeli funding, and need to make complicated decisions about how to communicate their opinions in public. Awad may often be the target of a delegitimizing labeling as a "good Arab" or a "token Arab." At the same time, she has repeatedly spoken out against political injustice aimed at Palestinians and the discrimination of Palestinian citizens of Israel. For this, she has been the target of critiques from both sides of the divide. "I am used to that. This is the story of my life, standing in the middle and getting confronted from both sides," said Awad, during our meeting at a café in her Tel Aviv neighborhood. Her music and her roles in acting have partly reflected this position of being in between, and Tel Aviv has been the only possible place for her to fully live that ambivalence, according to her.

Awad began her musical career at the age of sixteen as a lead singer in an Arabic rock group and graduated from an Israeli school of jazz and contemporary music. Her first album was *Bahlawan* (*Acrobat*), although no Israeli record label wanted "to take on the risk of promoting this album" until her association with Achinoam Nini increased her media exposure.[38]

The English translation of the Arabic song "Bahlawan" are as follows (author's translation, confirmed by the artist):

Walking on a thin string,
my arms stretched to the sides,
no guarantee, no safety net,
an acrobat.
Hanging between earth and sky and a crazy wind,
one step after the other,

still keeping my balance,
whatever happens,
any small mistake,
I fly.
I was always like this,
always on the edge,
and you were always afraid,
maybe afraid everyone will know,
that I'm an acrobat,
with no safety net,
whatever happens,
any small mistake,
I fly.

The song reflects what she sees as a life in between, as a Palestinian woman, as an Arab in Tel Aviv, as an Israeli abroad. "I am the ultimate acrobat, walking the thin line between everything," said Awad, adding: "It started with me being a woman in a patriarchal society that discriminates me by gender. Then into a racist society that discriminates me by nationality. And everywhere you have this thin line to walk. As a woman in the Arab world, as an Arab in the Jewish world, as an Israeli in the Arab world."

Tel Aviv has played an important role as the space within which this acrobatic balancing unfolded. At least with the right socioeconomic situation, Awad explained, the city offered something particular to her: "It's some kind of bubble where you can sometimes rest from the political, from the absorbed life that we have. I am a person who is in the headlines, so everything is political. Everything I do is political. Everything I do is, 'the Arab who is,' 'the Arab who wonders,' 'the Arab girl who got this role,' 'was invited to sing here and there.' This is always following me around. *Tel Aviv gives me a break.*"

To say "Tel Aviv gives me a break" is to invoke the city's image as a bubble that shields its residents from political turmoil and extremism. While Awad saw Tel Aviv as a city where she can immerse herself to escape the constant politicization of her identity, this hope somewhat contradicts Palestinian experiences with racialization and stigmatization as part of such immersion. Even if they meet the conditions of being a "good Arab," they always remain potentially "bad."

Awad knew that her access to the liberal aspects of Tel Aviv was based on certain privileges and demanded sacrifices. She first came to Tel Aviv in 1996 and describes the beginning as "difficult," until one is in the right economic situation. When she was a poor student, "Tel Aviv seemed like a tough and hard place to be." With her growing success came more money and a desire to live in Tel Aviv. She used the city as the place to wage a personal and individual struggle, rather than primarily a national Palestinian one. "I was rebelling in loneliness in a way. Today, I know that I am not alone. I know a lot of women are doing this quiet revolution of personal achievement. I strongly believe in personal achievement as a revolution."

Although this "revolution" clearly involves complicated balancing acts, this approach also mirrors the limited regime of conditional inclusion that "liberal" Tel Aviv offers for Palestinian citizens. A struggle for "personal achievements" works only on the condition of reducing the Palestinian collective cause for national rights to a level of liberal Israeli individual rights. In this sense, an individual artist's position in between requires a balancing act that stays within the framework of acceptable inclusion and does not challenge the settler-colonial structures that subordinate all Palestinians. The promise of individual liberties in Tel Aviv has been especially resonant among female and queer Palestinians, but it often leads to the co-optation of Palestinians as an individual success story of personal liberation.

This personal liberation for Awad involved an ongoing tension between urban immersion and recognition. The more she participated in the Israeli public sphere, the less she would be recognized as someone who represented the Palestinian political reality and identity; but the more she spoke out against Israeli policies, in fulfillment of that Palestinian expectation, the more difficult it became to blend into Tel Aviv and meet dominant Israeli expectations. As a celebrity living in Tel Aviv and representing Israel on the international stage, she earned accusations of being a normalizer, depicting a false picture of reality.[39]

In an interview with *The Guardian* newspaper, she said: "Each side wants me to align myself with them. Israelis would like me to show alliance with the Israeli state, to prove my loyalty. On the other side, I have to prove my loyalty to the Palestinians who ask if I have forgotten my father was kicked out of his village in 1948."[40] Her song *Bahlawan*, meaning "acrobat," may well be retitled "the impossible acrobat," because Israeli liberalism inscribes an unresolvable tension between the two polarized positions of being Palestinian and being in Tel Aviv.

Similar to Ashkar's insistence that her facial art equaled a political demonstration, Awad suggests that by merely making Palestinian citizens more visible, some kind of transformation occurs. "Look at TV in Israel today. You have never had that many Arabs on TV. They are opening little windows between the cultures here," she said over a drink at the Tel Aviv café, where she usually was the only Arab customer. Those who accused her of normalization would say that increasing visibility of "Arabs" on TV, outside of the proper political context, merely served to legitimize Israel and its image as a democracy. Referring to a cooking show, she said: "The Israeli audience was exposed to Salma, a Muslim girl with a headcover. It got used to her and the way she talks and her family and her village. I see these things as eye-openers. What if we don't get Salma on TV, what would be missing? Ok, so let's go and tell Salma not to cook for Jews and participate in the show. And? Ok . . . so that's the normalization you want? No Jews, no Arabs together anywhere?"

In making the dialogue between Arab and Jewish citizens a centerpiece of her activism and work, while living in Tel Aviv, Awad became a target for Palestinian critics and simultaneously faced Israeli pressures to be a moderate "good Arab." As a Palestinian celebrity in Tel Aviv, she symbolizes the impossible acrobatic act within the Israeli regime of conditional inclusion: a struggle of personal achievement that nevertheless fails to escape the cunning logic of co-optation that determined such individualism for Palestinians in Israel.

How easily Palestinian artists can be co-opted by the Israeli regime, even with the best intentions, becomes clear when one considers the way Israel instrumentalizes any sign of "co-existence" and showcases a small number of "good Arabs" internationally. Indeed, "the Israeli state invests in cultural exports as a means of improving its damaged international image, as well as gaining political and economic capital, utilizing culture as a diplomatic tool to divert international attention from Israel's aggressions."[41] This does not make "rebelling in loneliness" and the "revolution of personal achievement" less important or significant for the individual artists and parts of the public, but it does mean that any important gains and achievements are made under the implicit condition of remaining within the limits of a "good Arab," which precludes the potential for art to challenge Israel's false liberalism and inspire substantial radical transformation.

A CULTURAL EXILE IN THE SETTLER CITY

The three portrayed artists offer three distinct perspectives on the possibilities and limitations of Palestinian immersion in a self-identifying "liberal" urban space that is dominated by the Jewish Israeli majority. Each in their own way incorporates their personal experiences with this immersion into their creative works of art. Ashkar visibly tagged herself as Arab with facial calligraphy, Awad made sense of her balancing acts in the city as an "acrobat," and Bathish wrote in Arabic about the experience of being a queer Palestinian in Tel Aviv. Although each of them used their work as an artist to challenge the invisibility of the Palestinians in Tel Aviv, they were also unable to escape the eliminative logic that defines the frequent co-optation of Palestinians in Israel as individuals who are accepted and included under certain conditions of political compromise.

Ashkar's facial calligraphy demonstrates her Palestinian identity publicly and thereby counters misrecognition by Jewish Israelis, turning her face into what she called "a political demonstration." Yet, tagging oneself with art to demonstrate, "I am Arab," forms part of an individualized struggle for recognition that does not pose a fundamental challenge to the depoliticization and decollectivization of Palestinians in Tel Aviv. As an artist who exhibits in Israeli museums and communicates to Jewish Israeli audiences, she could only be included within this space under the condition that she operate within the framework of what is deemed tolerable. The possibility of demanding a radical political transformation through art is foreclosed by the very process of conditional inclusion that triggered the critical art in the first place.

Bathish delved deeply into Tel Aviv's life and tried to position himself as a Palestinian writer. His experiences of living in the quintessential Zionist city as a queer Palestinian inspired his writing at the time, but the Jewish Israelis who surrounded him were unable to read the Arabic texts he produced. The only possibility of communicating this work involved his co-optation by the Jewish Israeli left as a "token Arab," translating his Arabic texts into Hebrew during public presentations. The "city that hates the Arabic language," which "is afraid of the language you think in," as the writer phrased it, offers inclusion into its Jewish Israeli art scene but only under the condition of overwriting the Arabic language with Hebrew. In this context of a settler-colonial city, being forced to translate an indigenous language, which also happens to be the main language spoken in the Middle East, resembles much more than just linguistic conversion: it exemplifies how this settler city continues to erase the visibility and presence of Palestinians, their political identity, and their language, in the cultural sphere. This continuous exiling of the Arabic language from Tel Aviv exemplifies the wider distancing of Jewish settlers from Arabic for more than one hundred years, as they continue to view the language with "negative intimidating and security-based associations."[42]

Awad emphasized the ambivalent role of Tel Aviv in her balancing act between the competing senses of identity and responsibility, as a Palestinian, as an Israeli citizen, and as a woman. This balancing act opens up spaces for personal maneuvering and individual struggles, while also involving Jewish Israeli attempts at co-opting her as a quintessential "good Arab." It is precisely this hopeful struggle for individual sovereignty and flexibility within Tel Aviv's liberalism that simultaneously forecloses the possibility of a radical artistic position rooted in Palestinian national identity. To say that Tel Aviv gives her a "break" from the constant politicization of her life is to say that she deliberately immersed herself in Tel Aviv in search of a depoliticized urban space, thereby implicitly fulfilling the underlying criteria imposed on Palestinians who want to access Tel Aviv's "liberal" urban qualities.

The selection of three artists who are either women or gay further reveals the logic by which Israel often looks at Tel Aviv as a modern bubble in opposition to "traditional" Palestinian society. The dominant discourse suggests that the city is a safe haven for "victims" of conservative oppression who can use Tel Aviv to be free and liberate themselves from the constraints they face elsewhere. The key problem with Palestinian art in Tel Aviv is that despite its role as a critical tool for making marginalized perspectives visible, Israeli liberalism neverthe-less appropriates these artists and their artwork and uses their symbolic value for political purposes. "Arab" art has often been showcased locally and inter-nationally as proof of Israel's ostensible respect for diversity.

Broadly speaking, we can look at Palestinian art and literature in Tel Aviv as an expression of the wider predicament of cultural exile on one's homeland. This cultural exile illuminates the enduring impact of settler-colonial erasure and political displacement on the personhood and subjectivity of Palestinians. It explains not only how people are forced to move but also how a colonial-settler project is imposed on people on their homeland, causing a rift between their political identity and language, on the one hand, and the national-cultural character of the settler space that surrounds them, on the other.[43] As Pales-tinian artists, writers, and musicians juggle Palestinian identity and culture with life in the Israeli state and its foremost Jewish city, they simultaneously challenge aspects of their marginal position and incorporate its contradictory experience into their work.

This complex relationship between Palestinian art and settler-colonial ur-ban space somewhat challenges the idea of a bifurcated double vision, as a split between a colonial vision of art and an indigenous one.[44] The art and lived experience of the three portrayed Palestinian citizens is heavily influenced by their presence in a settler city that considers them outsiders and strangers. This settler-colonial reality not only limits and influences the content of art but also determines the means and language through which it can be expressed. While indigenous art is often framed as a form of resistance, and as a struggle for self-representation and visibility,[45] its role in this context of urban invisibility is fraught with ambivalence between participation and recognition. Although Palestinian art in Tel Aviv often counters the silencing of their presence, the artists' experience shows how participating in the Israeli art scene and recognition as Arabic-speaking Palestinians become two mutually exclusive desires. The figure of the acrobat in Awad's song symbolizes this ambivalent and unstable position of Palestinian artists who must "rebel in loneliness" because the city makes their inclusion and acceptance conditional on the absence of a visible Palestinian collective of radical artists.

NOTES

1. Spencer, *Anthropology, Politics, and the State*, 17.
2. Goldstein, "Dancing on the Margins."
3. Peters, "Loaded Speech."
4. Slyomovics, "Who and What Is Native to Israel?"
5. Most inhabitants of the original Palestinian village of 'Ayn Hawd were displaced into refugee camps with only about 150 of the villagers remaining inside the borders of what became Israel. In 1953, after most of the Palestinian villages depopulated by Israeli forces during the war had been razed, the village of 'Ayn Hawd was designated for preservation as an artists' colony (Al-Hayja' and Jones, "'Ayn Hawd and the 'Unrecognized Villages'").
6. Slyomovics, "Who and What Is Native to Israel?" 44.
7. Regev, "Present Absentee."
8. LeFevre, "Representation, Resistance and the Logics of Difference."
9. Strohm, "Impossible Identification," 19.
10. Lee, "'Anybody Can Do It.'"
11. Jenkins, "Categorization."
12. Strohm, "Impossible Identification," 10.
13. Tawil-Souri, "Where Is the Political in Cultural Studies?" 11; Strohm, "Impossible Identification."
14. Aviv, "Tsumud," 153.
15. Hilmy, "'ID Card' by Mahmoud Darwish—A Translation and Commentary."
16. Aviv, "Tsumud."
17. Alkhateeb Shehada, "And Acre Will Remain," 132.
18. Alkhateeb Shehada, "And Acre Will Remain," 128.
19. Strohm, "Impossible Identification," 21.
20. Sela, "Fawaran."
21. Christmann, "Nahum Gutman aus Tel Aviv."
22. Sela, *Effervescene*.
23. Yahav, "Intifada Substitute."
24. Du Bois, "Strivings of the Negro People."
25. Bayoumi, *How Does It Feel to Be a Problem?*

26. Hirose and Kei-Ho Pih, "'No Asians Working Here,'" 1498; Yan and Almeida Santos, "'China, Forever.'"

27. Boullata, "Artists Re-Member Palestine in Beirut."

28. Mendel, *Creation of Israeli Arabic*, 8.

29. Monterescu and Schickler, "Creative Marginality."

30. Monterescu, *Jaffa*, 283.

31. Hackl, "Key Figure of Mobility.

32. BBC, "Gaza Crisis."

33. Belkind, "Message for Peace or a Tool for Oppression?" 15.

34. Cohen, *Good Arabs.*

35. Hackl, "Good Arab."

36. Levy, " Jewish State."

37. Belkind, "Message for Peace or a Tool for Oppression?" 21.

38. Belkind, "Message for Peace or a Tool for Oppression?" 13.

39. NPR, "Arab Singer Joins Israeli."

40. Sherwood, "Mira Awad."

41. Belkind, "Message for Peace or a Tool for Oppression?" 23.

42. Mendel, *Creation of Israeli Arabic*, 223.

43. Hackl, "Key Figure of Mobility."

44. Thomas and Losche, *Double Vision.*

45. LeFevre, "Representation, Resistance and the Logics of Difference."

SIX

—∙∿∙—

THE URBAN POLITICS OF (IN)VISIBILITY

Marginalized Activism and the Nonrecognition of Palestinian Tel Aviv

PALESTINIANS ONLY RARELY BECOME VISIBLE as a collective in Tel Aviv, but, when they do, their presence disrupts the city's normalized erasure of Palestinian identity and history in unexpected ways. Several flash points of political activism challenge this erasure and invisibility, including spontaneous forms of activism, organized protests, and guided tours about the city's Palestinian past. These are mostly the isolated initiatives of specific activist groups that appear somewhat disconnected from the everyday lives of Palestinians and Palestinian citizens of Israel who focus on working, studying, or playing in Tel Aviv. What I have described as *immersive invisibility* throughout this book suggests that Palestinians in Tel Aviv feel pressured to maintain a political low profile and must often mediate the visibility of their identity in exchange for access to the city's socioeconomic opportunities and leisure spaces. Yet, various kinds of Palestinian political activism have always existed at the city's margins, both within Tel Aviv proper and farther south in Jaffa.

Paying close attention to the encounters between Palestinian activists and the Jewish Israeli public in the city shows how this urban space continues to suppress and fend off the visibility of any such collective political presence. Let us look at one rare Palestinian protest in the heart of Tel Aviv that was organized in 2014 by Balad, the National Democratic Assembly, a Palestinian nationalist party in Israel. The event included around two dozen activists who protested against attempts by the state to draft Christian Palestinian citizens into the army. The protest took place at the heart of the city, where Israel's Ministry of Defense was located, and did not involve any particular claim for recognition as Palestinians in Tel Aviv. Waving Palestinian flags and chanting slogans in Arabic, while holding up signs in Arabic and Hebrew, they staged

Figure 6.1 Palestinian citizens in Tel Aviv protest Israeli attempts to draft Christian Palestinian citizens into the army.

Source: Andreas Hackl.

this protest strategically in front of the ministry and interjected a Palestinian collective presence into Jewish Israeli Tel Aviv.

The staged protest at the heart of the city strategically interfered with the routine of those driving by or walking past in sports outfits or business suits, leaving some in shock, some wondering, and others in anger. One passerby shouted, "Die Arabs!" toward the demonstrators. Another angry man spit at them from his car window. Other verbal attacks included, "Go back to Gaza," and "Be happy that you are not in Syria." The fierce reactions highlighted the way some residents of the city actively fend off any visibility of a Palestinian collective that articulates a political opinion.

The protest stood out but some of the participating Palestinian citizens struggled to find it in the first place. In the run-up to the demonstration, my friend Lina told me about her experience of searching for the protest. The meeting point was announced on Facebook as outside the ministry, which is a large complex of buildings covering an extensive area. Getting off at a nearby train station, she found herself walking around, looking out for signs of a protest, hoping to spot any other Palestinians. Then, she finally heard a group of people speaking Arabic, on the other side of the street, who were themselves trying to find the demonstration. They searched on together until they finally spotted the organizers and a Palestinian flag, which was an unusual sight in Tel Aviv.

Ordinary residents of Tel Aviv fiercely fended off this Palestinian protest, thereby revealing the contradictions of the city's liberal "Arab-free" utopia. Many of its residents, who would probably proudly defend the city's liberal and diverse outlook in a different situation, appeared to feel threatened by the expression of this alternative political opinion. Half an hour into the protest, one agitated urbanite approached the police in an effort to break up the demonstration. I stood watching the conversation between the man and the police. Next to me was Awad Abdel Fatah, the general secretary of Balad at the time, who said: "He wonders how the police can allow us to be here. When they see a Palestinian flag in the heart of Tel Aviv, they are shocked."

This "shock" had to do with the fact that Palestinian-led demonstrations rarely happened within Jewish areas of Tel Aviv. Other groups of activists have occasionally staged informal protests and public gatherings outside of the realm of party politics. One of these informal events was a seemingly spontaneous dance of *dabkeh*, the traditional Palestinian folk dance, staged by a crowd in central Tel Aviv. Titled *Palestinian Dabkeh in the Middle of Occupied Tel Aviv* (in Arabic), the video footage of the dance, available online, shows a number of Palestinians and other people dancing to loud Arabic Dabkeh-Music in a large circle on the middle of a street.[1] Using a mobile speaker, they interjected a Palestinian presence momentarily into the urban space with no particular political message attached to it, apart from the implicit message: Here we are, and we are "Arabs"! The dance lasted for only a few minutes amid the honking of agitated taxi drivers who impatiently waited for the whole performance to end. Then, it dissolved as quickly as it had appeared minutes earlier. Spectators in cars kept driving by and passersby walking past, probably wondering where these people came from and what it was all about.

The precarious presence and fluctuating visibility of these isolated events are symptoms of an urban environment that perpetuates the erasure of the Palestinian political identity from the liberal surface of the city. These urban encounters situationally disrupt the "invisibility bargain" constraining the identities and political participation of urban outsiders: a bargain defined by an unwritten set of expectations for the acceptance of their presence as long as they are "seen to bring economic benefits to the country and maintain political and social invisibility."[2] Although visible activism challenged this understanding of conditional inclusion, it did not overcome the underlying characteristics of a largely invisible and marginalized Palestinian urban presence.

As a visible presence of small disconnected collectives, Palestinian activism in Tel Aviv is essentially a "nonmovement" because these activities are highly fragmented and do not have any overarching leadership or coherent ideology.[3] More than that: some of the "real" Palestinian activists who protested in front of the Ministry of Defense in relation to a national issue did not recognize the Palestinians in Jewish Tel Aviv as a legitimate part of this national struggle, as we see in the case of Jaffa's local activists later on in this chapter. Therefore, some Palestinian activists contributed in their own way to the nonrecognition of Palestinians in Tel Aviv by not deeming them a legitimate part of the Palestinian "community."

Cities always leave their unique imprint on the nature of social struggles and agency that can be expressed within it.[4] The settler-colonial history of Tel Aviv imprinted its own limitations onto the Palestinian presence in both space and time: in space, through the destruction of Palestinian areas and the rise of Jewish Tel Aviv in opposition to historic Palestinian Jaffa; and, in time, through the strategic erasure and overwriting of Palestinian identity and historical narratives in the "new" settler city. As Palestinian collectives take on a visible form in isolated and sometimes spontaneous ways, they simultaneously challenge this erasure and exemplify its marginalizing effects. This erasure becomes the target of another kind of activism in Tel Aviv: guided tours about the Palestinian history of displacement and destruction in this urban space.

MEMORY POLITICS: UNEARTHING THE PALESTINIAN NAKBA IN TEL AVIV

In guided tours that follow the traces of Tel Aviv's hidden Palestinian past, activists have unearthed a history of violence and displacement that lies buried underneath the surface of the city. These initiatives aim to reveal the "black city" of historical violence and displacement that lies hidden behind the myth of the "white city" and its celebrated modern architecture.[5] The tours are a kind of memory politics that reveal the dynamics of in/visibility in settler-colonial urban space, whereby people compete over definitions of historical memory within and about cities.[6] Achieving a uniform portrayal of history in Israel/Palestine is close to impossible even within a local setting, amid the "existence of collective pasts and the pasts of different collectivities."[7] Aimed at Jewish, Palestinian, and international audiences, these tours reinscribe an erased and alternative history into the contemporary urban space of Tel Aviv.

If one looks closely enough, this history is scattered all over Tel Aviv: an old Palestinian mansion turned into a university club, a hidden graveyard in front of a beachside Hilton Hotel, and the old black-and-white photographs that bear witness to an overshadowed past. The traces of Palestinian history and identity within the space of Tel Aviv are layers of subjugated knowledges, namely blocs of knowledge that are present but disguised or disqualified by the dominant systems of knowledge.[8] As one possible way of unmasking this disguise, activists took the story of the Nakba online, in 2014: the Israeli NGO Zochrot, dedicated to promoting awareness of the Palestinian Nakba ("catastrophe") of 1948 within Israel, launched the smartphone application iNakba in their Tel Aviv offices. Their release event coincided with the fireworks throughout the city marking Israel's Independence Day celebration. The message was clear: the birth of Israel and the modern city of Zionism was paralleled by mass displacement and the death of Palestinian urbanism.

What we put on a map is a deeply political issue, one of Zochrot's representatives in the crowded meeting room at the launch of iNakba indicated. Termed a *mnemonic device* used as "a reminder for a society that seeks to forget,"[9] the software was designed to replace the bulky atlases of historic Palestine. Integrated into the interface of Google Maps, it allows users to discover and learn about former Palestinian villages and neighborhoods in real time as they walk through places such as the city of Tel Aviv. Users can contribute their own content by sharing memories and photographs. The program operates in Arabic, English, and Hebrew.

"Maps can't be stopped by tanks," said Yousef Jabareen, a prominent attorney and member of the Israeli parliament, at the launch event. He recounted how his parents refused to talk about "the war" when he was young. "Now," he said, "members of the fourth generation [since the Nakba] can discover the stories themselves." This is important for young Palestinians who move into Israeli cities without even knowing that their own cultural and national history is connected to that particular space. According to Jabareen, "In a city like Tel Aviv, there is a total difference between our identity and what is inscribed into the space, or the names of places."

These memory politics are part of a growing movement to redefine and reclaim the connection between identity and space among Palestinians in Israel. Similar to other homeland minorities, Israel's exclusive ethnic character has led some activists to raise claims that go beyond liberal notions of cultural rights, equality, or distributive justice. They seek to revitalize issues of historical, national, and political rights and maybe even to revolutionize the political and cultural status quo.[10] Although initiatives like iNakba are unlikely to shift Jewish Israeli public opinion and revolutionize ideas about Tel Aviv, they become meaningful for its users and the Palestinians who trace their history through an augmented reality.

In their guided tours, Zochrot led groups of Palestinian and Jewish citizens to places where the history of Palestine was still visible, if only barely. For newly arrived students, the realization that Tel Aviv University was built on the land of a former Palestinian village under the same name as the area today is often eye-opening: Sheikh Munis was originally al-Sheikh Muwannis. Its only remaining mansion was turned into a social club, now called the Green House, for university members. One of the tours I attended took a group of Palestinian students from Tel Aviv University to other locations of former Palestinian places and villages throughout the city. One of them was the former neighborhood of al-Manshiyye between today's Jaffa and Tel Aviv.

Standing where al-Manshiyye once spread, the guide showed us photographs of the former neighborhood before inviting the students to imagine a future return of Palestinian refugees who have lived in exile since the Nakba of 1948. Equipped with flip chart paper, we formed small groups and sat down in circles in the park along the seashore. The participants' imaginations were supported by Zochrot's detailed map, which marked out former Palestinian built-up areas overlaying today's Tel Aviv city map. One group designed an environmentally sustainable town for returnees, and another suggested restoring the pre-1948 order and imagining the Palestinian refugees' return "without Jews." However, most groups emphasized that any solution would need to take the status quo into account. Discussion focused on housing, financial issues, and the possibility of utilizing yet unused land for the returnees' new villages, which some suggested should be fashioned based on their old ones. "We don't want to expel the Jews because we don't want to cause another tragedy through return," said one young woman. "So, where do you put the refugees then?" challenged a young man. "We will see. But we don't want another crisis," she answered. For the time of the exercise, the students appeared to indulge in some kind of augmented reality that made the urban space of Tel Aviv potentially Palestinian again. They used memory as a "prism" through which the city gained new meaning.[11]

This augmented reality of a lost Palestinian past contrasted with the Palestinian citizens' ambiguous lives in Israel and within Tel Aviv. Well-educated and probably from mostly middle-class families, they all studied at Israeli universities. As one group wrote down its outline of a refugee return in Hebrew instead of Arabic, another participant quickly denounced them as the "shabak" group, referring to Israel's Internal Security Agency, which is notorious for blackmailing Palestinians into collaboration. For some Palestinians, immersion in Tel Aviv symbolized the prevalence of Hebrew over Arabic, and this is sometimes associated with a loss of national identity and integrity. Although the tours offered temporary respite from immersive invisibility in the Jewish Israeli city, the city's hegemonic narratives were difficult to escape. Only a few meters from where the groups sat and discussed the return of Palestinian refugees, the inscriptions outside the so-called Etzel House showed the prevalent settler-colonial narrative beyond this augmented reality: "Etzel House: in memory of the *liberators* of Jaffa." Etzel was a unit of the Jewish Haganah, the prestate Jewish militia.

"This was a Palestinian house and in 1948 they expelled the people from here and now they have a museum for the forces that expelled them," said the guide, as we stood at the building. For the participants, these "liberators" were more accurately described as conquerors and colonizers. Standing outside this memorial site, which lies between Tel Aviv and Jaffa on the long stretch of public park that connects the two along the seashore, Zochrot's guide added: "Imagine Jaffa before 1948, it had seven newspapers, cinema and theatre, it was a center no less than Beirut. Like Tel Aviv is a place for Israelis today, Jaffa once was for Arabs."

A few weeks later, I attended another tour through former Palestinian areas in today's Tel Aviv. It began at the university and was led by the activist and architect Michael Yacobson and Omar al-Ghubari of Zochrot. The tour revealed a conflict between the aim of inscribing Palestinian identity into this urban space and the complexities of the present situation, meaning that the attempt to revitalize an essentialist, unified Palestinian history faces the struggle of freeing this history from the many layers of colonial history that define the present. In the neighborhood called Bavli, which was once called al-Jammasin al-Gharbi, a complicated issue came up: many of the remaining structures of former Palestinian houses had been resettled by Jewish immigrants. Ironically, under contemporary pressure by the city's authorities and investments in real estate, they too faced threats of eviction. Yacobson said, at the site, that "you can see what they used to do to the Palestinians they are now doing to the Jews." It did not take long until a Palestinian participant protested, saying the two things were not the same, criticizing the Israeli researcher for his "tone" when talking about the Nakba.

Some tension remained but the bus drove on to the former village of al-Mas'udiyya (commonly known as Summayl), an area earmarked for luxury real estate development in the heart of Tel Aviv. It was surrounded by some of the main traffic arteries and most expensive neighborhoods in town. Originally a mostly Palestinian settlement, it soon became mixed Jewish-Arab, with reportedly good relations before the Nakba. Jewish refugees then moved to the little piece of land that the former Arab residents had left in 1948, and the mosque was turned into a synagogue. Here, too, the Jewish residents now faced the threat of eviction.

We walked up a stairway onto an elevated plateau hidden away from the street by altitude and plants. Rusty old bicycles, which must have been parked there years ago, had become swallowed up by wild growth and bushes. When the guide began to talk about the history of this strange place, one elderly woman who was a local resident walked toward the group and asked bluntly: "Which organization?"

"Zochrot," my friend Lina, a Palestinian citizen, told her. The woman said: "Aha, remembering the Arabs! So, because you didn't succeed in bringing the Arabs here to take this land, you are now bringing the (real estate) tycoons here. The tycoons are only another kind of Arabs!" Lina then said that they had nothing to do with the tycoons but that it would be nice to turn the place into a memorial site of Palestinian displacement. The woman responded with a frantic loud voice: "We should have built a fence around this place a long time ago. Long ago . . . now they are trying to expel us too."

The woman walked back into her house, grumbling. When the group passed by her house later on, the argument between her and Lina erupted once again. The woman shouted and gesticulated and, eventually, began to cry. She seemed exhausted and desperate but did not quite want to give up on the matter, saying: "I don't have any problem with Arabs. That's for the government, thinking about how to kill them. But don't you live in this state too; get the services of this country? Did you go to an Israeli university?" she asked Lina, who was, indeed, a former student of Tel Aviv University. "It has nothing to do with services," she responded, upon which the resident shouted, "My problem with you is that you call yourself Palestinian."

"So what?" Lina responded, "This is Israel and its government is Israeli, and you are Israeli, right? And what do you get from Israel? Not much it seems! They want to expel you. Aren't we both suffering?" After a few seconds of thinking, the woman just said "yes," and both looked at each other with tears in their eyes, until the group walked off to the bus, which brought us to the next destination. The row made clear how a demand for recognition of Palestinian history was complicated by the contradictions of this urban space and its multiple layers of inequality and marginality. The invisibility of Palestinian Tel Aviv was a consequence not only of the gradual erasure of Palestinian space but also of its appropriation and reconstruction.

Figure 6.2 The 'Abd al-Nabi cemetery, where Jaffa's Muslim cholera victims are buried.
Source: Andreas Hackl.

The tour's last destination was the 'Abd al-Nabi cemetery, next to Tel Aviv's seaside Hilton Hotel, where some of Jaffa's Muslim cholera victims are buried. Like many other properties of the Islamic trust in Palestine (*waqf*), it was covertly sold off to an Israeli investment company and effectively confiscated by Israel under the Absentees' Property Law.[12] When I visited the cemetery, the grounds were hidden behind shrubbery next to a public park, where a group enjoyed sundown aerobics on the green meadows, with the hotel in the background. The gate to the cemetery was difficult to spot. "People don't ask themselves what happened here," said Omar, the guide. He added while smiling: "But they built Hilton Hotel here in the 60s and many of the photographs of the hotel show the graveyard."

As a challenge to Tel Aviv's exclusive identity, the Nakba tours are often directed at Jewish Israeli citizens and audiences but also provide an opportunity for the Palestinian citizens of Israel to retrieve their people's history and perhaps strengthen their sense of belonging to the Palestinian dimension of the space. As a form of "memory activism," they appropriate global models of truth and reconciliation and utilize tours to make the silenced Palestinian histories visible.[13] In moving through Tel Aviv, they access an alternative dimension of the city and gain the opportunity to redefine their own relationship with it, by ways of inscribing an alternative past onto the present material they encounter. Bringing the Nakba back into this city to raise awareness about it is one form of bringing a Palestinian voice to Tel Aviv, rather than accepting the idea that Palestinians belong "elsewhere." But, because the settler-colonial history of the city shapes multiple forms of marginality in former Palestinian spaces, the attempt to reestablish a direct link between pre-Nakba Palestine and to-day's Palestinians in Tel Aviv is complicated by a highly ambivalent reality that undermines claims for recognition of a "Palestinian Tel Aviv." This becomes particularly clear among Palestinians in Jaffa, who wage their own struggle for urban recognition as a marginalized urban community vis-à-vis Tel Aviv: a struggle that is disconnected from the reality of dispersed individual Palestinians and Palestinian citizens who live, work, or study in the "Hebrew City."

LOCALIZED ACTIVISM IN JAFFA AND THE NONRECOGNITION OF PALESTINIAN TEL AVIV

The idea that Palestinian citizens and Palestinians do not belong in Jewish Tel Aviv is widespread among activists in Jaffa, a place widely associated with Palestinian identity and a political struggle. Jaffa-based activism has no interest in highlighting the presence of Palestinians in Tel Aviv as a policy issue, because their political position in relation to Tel Aviv is based on a clear boundary and hierarchy: Jewish Israeli Tel Aviv overshadowing, marginalizing, and gentrifying what is left of the Palestinian community in Jaffa. In this sense, localized political activism in Jaffa plays a role in maintaining the invisibility and non-recognition of Palestinian Tel Aviv.

Some two kilometers south of Jaffa's Old City, dedicated Palestinian activists and their Jewish coalition partners came together to discuss the upcoming municipal elections in Tel Aviv in 2013. Tables and chairs were set up, and ash-trays, tea, and water were made available. It was August and a little more than two months to go until election day. In order to succeed in getting a seat on the city council, they needed to unify the local Palestinian voters behind one list of candidates and gather some additional Jewish votes on top. Sami Abu Shehade, who headed a coalition called Yafa List that year, hoped he could once again take up a seat on the council to advocate policies that benefited his Jaffa constituency.

"We try to bring the causes of Arab-Palestinians from Jaffa into city politics," said Abu Shehade at the coalition meeting in August 2013. A knowledgeable and calm man, Abu Shehade possessed a very friendly face with a curious yet demanding glance. Counting the heads of activists that showed up to the election planning meeting, he noted with a more serious air: "If we are not strong together, how do we want to get our votes on election day?"

Anxiety about the challenges that lay ahead could be felt around the table, though there was little time for complaints or regrets. Campaigns had to be organized and strategies agreed on. Although, at heart, the campaign was about local issues, in actuality, it was about much more than that. Abu Shehade was part of Balad, for which he could later become a member of the Israeli parliament under the unified Joint List of Arab parties. Balad has been the main nationalist Palestinian faction in Israeli elections and is widely seen as supporting the establishment of one binational democratic state in all historic Palestine, although this position is not official.

Sami Abu Shehade said his family has lived in the Jaffa area for at least five generations, and his grandfather was a farmer there who served in World War I. When the majority of Palestinians were exiled from their homes in Jaffa, his grandfather would have "died rather than leave." But soon his parents moved to Lydda (Lod), a mixed Arab-Jewish city southeast of Tel Aviv, where Abu Shehade grew up in the infamous train station neighborhood that has been the site of official neglect and pervasive crime. He returned to Jaffa as a pupil in a Christian private school and later became a student at Tel Aviv University. Although he was not born in Jaffa, the entanglement of his family history with the history of Palestinian displacement in the area made it rather difficult for him not to think about Tel Aviv-Jaffa through the prism of a national struggle against colonization and expropriation along a rigid urban boundary of political alterity. This struggle in Jaffa was rooted in the particular historical relationship this place has had with Tel Aviv, its Jewish Israeli Other.

After its founding, in 1909, Tel Aviv overshadowed Jaffa economically and demographically by the 1930s.[14] At the end of the Arab-Israeli War of 1948, all but thirty-five hundred of Jaffa's prewar Palestinian population of seventy thousand were displaced, twenty-six Palestinian villages in Jaffa's subdistrict were destroyed, and Israel's first prime minister, Ben-Gurion, expressed his vision by stating, "Jaffa will be a Jewish city."[15] Tel Aviv gradually encircled this former Palestinian port city, which then became a neighborhood in an ostensibly unified municipality in 1950, under the new name of *Tel Aviv-Yafo* (Tel Aviv-Jaffa). This erasure and subsequent encompassment of Palestinian Jaffa into the city that symbolizes the success of the entire Zionist project rendered it a marginalized space of Arab otherness. The relationship between Jaffa and Tel Aviv reflects a contest between tendencies of assimilation and Judaization, on the one hand,

and distinction, on the other, with simultaneous processes of connection and separation.[16] While Tel Aviv came to symbolize a dynamic and modern Jewish identity oriented toward the future, Jaffa remained inseparably linked to a lost Palestinian essence in the past. This loss had catastrophic implications for the Palestinians. Although faced with the contradictory reality of living as Palestinian citizens in the complex binational space of Jaffa, many of its older residents still hold on to a romanticized idea of localized nationalism.[17] From this perspective, the ambivalent reality of immersive invisibility among Palestinians in Tel Aviv was neither part of Jaffa's local nationalism nor part of Jewish Tel Aviv.

Rooted in the asymmetric relationship between the two national poles of the city, Abu Shehade and his coalition partners struggled for political representation of marginalized Palestinian Jaffa inside a more powerful and centralized Jewish Tel Aviv. This followed a logic that appeared similar to that of colonized territories seeking representation within the capital of the colonizer. The Palestinians who lived, worked, or studied within Jewish Tel Aviv did not really have a place in this relationship. As inside outsiders, they straddled both worlds, being Palestinian and in Jewish Tel Aviv, while, at the same time, being politically invisible and peripheral to both, the city of the political "Other" and their own ethnonational community.

The activists who campaigned for Jaffa's Palestinian population were primarily occupied with problems that were specific to the space of Jaffa. "We are the only list whose basis is Jaffa. We focus on the problems in Jaffa and on the Arab-Palestinian community," as Abu Shehade assured me at the election meeting in 2013. Other deeply rooted reasons were behind the invisibility of Palestinian Tel Aviv from the viewpoint of Jaffa: these individuals were seen as anomalous and without a community.

In an earlier meeting with Sami Abu Shehade at his office at the city council, I asked him what he thought about the Palestinians in Tel Aviv who lived, worked, or studied outside of Jaffa. Were they not relevant to his political program? Could they possibly wage a unified struggle for Palestinian recognition and equal citizenship within all of Tel Aviv-Yafo?

> Look, Andreas, their numbers are marginal. Most of those Arabs who are staying in Tel Aviv are different victims of our society. Either they are from the homosexual community and our society can't deal with them, or young female students who did not get married and it's hard for them to live normally in their cities and towns. So, they come here. Or, young people who don't have work in their areas and they come to work in Tel Aviv and live here because they work crazy hours. . . . So, you don't find a community anywhere in Tel Aviv.

Significant in several ways, this assessment justified the political irrelevance of Palestinians in Tel Aviv due to their lack of community, their low numbers, and their perceived status as seemingly anomalous *victims* of society. This view juxtaposes the cohesiveness and rootedness of Jaffa's identity and its many socioeconomic problems with the uprootedness and seeming incongruity of the Palestinians in Tel Aviv. The construction of Palestinian Jaffa as a coherent political space in opposition to Tel Aviv contributed to the invisibility and marginality of the Palestinian story within Tel Aviv.

That Jaffa's own Palestinian community was in reality not as unified as it was in theory became clear with the defeat of the Yafa List in the election results of October 2013, when it only garnered 2,195 votes, which was not nearly enough to secure a seat on the city council. For the first time in twenty years, not a single Palestinian member was on the council. The "Voice for Jaffa," their lead slogan, fell silent with this sobering outcome. "All Arabs need to support one list, so winning is almost like a miracle," said Abu Shehade when I called him after the defeat. One of the reasons behind this defeat was the political fragmentation of the Jaffa constituency into several lists, including the cross-party platform called "City for All," which was supported by the Arab Communists. It defined urban politics mainly in social and economic terms and in opposition to the mayor Ron Khuldai.

Not recognizing the Palestinian presence in Tel Aviv as part of the political agenda allowed Jaffa to be the placeholder for Palestinian issues on the urban level. This, in turn, made it easier for the municipality not to accord the phenomenon of Palestinians in Tel Aviv any official recognition. My meeting with the head of the municipality's affairs in Jaffa, Ami Katz, confirmed the suspicion that Jaffa-based Palestinian activism had no interest in recognizing the Palestinian presence in Tel Aviv. At Katz's office, I asked him why there are no festivals, community centers, or cultural fairs and similar events that target Palestinian citizens in Tel Aviv outside of Jaffa.

"If we open an Arab cultural center in Ramat Aviv, what will Abu Shehade say? He will say: why didn't you open it here in Jaffa? Why did you open one so far from the Arab community here?" Katz explained, adding, "of course," fewer Arabs lived in Ramat Aviv or other parts of Tel Aviv than in Jaffa, or at least this is what the available numbers said. But then, there are no reliable numbers, according to Katz: "About numbers . . . there are no official numbers we can provide really, because they don't exist. We only have numbers of those who are registered residents of the Tel Aviv-Yafo municipality. There are about 20,000 Arabs. Some 18,500 of them live in Jaffa, the rest in Tel Aviv." He admitted that the real numbers are probably far higher. This numerical invisibility of

Palestinians in Tel Aviv translated into a political invisibility that served the idea that Jaffa was the only truly Palestinian place in the city.

Yet, associating Jaffa's struggles with a Palestinian nationalist issue is rejected by the Tel Aviv municipality. "Are Jaffa's problems a political issue in national terms?" I asked Katz. After pondering for a few seconds, he said: "This is a town and not Israel, not the whole country. We are not doing national policy here. We can't solve the Arab-Jewish, or the Palestinian-Israeli conflict. Of course, there is a national conflict and this conflict constantly infects the relations between Arabs and Jews in the city. Anything done by the city towards the people here is immediately seen as part of the Zionist plan to drive Arabs out of Jaffa. But this is not the policy."

Ami Katz appeared to be a thoughtful man who earned respect from Sami Abu Shehade and other activists who spoke fondly of him. Some forms of cooperation on the municipal level transcended the boundaries of a national conflict, although this conflict was always there. Katz enthusiastically called Tel Aviv-Jaffa the "most pluralistic and diverse city in Israel" and added that "it would be a shame if we wouldn't manage to live together in this city."

The Palestinians who live, work, or study in Tel Aviv are not commonly seen as a part of this "diversity" and "pluralism," because their urban inclusion is made conditional on the situational suppression of the very senses of identity and difference that define true diversity. Somewhat complicit with this dynamic, the localized political activism of an urban indigenous minority in Jaffa intersects with the urban strategy of erasure to coproduce the invisibility of those members of that minority who find themselves on the wrong side of a reinforced rigid urban boundary. Politically invisible and external to the political space of two competing ethnonational ideologies, the contradictory urban immersion of Palestinians in Tel Aviv renders them urban outsiders twice over.

LOCALIZED ESSENTIALISM AND THE CONSOLIDATION OF THE BOUNDARY BETWEEN JAFFA AND TEL AVIV

The formation of a local Jaffan identity has played an important part in its framing as a coherent political space vis-à-vis Tel Aviv. Even those newcomers who came from the Triangle or Galilee regions to settle in Jaffa in the 1960s, as well as those who came from the West Bank, often readily adopted this local identity: the overall majority of the fifteen thousand or so Jaffa-born Palestinians has expressed an "urgent need to maintain community cohesiveness and rarely choose to reside elsewhere."[18] Due to the historical opposition between Jaffa and Tel Aviv, Jaffans never expanded the boundaries of their Palestinian identity toward those Palestinians who immersed themselves in the adjacent Jewish metropolis, many of whom were recent arrivals from other regions.

Jaffa's boundary to the Hebrew City also solidified after the destruction of those parts of Jaffa's former urban expansion area that would be within the southern areas of today's modern Tel Aviv, which is lined with beachside boulevards and high-rise holiday apartment blocks. This was mainly the mixed Jewish-Arab neighborhood of al-Manshiyye that stretched north of Jaffa along the seafront and has attracted mainly low-income renters.[19] Albeit geographically within today's space of southern Tel Aviv, the area forms part of Jaffa in practice and in memory. With its destruction and the overall displacement of most Palestinians from Jaffa, Tel Aviv's boundary moved southward while Jaffa's initial residential expansion northward was reverted in space and, seemingly, also in time: Tel Aviv came to represent Zionism's future, while Jaffa remained shrouded in nostalgia about the past.

The demolition of al-Manshiyye in 1948 was not, as is often portrayed, a side effect of the circumstances of war but rather a deliberate exploitation of wartime confusion through an ambitious and illegal modernization project for southern Tel Aviv, which included slum clearances of Jaffa's poor outskirts.[20] This violent restructuring of Jaffa's space and Tel Aviv's ongoing expansion into Jaffa have contributed to a siege mentality among its marginalized Palestinian population, many of whom have waged a struggle for survival in the heavily gentrified and fragmented space.

The clearances went hand in hand with a consolidation of an ethnonational border between the two cities. From the 1890s to the late 1920s, Hebrew speakers perceived northern Jaffa as a southern suburb called Neveh Shalom and a poorer area called Harat al-Tanakh. But, within a few years, these spatial distinctions of socioeconomic differences turned into a "national" division between the urban and modern fabric of Tel Aviv and the urban al-Manshiyye: as a division based on the borderline drawn between Jaffa and Tel Aviv in 1921, this "paper boundary" came to symbolize to Jews an "imaginary confrontation" with the Arab neighborhood of al-Manshiyye as an extension of Jaffa.[21]

Standing today at the edge of Jaffa's old port, one can take in the view toward the modern skyline and beaches of Tel Aviv. This view symbolizes the Tel Aviv-Jaffa boundary and echoes the feeling among many Palestinian Jaffans that Tel Aviv felt like "another world" or "a foreign space." Viewed from the other perspective, in the case of a Palestinian lawyer who had his office in one of the high-rise towers visible on that skyline, Jaffa's Palestinians appeared isolated and equally distant, as he told me: "Only because they are born in Jaffa does not make them more involved in Tel Aviv."

Nationalist Palestinian political activism in Jaffa operated within the limits of this predetermined boundary between the two cities, locating the Palestinians in Tel Aviv not only geographically but also politically outside of Jaffa. Even those Palestinian citizens who came from elsewhere to work or study in Tel Aviv, but chose to reside in Jaffa, reinforced the idea that Tel Aviv absorbs isolated individuals while Jaffa harbors a real community. According to Rafa, who chose to live in Jaffa rather than in nearby Tel Aviv, because she needed "Palestinian atmosphere": "In Israeli society it's all about the individual and in Arab society about the community. I like Jaffa, but there is nothing that connects me to Tel Aviv."

Although some look at Jaffa in a romanticized way, as a place with a "real" Arab community, most Palestinian citizens, who moved into Tel Aviv for work or studies from the Galilee and Triangle regions, felt like they had little in common with this enclosed community. This feeling was mutual. Political activists and many Jaffa-born residents viewed with suspicion how young middle-class Palestinian citizens of Israel used Jaffa as a gentrified leisure space, drinking alongside Jewish citizens in bars and dating girlfriends and boyfriends openly. Many of them came down to Tel Aviv and Jaffa from the north and often had a better education, more opportunities, and their own preferred bars and clubs, places to which most local Jaffans usually did not go. In the words of Abed, a young activist and relative of Sami Abu Shehade: "Many people from Jaffa never heard about [the bar] Anna Loulou. It's something for those from outside. The people in Jaffa have their own problems. But those in Anna Loulou coming from outside don't want to see these things."

Jaffa has, indeed, had serious problems. One of them is crime, said Abed: "The crime here, for a long time the police said, 'crimes are OK, as long as it's between two Arabs.' But once there is a Jew involved as a victim, they will come. If a Jew is killed, everyone will come and things will go crazy. But an Arab, that has become normal." Just like Tel Aviv's leisure-focused residents usually do not think about Gaza being only forty miles south along the coast, when they are at the beach, they generally do not worry about what one journalist, in response to six murders that took place in Jaffa within a few weeks, called "a war zone in south Tel Aviv."[22] Although the reasons for such violence are complex, a lack of policing in Arab areas, family feuds, poverty, and racism are among them. Another major problem in Jaffa has been a severe housing crisis that led to a civil resistance struggle involving squatters and legal action, locally referred to as the "housing intifada." About 40 percent of the Palestinian population live in so-called absentee properties, designating formerly Palestinian properties that were taken over by the Israeli state.

Many have faced eviction orders because they were considered squatters in their own homes.[23]

Against this backdrop, Sami Abu Shehade calls Jaffa a "ghetto" and thereby invokes it as a metaphor for a besieged enclave, an outpost of Palestine that is close to ever-expanding Tel Aviv, and says that "the problem is a very small and weak community in Jaffa that is competing with the elites of Israel living in Tel Aviv." As Abu Shehade's nephew Abed put it: "If something happens [in Jaffa], people here stick together, like in a village. Here it's like in a village."

In this sense, localized Palestinian activism in Jaffa follows a logic of strategic essentialism, a tactic minority groups use to mobilize on the basis of their shared identity because such essentialism can be strategically advantageous.[24] Although the term *strategic essentialism* illustrates the necessity of identity-based claims and mobilization for the sake of political action, it also recognizes the impossibility of coherent essentialism. This contradiction becomes clear when immersing oneself in Tel Aviv as a Palestinian is associated with a loss of national and essentialist identity, as a person with no clear community within the city.

It is important to note that not all political activists in Jaffa base their agenda on a rigid boundary in relation to Tel Aviv. The socialist politician and workers' rights activist Asma Agbaria, for example, ran her own list in the Tel Aviv-Jaffa municipal elections under the campaign slogan, "City without borders." Rather than seeing Palestinian Jaffa and Jewish Tel Aviv as segregated opposites, she aimed to break up this boundary by making Jaffa "an equal part" of Tel Aviv. "Jaffa and Tel Aviv are two cities and it is time to change this," she told me in an interview. Rooted in the communist tradition of Jewish-Arab politics in Israel, she emphasized a common class struggle on the municipal level and contested the idea that Jaffa is a besieged "village" outside of Tel Aviv. However, her campaign was not very popular, judging by the election outcome. While this agenda of reframing Jaffa and Tel Aviv as a unified urban space could open up the possibility of recognizing the Palestinians and Palestinian citizens of Israel who immerse themselves in the Jewish Israeli city as politically relevant, the campaign did not address any of their particular challenges and remained firmly rooted in a small Jaffan constituency.

CONFINED IN SPACE AND TIME: LOCAL ACTIVISM AND THE COPRODUCTION OF PALESTINIAN INVISIBILITY IN TEL AVIV

The conditional inclusion of minority citizens in this settler city can prevent the emergence of a collective political space for ethnonational identity politics.

At the same time, the localized essentialism of ethnonational minority politics can further deepen the invisibility of the urban minority, excluding its seemingly anomalous members from a collective political space. This dynamic is one of the historical successes of the settler city, as it has undermined the creation of a unified politics of Palestinian indigeneity through colonization, urban fragmentation, and the strategic nonrecognition of a Palestinian component of Tel Aviv. Palestinian activism across the boundaries between Tel Aviv and Jaffa is, therefore, double *noncollective* because it not only is internally fragmented and incoherent but also involves some fragments delegitimizing the relevance of others.

City politics and some of Jaffa's activists maintained and coproduced a rigid boundary. This boundary divides the modern Jewish city from an essentialized "ethnic" suburb that becomes the locus for a marginalized Palestinian community that struggles for survival and for representation on the municipal level. As some indigenous spaces were erased, others were encompassed, and yet others are still in the process of being formed, the historical rooting of indigenous politics in localized essentialism shapes a political space that is fragmented and limited in both space and time.

It is fragmented in space because the boundaries between the two urban spaces marked as "Palestinian" and "Jewish Israeli" are rigidly constructed and mutually exclusive. The grounding of the communal Palestinian struggle of Jaffa in a history of colonization and displacement solidifies that spatial boundary and empties the "new" settler-colonial space of its Palestinian content. In terms of time, the historical rooting of Palestine and everything Palestinian in Jaffa, and in a buried history of the Nakba, becomes largely disconnected from Palestinians in Tel Aviv today. Palestinian time and history within Jewish Israeli Tel Aviv are, therefore, fragmented and discontinuous, whereby the nationalist glance into the past fails to see a new emerging Palestinian present at its doorstep. While Palestinians within Tel Aviv seemingly have no history in that space, and no "community" at that, Palestinians in Jaffa are burdened with too much history and community.

Neither recognized as a political constituency for minority activism nor a target of municipal minority politics, those members of the ethnonational minority that have moved into the settler-colonial city ultimately fall between the cracks: Palestinians in Tel Aviv, and the spaces they inhabit, are invisible both to Palestinian activists in distinctively Palestinian Jaffa and to the municipality of Tel Aviv-Jaffa as a whole. Classified as anomalous people lacking a community, the very logic of urban dispersion and immersive invisibility that defines their conditional access to the city becomes the foundation from which fellow Palestinians justify their political irrelevance.

The rare events of Palestinian collective action in Tel Aviv that I introduced at the beginning of the chapter only disrupt this invisibility situationally. In doing so, they trigger verbal abuse, fierce opposition, and a feeling of "shock" among Jewish Israeli urbanites who make clear that Palestinian politics belongs elsewhere, but certainly not on the streets of Tel Aviv. The Palestinians themselves also contribute to this political invisibility with the city through a variety of factors, including the individually enjoyed benefits of urban anonymity and the tendency to not seek out other members of the "community."

Yet, as the spaces of immersive invisibility are formed, and incoming students turn into employees and commuters become potential residents, questions are asked and claims will be made, if only on a small scale. Why are there no Arabic-speaking schools in Tel Aviv?[25] Why do employees come under pressure to avoid speaking Arabic and shut up any references to "politics"? Why are there hardly any Arabic-language books to be found in the city's bookshops? Could the mayor of Tel Aviv ever be Palestinian? These and similar questions are not usually asked openly, but they increasingly matter as the urban center of Tel Aviv attracts more and more working- and middle-class members of the Palestinian minority in Israel, alongside thousands of labor commuters from Palestinian towns in Israel and from the occupied West Bank. But, so far, the Palestinians in Tel Aviv are unseen partly because no one wants to see them.

Articulations of Jaffa as a marginalized Palestinian space ironically become complicit in renewing the myth that Tel Aviv proper was built in a space emptied of Arabs, which defines its utopian vision as an Arab-free Jewish city in opposition to Arab Jaffa.[26] Indeed, "the symbolic, discursive, and later physical erasure of the Palestinian hub [Jaffa] became a precondition for the symbolic and material emergence of Jewish-Israeli Tel Aviv."[27] Contemporary Tel Aviv lives with a mirage that hides Palestinians in time and space.

Memory activism that has uncovered parts of the buried history in the physical space of Tel Aviv challenges this dominant narrative, while offering an opportunity to reimagine the Palestinian relationship with the city through history. Yet, these tours are not really concerned with the contemporary reality of Palestinians in Tel Aviv and fail to connect history, the present, and the future in ways that go beyond imagining a return of Palestinian refugees. Ironically, the Palestinians that are already in Tel Aviv today seem to be far less visible and important to many activists than the remnants of destroyed buildings and the exiled generations of refugees that can be imagined in return scenarios. A history of war and colonization destroyed many parts of Palestinian urbanism, while subsuming others. Yet other spaces of Palestinian urbanism are in the process of being formed: the latter is not an anomaly of the former but rather a contemporary extension of an ongoing Palestinian struggle with and against the effects of settler-colonial erasure of indigenous identity and political visibility.

NOTES

1. Nawajaa, "Palestinian Dabkeh."
2. Pugh, "Negotiating Identity and Belonging," 984.
3. Bayat, *Life as Politics*, 16.
4. Bayat, *Life as Politics*, 13.
5. Rotbard, *White City, Black City*.
6. Freeman, "'Toronto Has No History!'"; A. Smith, "Settler Sites of Memory," 65.
7. Ben-Ze'ev, *Remembering Palestine in 1948*, 2.
8. Foucault, "Two Lectures," 82.
9. Tirosh, "INakba, Mobile Media and Society's Memory."
10. Jamal, *Arab Minority Nationalism in Israel*, 2–6.
11. Ben-Ze'ev, *Remembering Palestine in 1948*, 3.
12. Yazbak, "Islamic Waqf."
13. Gutman, *Memory Activism*.
14. Rabinowitz and Monterescu, "Reconfiguring the 'Mixed Town,'" 206.
15. Levine, *Overthrowing Geography*, 215.
16. Rabinowitz and Monterescu, "Reconfiguring the 'Mixed Town,'" 206.
17. Monterescu and Hazan, *Twilight Nationalism*.
18. Monterescu, *Jaffa*, 47–48.
19. Aleksandrowicz, "Camouflage of War," 178.
20. Aleksandrowicz, "Camouflage of War."
21. Aleksandrowicz, "Paper Boundaries."
22. Littman, "War Zone in South Tel Aviv."
23. Hackl, "Address Inequalities Facing Arabs."
24. Sylvain, "Essentialism and the Indigenous Politics of Recognition."
25. At the time of writing, an initiative to push for the opening of a Hand in Hand bilingual school in Tel Aviv, adding to the one already existent in Jaffa, emerged.
26. Levine, *Overthrowing Geography*, 219.
27. Rabinowitz and Monterescu, "Reconfiguring the 'Mixed Town,'" 206.

SEVEN

—⁓—

WHEN THE LIBERAL BUBBLE BURSTS

Violent Events and the Circular Temporality of Exclusion and Stigmatization

AS EMBODIED IN ITS NICKNAME, the Bubble, Tel Aviv is seen by the Israeli public as an urban buffer that maintains a liberal and lively atmosphere despite the surrounding political conflict and violent events. A series of violent events during the summer of 2014 and their repercussions within Tel Aviv unmasked this idea of a bubble as a fantasy. The violent events triggered a climate of fear among Palestinian citizens in Tel Aviv and intensified their need to remain invisible as "Arabs" at a time of anti-Palestinian sentiment and a polarizing political context.

On June 12, 2014, three young Israelis were kidnapped and, later, killed by Hamas-affiliated Palestinians outside a Jewish settlement in the West Bank. In response, Israel launched an extensive search-and-arrest operation that lasted until the bodies of the victims were found on June 30. On the morning of July 2, Jewish Israeli youths kidnapped a sixteen-year-old Palestinian near his home in East Jerusalem and, later, forced him to swallow gasoline and burned him alive. The murder was believed to be a revenge killing for the kidnapping of the three Israelis in the West Bank. As tensions in the West Bank and East Jerusalem ran high, anti-Palestinian rhetoric and protests by Jewish nationalists stirred up a climate of fear and confrontation in Israeli cities. On July 7, 2014, the Israeli army launched the military mission Operation Protective Edge in the Gaza Strip, with the stated objectives of stopping the ongoing rocket attacks by Hamas and destroying its capacity to conduct operations against Israel. This was followed by a ground operation and ongoing airstrikes until the operation officially ceased on August 26. At the end of the operation, 2,251 Palestinians, including 1,462 civilians, were killed, among them 551 children and 299 women. On the Israeli side, the conflict killed 6 civilians and 67 soldiers.[1]

On first glance, Tel Aviv appeared to be largely unaffected by much of this escalation: people still went to cafés and sunbathed at the beach, even as army helicopters were seen flying south toward Gaza. In one of the bustling cafés, I met Ziyad, a Palestinian citizen of Israel who studied at Tel Aviv University. Since his arrival in the city, he tried hard to reconcile his Palestinian political identity with life in the foremost Jewish Israeli city. A polarizing conflict now upset this fragile equilibrium amid Israeli bombardments of Gaza and militants' rocket fire into Israel. "Israelis usually don't confront me with their opinions, but now it all comes out," said Ziyad, who felt a strong sense of solidarity with Palestinians in Gaza. Suddenly, the sound of the city's rocket warning siren interrupted our conversation and the waiters hectically guided customers into a nearby residential building for shelter. As the wailing siren saturated the city, Ziyad and I stood there among Jewish Israelis without uttering a word, especially not in Arabic, for fear of the others' reactions. Then we heard the dull sound of an explosion, indicating that the rocket was just intercepted above the city, as if shielded by a protective bubble. Tel Aviv then returned to business as quickly as it had sought shelter a minute before: cars resumed driving, people continued their conversations, and customers went back to sipping cups of coffee. For the Palestinians, however, the moment brought a continuous seething tension to a temporary boiling point.

Tel Aviv's "bubble" makes Palestinians' urban presence conditional on their ability to blend in as apolitical and unmarked individuals. This Gaza conflict severely undermined their ability to blend in among the Jewish Israelis where they were living or working. Isolating the pragmatic aspects of their urban immersion from politics and conflict became increasingly difficult. These violent events and their repercussions made it impossible to ignore ethnonational differences in exchange for a culture of impersonal civility, which is a core feature of modern cities.[2] The Palestinians' access to the civil and impersonal qualities of the city was replaced by a polarization between friend and enemy, insider and outsider. However, it was not the actual exercise of violent conflict inside the city that destabilized liberal urban capabilities.[3] The bubble burst as a result of recurring violent events and moments of crisis that lay outside the city's space, while, in fact, becoming a constituent part of it through the politicization of otherwise pragmatic social relations.

Their daily efforts to reconcile being Palestinian and in Tel Aviv often suspended "politics" temporarily and situationally, in exchange for a focus on pragmatic urban immersion. But the circular and recurring polarization of Jewish-Arab urban relations in Tel Aviv show that antagonism is "an ever-present possibility."[4] The frequent recurrence of the political dimension polarized political identities and disrupted the liberal bargain of invisibility that defined Palestinian urban access in Tel Aviv. This mirrored important insights from the ethnographic analysis of an apolitical Palestinian refugee camp in Jordan.[5] Departing from theories on friend-enemy distinctions by Carl Schmitt and those who built on his philosophy, this research showed how the Palestinian refugees rejected camp politics because it intensified the very tension between being Palestinian and being Jordanian that they hoped to reconcile in their ordinary lives. Although their disengagement from politics attempted to "limit, control, and hold back the upsetting dynamics of the friend/enemy distinction," such accommodation is intrinsically fragile because polarizing events invariably occur that can push the dialectic of friend versus foe onto the surface.[6]

As I show later in this chapter, this fragility of the pragmatic social relations that suspend friend-enemy antagonism temporarily is not only due to the impact of exceptional events but also built into the very core of Israeli liberalism. The violent events of the summer of 2014 merely marked a specific peak in a circular pattern of stigmatization and exclusion that affected Palestinian citizens of Israel and other Palestinians within the bubble of Tel Aviv. Since the Israeli occupation and colonization of Palestinian lands have been ongoing, there has hardly been a month or year without military violence against Palestinians and publicized acts of racism against Palestinian citizens. Moreover, some polarizing events are structured into Israel's annual calendar, including public memorial days that victimize and commemorate fallen Israeli soldiers and "victims of terrorism" as well as events such as Israel's Independence Day that is marked as a day of mourning by most Palestinians. They experience the fluctuating intensities of threat, racism, stigmatization, and exclusion as a pattern of ebb and flow in a circular and recurring temporality. Rather than being an exception to the Israeli liberalism of coffee-sipping Tel Aviv, these recurring pressures lie at the core of its role in the ongoing settler-colonial domination of the Palestinian people and the suppression of their sovereignty.

A CLIMATE OF POLARIZATION, DISSONANCE, AND FEAR

The Gaza conflict created a tense and polarized climate between Palestinians and Jewish Israelis in Tel Aviv and other cities. Several days into Israel's military campaign in the Gaza Strip, the first protests were held around the country. Palestinian citizens of Israel concentrated their protests in mixed towns such as Haifa and Jaffa, where they were often confronted by aggressive counterprotests. One group of violent Jewish Israeli nationalists attacked the thirty-one-year-old Rami and his friend on their way to an antiwar event in

Haifa. "We spoke Arabic on our way to the demonstration," Rami told me, "And some guys came over, shouting 'Death to Arabs!' They were screaming terrible things. I think they wanted to kill us." Rami and his friend escaped with a broken nose and minor injuries, but such stories spread quickly among Palestinians living in Tel Aviv, where similar violent confrontations occurred between antiwar protesters and nationalists shouting, "Death to Arabs!" and "Death to leftists!"

Meanwhile, right-wing politicians polarized the public climate further. Avigdor Lieberman, then Israel's foreign minister, called on Israeli citizens to boycott Arab businesses that shut their doors in protest of Operation Protective Edge, as the Gaza offensive was called. Then deputy speaker of the Israeli parliament Moshe Feiglin called for a mass deportation of Palestinians from Gaza to places across the world. The state also stepped up its measures against Palestinian politicians in Israel, such as Hanin Zoabi, a member of parliament for the nationalist party Balad. She was banned from parliament for six months on suspicion of verbally assaulting police officers at a protest and for denying that the kidnappers of the three young Israelis (described above) were "terrorists."

Although the routine of daily life in Tel Aviv continued seemingly unaffected, this discursive polarization—together with violent confrontations on the ground—contributed to a climate of fear among Palestinians in Tel Aviv, who felt especially vulnerable as individuals in a large Jewish Israeli city. Moreover, the escalation deepened the rift between their senses of identity and solidarity with Palestinians and the urban culture that surrounded them.

For many Palestinians in Israel the Gaza conflict triggered extreme feelings of estrangement. As Muhammad Zeidan, the chair of the High Follow-Up Committee for Arab citizens of Israel, a national umbrella organization, told me in a conversation after the conflict: "This war was on Hamas, and Hamas is part of the Arab-Palestinian people. The violence was extensive.... This picture, without doubts, influences how we, the Arabs inside [Israel] feel. We carry Israeli IDs and Israeli citizenship, but Israel has yet to treat us like citizens. We are besieged and our treatment of this country is as if we were strangers on our homeland.... We do want coexistence, but only under the condition of equality."

In this sense, the conflict strengthened the feeling of being a stranger in one's homeland. Palestinians in Tel Aviv may have always felt like strangers and outsiders as far as the stigmatization of their identity in this city was concerned, but at least they could immerse themselves with tactics of invisibility to make use of its economy and lifestyle. The summer of 2014 made such tactical invisibility both more urgent and ever more difficult to maintain.

"I am afraid to speak Arabic now," said my friend Suheir, as we walked across a square in central Tel Aviv, where she worked for an NGO. She added, "I have reached a point where I prefer to speak English over Arabic. I feel I am in danger." We sat down on a public bench. Suheir pointed at the passing people and turned to me to say that she felt scared of being recognized as an Arab. It had been like this since the brutal murder of the Palestinian teenager in Jerusalem earlier that summer. Under the impact of Palestinian-Israeli polarization, she felt drained by living in this Jewish Israeli city. "I just sleep a lot, avoiding being outside here. I feel that I can't stand Jewish Israeli society anymore. I can't listen to them anymore. Not because of the Hebrew, but because of what they say, their conversations."

Fear and fatigue mixed with feelings of guilt: How, as Palestinians, could they live and work in Jewish Israeli Tel Aviv while the Israeli army bombarded their brethren in Gaza? As Suheir put it, it was hard "living here and continuing daily life while over there in Gaza they just die." While their hearts mourned the victims of Israeli airstrikes in Gaza, most Jewish citizens around them mourned the very soldiers they disdained. The regular rocket sirens heightened the tension further, to the point that some Palestinians were unsure what to fear more: the incoming rockets fired from Gaza or the often agitated Israelis they shared shelters with. One rocket warning siren went off while Sami Abu Shehade, the politician, was shopping with his children in a mall outside Tel Aviv. Instead of joining others in the shelter, he decided they should run "the other way," fearing someone might confront them if they spoke Arabic.

While the pressure grew on Palestinian citizens of Israel to keep a low profile, they also felt a growing desire to speak up. A rift that the Palestinian citizens usually straddled now seemed to tear them apart, causing severe dissonance between identity, political solidarity, and space. The problem was that, although they grew distant from the Jewish Israeli mainstream under the impact of this conflict, they still studied at the same universities or worked alongside the same colleagues.

One day in July 2014, I met the twenty-year-old Tel Aviv University student Leila. Although it was hard for her to spend time surrounded by Jewish Israelis that week, the relative anonymity of a bar in central Tel Aviv seemed like a good refuge. "I can't stand this duality anymore," Leila said, after she ordered a drink in fluent Hebrew. "My good friends are in Gaza, locked in and fearing for their lives, but the people around me support the army that bombards them." She said that the Palestinian-Israeli conflict was now much more on the surface of her life in Tel Aviv: "It was always there, but it has become more obvious."

The feelings she and other Palestinians in Tel Aviv experienced during these polarized times were difficult to bear and symbolized that their conditional inclusion in the city triggered recurring estrangement and frustration. Leila said that she walked around Tel Aviv and felt that everyone who was not visibly taking a side appeared to be "satisfied" with what Israel did in Gaza. "I can only say 'hi,' 'thank you,' and 'goodbye' to people, that's it. They simply don't understand me, and in addition to that I walk with self-hatred and feelings of guilt."

Although Leila was physically in Tel Aviv, her mind and heart were in the Gaza Strip. Staying updated about her friends in Gaza was paramount, so she set her smartphone on "high-alert," as she put it, allowing notifications for every single tweet from the people she knew there. "Every message on Twitter I get is a sign that they are alive," said Leila.

Most Palestinians in Tel Aviv are not primarily political activists, and some may even have little interest in politics, or simply try to get on with their daily lives. Leila, on the other hand, was studying to become a Palestinian filmmaker and had long been politically active, as her family has a history of being deeply involved in the Palestinian struggle for national liberation. Indeed, she was literally born into it: her maternal grandfather was a prominent leader of the Popular Front for the Liberation of Palestine (PFLP), who was assassinated by rockets fired into his office in Ramallah from Israeli helicopters. Leila's family moved to Ramallah after the second intifada in order to be "closer to political action," she explained. Today, however, they live in the quiet Arab town of Baqa al-Gharbiyyeh. This heritage of a deeply political family history only increased the feeling of dissonance for Leila. Especially during times of war, it made her feel guilty.

"I keep on justifying the fact that I am in Tel Aviv these days. But you know . . . my grandfather was . . . All that patriotism in my family comes from him," Leila explained. Although Tel Aviv behaved as if it were a bubble without history and a place without Palestinian identity, Leila's identity and family history represented everything that threatened the legitimacy of this liberal Israeli space. Her mother long struggled to obtain Israeli citizenship and only carried a laissez-passer. When she tried to obtain Israeli citizenship, it was refused for reasons "relating to my grandfather," said Leila. It is difficult to square this history of conflict and exclusion with the expectation of being an apolitical individual in Tel Aviv.

"These days I lost hope," Leila told me later about the Gaza conflict. "I felt like I don't belong here. I can't go back to school now and pretend that nothing happened, while half of my classmates may be reserve soldiers. It would tear me apart." She added that she usually tried "not to be in conflict with Jewish colleagues at university, constantly separating what I feel and hear." This tactic worked well during quiet times, but the recurring flare-ups of violence and polarization made it increasingly difficult. "I am also studying with people who don't say anything about what their country does," she said.

Moreover, many of her classmates did not talk to her because she openly defined herself as a Palestinian. She would tell them that she considered herself to be "one of those people they are bombing." On the other hand, she was somewhat bound to the daily life in Tel Aviv; the life of an Israeli citizen who studied cinema at an Israeli university and lived in student dormitories. "Here I feel like I am with my anger alone, alone in my room," said Leila, adding that she felt paralyzed by the entrapment in this contradictory position. Her anger also came from an inability to act amid a strong urge to do something. "But what can I really do?" she asked. While she studied in Tel Aviv, Palestinians died in Gaza.

WHEN WAR COMES TO WORK: COLLEAGUES BECOME "ENEMIES"

As political opinions became voiced more clearly, blending into Jewish Israeli workspaces became more difficult for Palestinian citizens. Recurring violent events posed a significant threat to them, especially in the face of frequent appearances of nationalist mobs who waited for an opportunity to attack "Arabs." This is clear in one particular memory of Bushra from Jaffa, who now worked with an organization supporting Palestinian women in their search for work in Tel Aviv and other towns and cities. As I showed in chapter 1 of this book, many of these Palestinian women in Jaffa fear working in Tel Aviv due to their hypervisibility as "Arabs" while wearing the hijab, or Muslim headscarf.

Long before she started her current job, Bushra once worked as a waitress in a Tel Aviv shopping center. One day, after a suicide bombing outside the center killed thirteen people, her manager hastily removed her name tag because it identified her as "Arab." As groups of enraged protesters began to gather outside and shout, "Death to Arabs!" the only safety for a Palestinian woman was in remaining invisible to them. She said she was lucky that, at the time, she did not yet wear the headscarf, as she adopted wearing it only later in life. Suicide bombings were common at a particular time of violent Palestinian-Israeli conflict, but a large number of recurring and periodic events have a very similar impact on Palestinians in Israeli workplaces today. The backdrop of polarizing events can inscribe tension into situations at the workplace that might seem entirely natural to Jewish Israelis.

The social worker Lina, who had previously studied and worked in Tel Aviv, was counseling young Arab pupils in Haifa's public school system during the violent summer of 2014. She shared an office with mostly Jewish Israeli colleagues during the Gaza conflict. When colleagues asked her to donate money for wounded soldiers, she was very upset but decided not to make a scene at work and did not immediately speak out against it. Swallowing frustration and opposition for the sake of pragmatic work relations became increasingly difficult for the Palestinian citizens. At the same time, professional success can depend on their ability to appear as moderates that keep political opinions and emotions under control.

One day in November 2013, a group offering workshops with dogs for children came to their office. Lina played with the dogs until one of the trainers explained that a workshop with these dogs among pupils will be an important preparation for the army. Slowly but surely, Lina began to understand. She talked about it with her Jewish Israeli manager, who told her that he used to work with dogs in the army, too, "as an object," a soldier performing the Arab "target" during training operations. Such an object wears armor and helps train the dogs to attack. "To attack Arabs," said Lina, adding, "I sat there and thought to myself: if a Palestinian is an object, I am a Palestinian, so I am scared of this dog!" At least, this is what she would have wanted to say in that moment, but she did not. She had to swallow it and tried to move on despite her frustration. However, several months into the polarized climate following the 2014 Gaza conflict, the tension reached a boiling point: she was asked to be involved in the workshops that promoted the Israeli national service in Arab schools and, eventually, handed in her resignation. The dissonance between her set of beliefs and the political context of her work had become unbearable.

It is clear to see that the 2014 Gaza conflict had an impact on Palestinian citizens' professional lives in Israel. One newspaper story discussed this impact and cited an attorney from the Nazareth-based Worker's Hotline, who stated that dozens of complaints were received in previous weeks from "Arab workers" who were either fired or threatened with dismissal for expressing what the attorney described as "thoughts outside the consensus" on social media sites.[7] In the same piece, Smadar Nehab, the director of the NGO Tsofen, which seeks to promote Arab employment in Israeli high-tech, is cited as saying that high-tech companies showed less willingness to hire skilled Arab engineers, with the common excuse being: "This is not the time. Let's wait until things calm down." The problem is that things never fully calm down for the Palestinians in Israel. After a series of knife attacks in late 2015, Tel Aviv and other Israeli cities banned the mostly Arab cleaning workers and other service employees from schools when students were present for fear of attacks.[8] These combined events show the fragility and conditionality of Palestinian inclusion in Jewish Israeli workspaces.

The Gaza conflict severely affected Palestinian citizens' work because it pushed opinions to the surface that would otherwise remain unarticulated. In this sense, it undermined the fragile balance between identity and anonymity that Palestinians in the city often established with the help of tactics of invisibility. Some conflicts at work thus became inevitable in recurring ways, as one conflict or political event followed another. This became evident when I talked to Ramzi, who worked at a start-up in Tel Aviv, about a previous position he held at an Israeli company for online security.

At the time, the Gaza flotilla incident took place, when an activist ship set for the Gaza Strip was raided by Israeli soldiers who killed nine activists on board. This had repercussions at the workplace not so different from the Gaza conflict, Ramzi told me, explaining: "One of my co-workers was a settler from the West Bank. He sent out an e-mail to everyone calling for a demonstration in support of the settlers. In the headline of the e-mail it said: 'All of us are Sayeret 13.'" This referred to the Israeli army unit that captured the boat and killed the activists on board. It was hard for Ramzi to swallow the email quietly, and so he replied with a message to every employee in the office, writing: "I don't think this is the right place to discuss these things. But if it is, tell me and I can speak a lot about crimes against humanity." Eventually, their manager told them not to discuss any political issues at work. In doing so, he aimed to restore the culture of apolitical civility between Jewish and Palestinian citizens at the workplace.

ISOLATED PROTESTS: POLARIZATION AND JEWISH-ARAB DISSOCIATION

The Gaza conflict made it more dangerous for individual Palestinians to be visible in certain situations. However, violent events that took place a week earlier had polarized relations between Palestinians and Jewish Israelis and provoked a number of protests within the city. One of the first protests in Tel Aviv took place on July 3, 2014, under the lead slogan "There is no solace in revenge." This was one day after the kidnapping of the Palestinian teenager in Jerusalem. Several thousand activists and supporters of Israeli left-wing parties filled one of Tel Aviv's main squares. "From inside pain and anger is rising, and a circle of revenge erupts," said Dov Khenin of the Communist "Hadash" Party (Democratic Front for Peace and Equality). He continued: "But [revenge] between who? Revenging the Arabs that are doing surgery at Echelov-hospital in Tel Aviv? Or revenge on the Arab from the Galilee who is studying at Tel Aviv University?"

Although there seemed to be few Palestinian citizens at that protest, Khenin's statement revealed a contradictory form of exceptionalism: their qualitative difference in relation to Palestinians was highlighted in their defense as hardworking "good Arabs"; yet no matter how hard they tried to be successful, and no matter how well they became immersed in Jewish Israeli workplaces or cities, nationalists could always stigmatize them and take "revenge" on them as Palestinian token enemies.

Amid the climate of polarization, joining anti-war protests alongside Jewish Israelis was as difficult for the Palestinians as working or studying with them. Students held a protest at Tel Aviv University while most other activities Palestinian citizens organized took place either in other cities or in Jaffa. Generally speaking, the polarization of the war appeared to make Arab-Jewish cooperation extremely difficult. Ironically, this lack of cooperation came at a time when all major antiwar demonstrations led by Jewish Israelis underscored a "joint" Arab-Jewish stand, suggesting that "Jews and Arabs refuse to be enemies." This hopeful idea seemed far from the reality at a time when the "co-existence" of Palestinian and Jewish citizens was experienced through the dichotomy of friend and enemy.

Even within the most dedicated joint peace organizations, Palestinian-Israeli cooperation was largely put on hold. Among them were Combatants for Peace (CfP), which coordinated several activist networks that included Palestinians from the occupied territories alongside Palestinian and Jewish citizens of Israel. "Each time there is an outbreak of violence we become more relevant, but at the same time less able to act," said Assaf, one of CfP's Jewish Israeli coordinators in Tel Aviv. This inability to act across Palestinian-Israeli divides also resulted from pressures on Palestinians not to cooperate or "collaborate" with Israelis. This was felt most strongly by activists in the occupied West Bank and in Jerusalem, where some faced threats from other Palestinians around them for collaborating in joint activities. The Palestinian citizens of Israel faced a similar dilemma. "As you probably noticed, most Jewish Israelis have recently become more and more right-wing," said Mohamed, a leading coordinator of CfP. He added that it has become difficult for him to speak about nonviolent cooperation at times when "the relation between Israel and Palestinians has become one of force; force that needs to be answered by force. I believe in it, but I can't do it anymore."

All this had severe implications for the Palestinians' ability to take part in daily life within a Jewish Israeli city, while the underlying contradictions also undermined their ability to voice dissent. For the most part, Jewish and Palestinian citizens did not participate in the same political demonstrations against Israel's Gaza operation in Tel Aviv. "I can't attend a protest under an Israeli flag," said the Palestinian politician Sami Abu Shehade. At the site of one weekly Tel Aviv protest, the Jewish Israeli city councilor Mickey Gitzin of the Israeli Meretz Party said that he would not want to take part in any "Arab protest" either: "I am Israeli and Jewish, emotionally connected to this state. I don't relate to Arab protests that speak Arabic and the language of Palestinian nationalism." These ideological differences were nothing new and invariably existed in the innumerable social relations between Palestinian and Jewish Israelis in Tel Aviv. Crucially, though, it was the impact of the conflict and the political polarization that pushed dissonance to the surface.

One logical consequence was that Palestinians in Tel Aviv avoided spending too much time in this Jewish Israeli city during the conflict, with some protests taking place in the old city of Jaffa. Associated with a local activist community and a sizable Palestinian population, the assumption was that protesting in the heart of Old Jaffa was safer and felt more familiar than doing so in Tel Aviv, where the threat of facing nationalist Israeli counterprotests was perceived to be higher. The protesters gathered on the small traffic refuge that surrounds the iconic clock tower at the entrance to the old city. Alongside a few dozen Palestinian citizens, some foreigners and a handful of Jewish Israeli activists joined in. Eventually about a hundred protesters stood cramped together on the narrow traffic island, some lining up along the edge of the elevated square, facing the road with signs. "Raise your voice the people in Gaza are dying," was one of the battle cries. The restricted space around the clock tower somewhat emphasized the marginalized spaces available for public Palestinian dissent in Tel Aviv-Jaffa. As the police watched, organizers grew increasingly cautious not to disrupt the traffic.

The Israeli riot police then arrived, and a handful of activists attempted to walk beyond the edge of the square down onto the busy street. The police force soon positioned itself in anticipation of an escalation. Then a fierce argument erupted between some of the older Palestinian activists and the younger crowd, who wanted to push things further and escalate. "They want to walk down there but it will only escalate," said one of the older men at the site, adding: "This is not Umm el-Fahm here! It's only Jaffa." Unlike his place of birth Umm el-Fahm, a major town in the northern Arab-Triangle region, the Palestinian community was vulnerable in Tel Aviv-Jaffa, especially during these times of escalating violence and polarization. Eventually, the youths' anger was kept in check and the protest ended quietly, leaving a sobering mood among many of the activists who felt that their voice had been contained while the war on Gaza continued. The event underlined the vulnerability of Palestinian citizens in Tel Aviv-Jaffa, which was a result of their systematic relegation into marginalized political positions, both as a small community in Jaffa and as dispersed individuals within Jewish Tel Aviv. Such "relegation" denotes the processes that thrust and maintain persons in marginal urban locations and positions.[9] Collective protests and Palestinian individuals were both rendered increasingly vulnerable to violence at that time; the former, for its hypervisibility, and, the latter, for its isolated position.

RECURRING RITUALS OF OTHERNESS:
DOMINATION THROUGH SIRENS AND FLAGS

As recurring violence and polarization follow a pattern of ebb and flow, these conflicts and moments of political tension come and go for the Palestinians in Tel Aviv. Moments of tension surfaced in especially regular fashion during recurring Israeli nationalist rituals and nationalist celebrations, which intensified the alterity between Palestinians and the Jewish Israeli city. Israel is not alone among modern nation-states in designating a particular day to celebrating its independence and another one to remembering those who sacrificed their lives for the existence of the state.[10] Along with Independence Day, most Israelis observe Remembrance Day, or, as its full name goes: The Day of Remembrance for the Fallen Soldiers of Israel and Victims of Terrorism. These national days are both ordered, not as a coincidence, sequentially in the Israeli calendar, proceeding from formal mourning to less formal and all-embracing celebration. Holocaust Memorial Day precedes both and contributes to a dramatic historic narrative from catastrophe to freedom and independence, which was and still has to be defended through the sacrifice of its people.[11]

While most Palestinian citizens recognize or at least tolerate the siren that marks Holocaust Memorial Day, they mostly detest Remembrance Day, both for its victimization of Israeli soldiers and for the all-embracing methods by which it enforces commemoration. Its countrywide siren calls on citizens to commemorate in silence, and by doing so visibly in public, to openly express their affinity to the nationalist ritual. For instance, in Tel Aviv, people answer this call by stopping their cars on the highway and stepping onto the street, or by standing up in trains, offices, and classrooms. It is a national Israeli ritual that troubles the Palestinians and involves a dilemma for their visibility: Should they stand up with the Jewish Israeli masses to blend in and retain their anonymity, while swallowing anger and frustration? Or should they stay seated and drive on when all others stop and stand up, thus making their opposition visible?

During one Remembrance Day, I experienced how this dilemma plays out in daily practice. I stood waiting at a train station in Tel Aviv, on my way to an alternative commemoration event, at which both Jewish Israelis and Palestinians shared narratives of loss and mourned together. However, I wanted to avoid being stuck in public space during the Israeli ritual, and so I nervously checked the time repeatedly and calculated beforehand how I would get there either before or after the siren marked the collective silence. My efforts were futile. The train arrived late and only a few minutes after I boarded it, the siren wailed and everyone around me stood up as if an external force commanded them to do so. I neither wanted to show allegiance, nor did I hope to make a visible statement against it. What saved me from having to make the decision was that a lack of free seats made me stand from the very beginning. The action of standing up would have been a statement, but already standing could hardly be seen as such.

Faced with similar dilemmas, most Palestinians in Tel Aviv that I knew tried their best to avoid the question altogether by staying away from public places during Remembrance Day. As the siren tries to synchronize everyone in the country, it expresses ideology as a force that interpellates or hails concrete individuals as concrete subjects.[12] In ways that upset the fragile balance Palestinians establish, similar to the impact of polarized conflict, the siren demands that people identify as either supportive or resistant, synchronous or asynchronous, friend or enemy. In this sense, it is very similar to the siren that calls on citizens to seek shelter as a warning of rocket attacks: it creates a sense of unity through the experience of a common threat. At the same time, it enforces a dichotomy of friends and enemies, sameness and otherness, making it ever more difficult for Palestinian citizens to navigate the space in between. As the actor and musician Mira Awad told me during one of the Remembrance Days in Tel Aviv, where she lived, its polarizing impact was similar to times of open conflict: "Everybody was tense. When you say something, they feel like you are attacking their heritage and history. . . . Everybody is so oversensitive, but also Palestinians are oversensitive. A million and a half Palestinians inside Israel make a big effort not to be outside when the siren goes off. . . . We have a problem with the memorial of soldiers because we feel it is one sided. So, we don't go outside. It is painful because we don't get the same recognition."

Overtly confronting Israelis during this ritual requires courage, but it does not necessarily lead to more recognition or less frustration. So, instead of protesting, most Palestinians in Tel Aviv hide and stay away when the siren wails.

This political ritual weaves the wider context of Palestinian nonrecognition in Tel Aviv into microstrategies of invisibility, whereby a lack of overall recognition makes invisibility both more necessary and more difficult to maintain in the face of these events. Many Palestinians in Israel would agree that it is not politically problematic to take off a necklace at work or deliberately avoid speaking Arabic to security guards. But standing up for a nationalist Israeli ritual is different. Concealing something is one thing, but showing political support for Israeli nationalism is quite another.

At least within the private sphere, some Palestinian citizens managed to achieve some sort of compromise, as did one Palestinian friend of mine who lived with a Jewish boyfriend in Tel Aviv, saying, "I didn't stand up when the siren wailed, but my boyfriend decided to go to the bathroom and commemorate there. He said, 'I know you are Arab.' So it was OK that I stayed outside and didn't stand up." Some relationships, at least, managed to resolve the tense dilemma the ritual imposed on the Palestinians.

What the siren did by means of sound, Israeli flags on Independence Day symbolized in visual terms. Once a year, the streets of Tel Aviv and other Israeli cities are filled with partying crowds waving national flags and accessories colored in Israel's national blue and white. While Jewish Israelis celebrate their state's inception and continuing existence, the Palestinian citizens of Israel look back at a history of dispossession and violence. It is a difficult day to be a Palestinian in Tel Aviv and not an easy one to be a foreign anthropologist either. My neighbors in Tel Aviv, who mounted a massive flag from their balcony, celebrated independence until the morning hours, shouting repeatedly in Hebrew through a megaphone: "Thank you Eretz Israel! Thank you Eretz Israel!"

For Ziyad, the nursing student, the national flag symbolized the historic process of erasing Palestinian identity and history. During a walk on the eve of Independence Day, he said: "I have a problem with this flag. I simply can't stand it. The flag is a symbol for the fact that this country does not consider me part of it, that I don't belong to it, that it is no home. Nothing about this flag belongs to me." For Ziyad and other Palestinian citizens, the flags add to feelings of estrangement in Tel Aviv, where a display of countless Israeli flags is less usual than in Jerusalem, for example. The display of flags makes one thing clear to the Palestinians in Tel Aviv: you may think that we accept you because this is liberal Tel Aviv, but let me remind you that this is still Israel, a Jewish state!

During the whole period from Holocaust Memorial Day through Remembrance Day to Independence Day, the entrance of the Tel Aviv cinema where Ziyad worked was lined with dozens of flags to both sides. "Everything looks different during these days," he explained, adding that Independence Day added tension to an otherwise already difficult situation. What made things worse for Ziyad was that his brother Saleh, who was gay and identified as a liberal Arab, rather than as a Palestinian, put up an Israeli flag in their apartment in Tel Aviv. "I told him he better remove it before I get home," Ziyad said, just after receiving the message with a picture of the flag from his brother.

Between sirens and flags, Palestinian citizens of Israel feel their status as outsiders in Tel Aviv more strongly than usual during these times of tension. The overall politicization of public spaces and the dilemmas it involves make it difficult to avoid conversations about "politics" and visibility as Palestinians. One morning after Independence Day, I met Salma, who worked as a section head nurse in a private clinic in Tel Aviv. After complaining about her neighbors' excessive independence party, she told me a story that exemplified how the period of flags and sirens affected daily interactions and undermined Palestinians' ability to blend in:

> Yesterday in the supermarket I went to buy vegetables and fruits. I decided to have a light dinner. The guy at the counter said: "Are you going out?" I looked at him and said: "No, I don't go out. You don't know that Arabs don't go out and celebrate on Independence Day?" He said: "So you are not celebrating the existence of Israel?" I said, quietly, not aggressive: "I don't feel like celebrating the day on which my grandfather and my father lost a lot of land. My family became refugees in Syria, Lebanon and Jenin in the West Bank." I said it without anger, saying just that this day is painful for me. He said: "You know what, you are right."

Similar to the impact of polarizing conflict, Independence Day and Remembrance Day brought questions to the surface that would otherwise remain hidden from casual daily interactions between strangers in the city. One way of putting it would be to say that these times bring the nationalist and settler-colonial dimension of Tel Aviv into the foreground of its liberal dimension, consequently undermining the Palestinians' ability to immerse themselves anonymously. This is not to say that no relationships exist that do not transcend this alterity, at least symbolically. For example, the long-term Tel Aviv resident Farah admitted that Israel's Independence Day was, in fact, "Nakba Day" for her, which is why Jewish friends no longer invite her and her partner to any celebrations, out of respect. "One of my friends once told me that he put down the flags right before Independence Day because he had Arab visitors. That's very nice," Farah said. However, it did little to address the underlying tension between Palestinian identity, urban space, and Israeli nationalism: "You feel that this is not your country on these holidays. It becomes clear that you are not actually part of this whole thing."

NOT AN OPEN CITY: VIOLENCE, POLARIZATION, AND RECURRING TENSION AMONG PALESTINIANS IN TEL AVIV

The Palestinian experience of recurring nationalist and violent events unmasks the ostensibly liberal face of Tel Aviv and lays bare the exclusive nationalism that hides behind the pragmatic bargain of conditional inclusion. Against the backdrop of Tel Aviv's well-crafted liberal image, observers may see it as an "open city" with a capacity to resolve differences and include diverse groups and causes; such an open city would be able to strengthen basic civic capabilities in the face of war and racism.[13] However, the experience of Palestinian citizens accentuates that Tel Aviv has a chronic incapacity to be open and inclusive. The liberal bubble of Tel Aviv bursts under the impact of recurring conflicts, annual nationalist rituals, and violent events as they frequently occur in circular patterns.

That the 2014 Gaza conflict was by no means an isolated event became clear seven years later. In May 2021, Israel and Hamas engaged in yet another round of heavy fighting. The launching of thousands of rockets from Gaza toward Israel was paralleled by sustained Israeli air and ground strikes in the densely populated Palestinian enclave. The flare-up followed a week of wider confrontations between Palestinians and Jewish Israelis. The tension had built in the lead up to an Israeli court ruling about evicting Palestinian families from the East Jerusalem neighborhood Sheikh Jarrah, to make way for Jewish settlers. Protests around Jerusalem soon turned into violent confrontations in the Old City, which escalated, especially, around the holy sites of the Al-Aqsa Mosque compound and the Noble Sanctuary, the holy esplanade worshipped by Jews as the Temple Mount.

These interlinked violent events may have followed familiar patterns, but they had a new level of intensity. The rocket barrages fired from Gaza toward Greater Tel Aviv were unprecedented in scope, although most of them were intercepted. One of the most significant shifts, however, occurred within Israel, as mixed Jewish-Arab towns such as Acre, Haifa, Jaffa, and Lod became the sites of what media soon called a "civil war." While Palestinian citizens staged protests and turned their frustration, anger, and violence toward their Jewish Israeli neighbors, far-right Jewish Israelis and settler groups, often armed with pistols and operating in full view of police, moved into mixed urban areas on the hunt for "Arabs." Israel's public security minister, Amir Ohana, encouraged "law-abiding" Jewish citizens to carry weapons, and so the government openly supported the vigilantism of Jewish mobs attacking Palestinian citizens.[14] One of these attacks was caught on video, showing an angry Jewish group pulling a man they thought to be Arab from his car and beating him up in the Bat Yam area south of Tel Aviv.

Although most of these confrontations were concentrated in mixed towns and neighborhoods, they once again have serious repercussions for Palestinian citizens who live in Jewish cities such as Tel Aviv. The rapid spread of violence and polarization highlights in the most apparent fashion that the liberal bubble of Tel Aviv is a mirage and that the city's ambition to be open and inclusive continues to be undermined by the core dynamics of an unresolved conflict and an ongoing settler-colonial occupation of Palestinian territories.

Recurring polarizing events restrict the Palestinians' ability to circumvent the stigmatization of their identity and blend into workspaces and cities, because the circular politicization of Jewish-Arab relations in the city inscribes antagonism into otherwise depoliticized pragmatic interactions. This limits the possibilities and spaces available for safely expressing opposition through voicing their opinions and articulating their political differences, which is the basis for peoples' right to a city.[15] Recurring Jewish-Arab polarization means that Israeli urban space pressures those who become visible as Palestinians through the threat of exclusion and potentially violent repercussions. It enforces stigmatized otherness and simultaneously restricts anonymous urban immersion.

This threatening component of urban life brings the Palestinian experience of Tel Aviv in line with the tactics employed by other threatened minorities, who are pressured to dissimulate as majority members for their own protection during times of adversity.[16] Palestinians who immerse themselves in Tel Aviv's economy with the help of tactics of invisibility, such as taking necklaces off and avoiding the Arabic language, soon find that they must use similar tactics to evade tension and potential threats during polarized times. The frequency and intensity of surfacing nationalism, violence, and categorical exclusion within Tel Aviv shows that it is closer to Gaza and Palestine than its citizens would like to recognize.

The sophisticated air defense system that Israel dubbed the "Iron Dome" intercepted most rockets headed for Tel Aviv, thereby complementing the metaphoric "bubble" with a "dome." However, the deaths and destruction in Gaza have long penetrated the city's boundaries, because they became manifest in the fears and frustrations of the Palestinians who lived, worked, or studied in the city. The killing of Palestinian youths in East Jerusalem, the bombardment of the Gaza Strip, and annual nationalistic celebrations transform experiences of conditional urban inclusion into experiences of estrangement and outright hostility. This makes Tel Aviv's ostensible liberalism look like a fantasy that only survives because it protects itself from many uncomfortable truths. No bubble or dome can shield the people of Tel Aviv from the reality that their city stands at the center of an ongoing settler-colonial project that continues to control the freedoms of the indigenous Palestinian population by a variety of means. Along with war and occupation, enforcing Palestinian invisibility as part of their urban inclusion is one of these means. Consequently, this colonial-liberal city cannot be fully inclusive and open without resolving the ongoing Palestinian-Israeli conflict and without addressing its key role in the past and current forms of Israeli settler colonialism.

NOTES

1. UN, "Report of the Independent Commission."
2. Sennett, *Fall of Public Man.*
3. Sassen, "Urban Capabilities," 90–91.
4. Mouffe, *On the Political,* 16.
5. Achilli, "Disengagement from Politics."
6. Achilli, "Disengagement from Politics," 253.
7. Maltz, "Gaza Effect."
8. AFP, "Two MKs Charge Discrimination."
9. Wacquant, "Revisiting Territories of Relegation," 1078.
10. Handelman, *Models and Mirrors,* 191.
11. Handelman, *Models and Mirrors,* 198.
12. Althusser, "Ideology Interpellates Individuals as Subjects"; Handelman, *Models and Mirrors.*
13. Sassen, "Urban Capabilities," 87.
14. Holmes and Kierszenbaum, "Far-Right Jewish Groups."
15. Blokland et al., "Urban Citizenship and Right to the City"; Harvey, "Right to the City."
16. Kohlberg, "Some Imāmī-Shī'ī Views on Taqiyya," 395; Sözer, *Managing Invisibility.*

CONCLUSION

—ᴧᴧ—

A SETTLER-COLONIAL CITY FOR ALL ITS RESIDENTS?

Palestinian Tel Aviv and the Future of Liberal Urbanism in Israel/Palestine

Tel Aviv is called the land of opportunities.
People come without political consciousness.
But with time, they start to ask questions and build their opinion.

—Saleh, a Palestinian citizen living in Tel Aviv

THIS BOOK OFFERS, FOR THE first time, a comprehensive take on Palestinian life in Tel Aviv: a city that embodies the success of the entire Zionist project and symbolizes modern Jewish urbanism. I have grounded this ethnographic exploration of contemporary urban life in the history and ongoing relevance of settler colonialism as a structure of elimination and erasure, which contributes to the invisibility and marginality of Palestinians in Tel Aviv today. Historically, such elimination involved the forced removal and expropriation of indigenous peoples, as in the mass displacement of Palestinians in 1948, the prevention of their return, and the destruction of Palestinian urbanism. Importantly, this strategy of colonial elimination continues in the "positive" sense of erecting a new society and building new cities on the expropriated land base.[1] Colonialism, therefore, survives in "settler form."[2] Palestinian citizenship in Israel has been one such form: an inclusive version of settler-colonial elimination, highlighting that the urban inclusion of indigenous people does not necessarily mean the end of their colonial domination. Citizenship itself functions as a liberal "technology of governance through which settler states control, manage, and contain indigenous peoples and their claim to sovereignty and self-determination."[3] This logic on the national level of citizenship is reflected in Tel Aviv on the urban level, showing how a "liberal" city both enacts and conceals colonial domination through forms of liberal incorporation that negate any sense of sovereignty, self-determination, and urban citizenship.

After all, the city of Tel Aviv was ostensibly built on empty land and constructed in opposition to Palestine and the Palestinians.[4] It could fashion itself as Arab-free and, essentially, Jewish, in part because of this forced removal of the indigenous Palestinian population. Today's invisibility of the Palestinian presence in the city reveals both a victory and a failure of settler-colonial elimination. It is a victory because the ongoing invisibility and nonrecognition of an indigenous urban minority continues the eliminative mandate of colonialism by means of liberal incorporation. Yet, the Palestinian presence also represents a failure of colonial elimination because the Palestinians keep on coming and making use of the settler city with the help of tactics of invisibility and creative adaptation. Although dispersed, noncollective, and often conditioned on de-politicization, this ongoing immersion of indigenous Palestinians in the settler city involves claims to urban access and inclusion.

As Audra Simpson writes in the context of the native Mohawks in Canada, "Like Indigenous bodies, Indigenous sovereignties and Indigenous political orders prevail within and apart from settler governance."[5] The Palestinian immersion in Tel Aviv is different from this context because it does not form a coherent political order. Nonetheless, these numerous struggles for urban access and inclusion represent islands of Palestinian indigeneity and survival, even if the city pressures them to make their Palestinian identity invisible. On the one hand, the urban incorporation of Palestinians into the settler city of Tel Aviv is a mode of settler-colonial control. On the other hand, it also challenges such control through the ongoing struggles for urban access and inclusion.

One main purpose of this book is to build a better understanding of the particular practices and characteristics behind the Palestinians' ambivalent urban immersion in Tel Aviv, against the backdrop of eliminative inclusion as a settler colonial urban strategy. Rather than bluntly excluding Palestinians and Palestinian citizens, Tel Aviv includes them selectively under certain conditions of invisibility: they are expected to be hardworking, "good Arabs" who know when to conceal their ethnonational identity and when to suppress political opinions. Each chapter shows in its own way how a regime of colonial elimination manifests itself in diverse forms of conditional inclusion and invisibility. One layer in this regime of conditional inclusion is the bounded mobility that connects Palestinian citizens of Israel and Palestinians from the West Bank to this urban space. Considering this mobility within and beyond the city (chap. 1), I suggest that the bounded nature of Palestinian mobility in relation to Tel Aviv is key to our understanding of how an urban regime of inclusion limits the entitlements and citizenship of its subjects and how it renders their presence invisible and marginal. Such restricted mobility contributes to the durable marginality of an indigenous minority within this settler city.

We have seen that these Palestinian *journeys* in Tel Aviv are often limited in time and depth, lacking a sense of arrival in and belonging to the city. Yet, Palestinian journeys into Tel Aviv also entail individual tactics and balancing acts that negotiate this space of conditional inclusion and actively seek access to its social life and economic opportunities. As Palestinians are using and accessing the educational and professional spaces of Tel Aviv (chaps. 2 and 3), tactics of immersive invisibility emerge as a key component in the balancing acts of individuals. Especially middle and upper-class Palestinians who hold the right privileges and aspirations often use these flexible tactics and make pragmatic compromises. They do so in order to access socioeconomic opportunities like higher education and professional careers, or simply to roam in public while retaining privacy and anonymity. Such immersive invisibility supports the settler-colonial strategy of eliminating any visible collective presence of Palestinians from the city. At the same time, this immersive invisibility also becomes an individual aspiration because it helps the Palestinians to evade stigmatization and allows them to redistribute urban access in the absence of recognition. As it is employed to evade disadvantaging stigmatization and discrimination, such accommodating immersion enables an urban minority to make use of a city that fends off its ethnonational identity. This serves the city, too, which makes good use of Palestinian labor but does not want to recognize this Palestinian presence politically. Tel Aviv uses the Palestinians as much as the Palestinians use Tel Aviv.

Unlike their relatively privileged and successful middle-class contemporaries, a marginalized Palestinian working class remains largely invisible within Tel Aviv, not by choice but by compulsion. Although Palestinian class formation in Tel Aviv is partly dynamic and takes divergent ways, the settler-colonial dimension of this political economy effectively racializes citizenship and class mobility on multiple levels. It does so through the forced invisibility of the working class and by creating a sense of isolated anonymity among the middle and upper classes, who find that their "success" in the city remains conditional on their ongoing invisibility as a Palestinian collective.

The diverse stories and circumstances that make up these scattered and temporarily immersed spaces offer an alternative perspective on how marginalized and stigmatized minorities can make use of cities. This perspective challenges approaches that look at visible claims to urban citizenship as a necessary expression of differences and identity politics in order to *transform* the city.[6] Some minorities around the world are much less concerned with transforming a city than they are with making good use of the available opportunities and spaces.[7] Moreover, they often do so not because they seek distance from "who they are" in ethnonational or religious terms, but as a way of maintaining a feasible balance between identity and participation in adverse cities and potentially hostile regimes. By and large, Palestinians make use of Tel Aviv and seek access to its social and economic spaces rather than seeking to transform their rights and claim recognition as a distinct urban minority. Importantly, though, these innumerable encroachments into the city of the political Other will undeniably contribute to new relationships between Palestinians and this city, driven by quiet claims for urban access and inclusion.

Outside of workplaces and students' classrooms, Tel Aviv is renowned as a city of fun and leisure (chap. 4). As the popular saying about Israel's three major cities goes, "Haifa works, Jerusalem prays, and Tel Aviv plays." From nightlife to conviviality and spontaneous encounters, Palestinian leisure and fun in Tel Aviv express a key dilemma of their urban immersion: this liberal city inspires a hope for freedom of expression but forecloses this freedom the moment it inspires it. The visibility of one aspect of identity often depends on the invisibility of another, and this becomes especially clear in the often public and boundary-transgressing practices of fun and leisure. Within Tel Aviv, spaces of collective Palestinian fun are marginalized, while individual Palestinians who immerse themselves in its Jewish Israeli spaces struggle to blend in without recurring misrecognition and feelings of estrangement. In this contradictory regime, invisibility becomes both an individual desire and a product of systematic urban marginalization. Although rarely discussed as such, the freedom to have fun and enjoy leisure visibly and collectively, without hiding one's identity and its multiple dimensions, is a key component of equal urban citizenship. The particular dilemma of this settler-colonial context is that enjoying the city of the ethnonational majority is also deemed illegitimate by members of the Palestinian community, resulting in a condition of dual exile that demands tactics of invisibility in both directions: vis-à-vis other Palestinians and Jewish Israelis.

This ambivalence while immersing in the city's leisure spaces also defines the experiences of the three portrayed Palestinian artists in Tel Aviv (chap. 5). While producing alternative narratives and Palestinian perspectives on the city, the three artists incorporated some of the contradictions they experienced into their work. Although they each used their creative work to challenge the invisibility of the Palestinian experience of Tel Aviv, they have often been co-opted as "good Arabs" who are accepted and included under certain conditions of political compromise. Despite the potential of art to make marginalized urban perspectives visible, Israeli liberalism appropriates artists and their artwork and utilizes their symbolic value for political purposes. Overall, the life of Palestinian artists in Tel Aviv reveals the predicament of living in cultural and political exile while still being on one's homeland. As the Palestinian writer Raji Bathish told me, explaining why he left Tel Aviv, "it's very hard to live in a place that is afraid of the language you think in."

Tel Aviv's settler-colonial character not only erases the Arabic language from within its space but also actively fends off collective manifestations of Palestinian identity and politics (chap. 6). Apart from the occasional protest and spontaneous activist event, Tel Aviv's residents are not used to seeing Palestinian citizens who break with the invisibility bargain of their urban inclusion and surface as visible collectives instead. Palestinian protests are, therefore, received in a kind of "shock" by some of the city's Jewish Israeli urbanites, who sometimes react with verbal abuse and confrontation. This is different in Jaffa, the former port city that has been enveloped by Tel Aviv and still features a solid Palestinian community while being recognized as an activist space on the municipal level.

Maybe ironically, this localized activism contributes to the invisibility and nonrecognition of the Palestinians in Jewish Israeli Tel Aviv. It operates with a rigid boundary between a local besieged Palestinian community in Jaffa and the modern city of Jewish Tel Aviv. Such Palestinian activism ends up coproducing the urban invisibility of the Palestinians in Tel Aviv together with the policies of the city. The rooting of Palestinian urban politics in the localized essentialism of Jaffa, as a flag-bearer of the Palestinian national community, creates a political space that is fragmented and limited in spatial and temporal terms. It is fragmented in space because the Palestinians in Tel Aviv are not seen as a part of Palestinian political space, and it is limited in time because the nationalist glance into a Palestinian past fails to see a new emerging Palestinian present at its doorstep. This exclusion of today's Palestinian Tel Aviv from Palestinian temporality becomes evident in the memory activism that uncovers the buried Palestinian history within the physical space of Tel Aviv. Although these guided tours offer participants an opportunity to reimagine the Palestinian relationship with the city through national history, their vision is more concerned with imagining the return of exiled refugees than with connecting the current ambivalent immersion of Palestinians in Tel Aviv to this alternative national history. As urban exiles in their homeland, the Palestinians are unrecognized twice over: as Palestinians in Tel Aviv, and as Tel Avivians among Palestinians.

Ultimately, the recurring experience of political polarization and violence that impacts Palestinians in Tel Aviv reveals the structural limits of their urban immersion (chap. 7). These limits are structural because the threat of violence, contentious politicization, and Jewish Israeli nationalism regularly infect otherwise civil urban relations in a self-consciously liberal and open city. While the impact of the 2014 Gaza conflict marked one particular peak of estrangement and insecurity among Palestinians in Tel Aviv, annual nationalist rituals, such as Remembrance Day and Independence Day, follow a circular temporality of exclusion. These polarizing events turn relations between urbanites and colleagues into relations between friends and enemies, insiders and outsiders, "us" and "them." They upturn the fragile balance Palestinian individuals establish between their identity and a potentially hostile urban space, confronting them with difficult decisions: remaining silent and safe but swallowing the anger and frustration that boils up inside, or making one's opposition and difference visible in the face of stigmatization and violent threats. This tense experience with recurring antagonism highlights Tel Aviv's chronic incapacity to be open and inclusive toward Palestinian citizens.

Yet, even during any normal day, Tel Aviv triggers feelings of deep estrangement among Palestinian citizens despite their longing for urban life. The Palestinian citizen Rafa, who, as a young woman, moved to Jaffa to work and live because she rejected Tel Aviv as a place of residence, put it the following way during our meeting in a local cafe: "The problem, the political problem is that we don't want Tel Aviv. I want Jaffa to return to its old stage how it used to be. I don't want Tel Aviv. Tel Aviv is like a settlement. But on the other hand, I want places in Arabic and Hebrew, signs in Arabic and Hebrew. But Tel Aviv itself, as a town that rose from Palestinian lands, I don't want her. So that's the conflict. I want Tel Aviv as a city, for its urban atmosphere, but Tel Aviv as a Jewish city, I don't want."

In many ways, this statement encapsulates the ambivalent relationship the Palestinian citizens of Israel have with Tel Aviv. They desire access to a large urban space with opportunities for work, education, and leisure, but they also realize that Tel Aviv is essentially Jewish Israeli in highly exclusive ways. This lack of equality and urban citizenship among Palestinians in Tel Aviv is not an unintentional failure of its liberalism; the exclusion of Palestinians lies at the core of what the city is and always has been. Its liberalism was never meant to include the Palestinians. Like Palestinian citizenship in Israel, such unequal urban citizenship "is doing what it was created to do: normalize domination, naturalize settler sovereignty, classify populations, produce difference, and exclude, racialize, and eliminate indigenous peoples."[8]

PALESTINIAN JOURNEYS AND THE
FUTURE OF LIBERAL TEL AVIV

"First Hebrew City" and "Bride of Palestine" are nicknames for Tel Aviv and Jaffa, respectively, that express how people imagine the relationship between space and their national identities. In a similar vein, national majorities often utilize cities politically to express some kind of essence about their nation and their identity. But beyond the powerful labels that distinguish cities through such identity politics often lies a much messier and incoherent reality. By unveiling a shrouded world of Palestinians underneath the surface of the quintessential modern Jewish Israeli city, this book makes such contradictions and incongruities visible, rather than delineating yet another fictional space with an ostensibly cohesive identity. Indeed, there is not much cohesiveness in the experienced reality of Palestinian Tel Aviv.

As people of diverse legal statuses, class backgrounds, and gender identities, with very different aspirations toward the city, the Palestinian citizens of Israel and the Palestinian laborers from the West Bank do not invite us to presume a closely knit urban minority. This urban ethnography has offered an important alternative vision about how indigenous people can use settler cities within limits despite their categorical stigmatization. Indeed, most dominant ideas about how urban minorities can struggle for justice and equality, for example by claiming visibility, seeking recognition, claiming a right to the city, or mounting urban protest, make little analytical sense in the context of immersive invisibility among Palestinians in Tel Aviv.[9] One may even question the usefulness of the term *urban minority* in this context, given the large diversity of Palestinians and Palestinian citizens of Israel and the varying degrees of depth in their urban presence.

This reality of noncollective immersion reveals a new kind of nested urban space in the making. This nested space is defined by the systematic dispersion of indigenous people into disconnected islands of individual struggles for inclusion and access in a settler city. The history of dispossession and an ongoing settler-colonial conflict continue to shape this particular representation of conditional urban immersion in an ostensibly liberal city. Unarticulated, yet present, the ashes of the Nakba of 1948 and with it the Israeli destruction of Palestinian urbanism reverberate in the Palestinians' quiet struggles today for inclusion in Tel Aviv, which is the one large city in an absence of any major Arab city to claim. Because the city renders them categorical outsiders, even if they are invited to access socioeconomic opportunities under certain conditions, most Palestinians and Palestinian citizens of Israel have long resigned themselves to focusing on *using* the city rather than claiming recognition and rights as an urban minority.

However, simply because there is no collective *struggle* or recognized *community* of Palestinians in Tel Aviv does not mean that there are no significant claims or struggles at all. Each story explored throughout this book involves certain claims and struggles: claims for access to jobs, careers, and education, struggles for privacy and individual control, and individual claims for recognition of gendered identities and other urban freedoms. This includes even the most basic desire for recognition, to be recognized as human, which represents an ongoing struggle in the face of racism and degradation. While the Palestinians in Tel Aviv employ tactics to avoid stigmatization and being disadvantaged in a compromise with the urban regime of conditional inclusion, they must also employ tactics of invisibility around other Palestinians to protect situational privacy and anonymity. This complex encounter between Palestinians and the quintessential Jewish Israeli city begs two main questions that I have answered in a variety of ways throughout the book: What does the prism of Tel Aviv tell us about the Palestinians, and what do the Palestinians there tell us about Tel Aviv?

Viewed as journeys, the lives of Palestinians in Tel Aviv pass through many places and states of being, from the challenges of arrival and commuting to apartment searching and job finding as well as the balancing acts that make successful careers and work life in Israel's economy feasible for them. Artists come and creatively engage with the city, appropriating some of its characteristics and challenging others. Some leave again, unable to blend in without losing their sense of dignity and cultural integrity. The city inspires hope for urban inclusion but often shatters this hope as a part of that inclusion.

The *conflict*, a wholesale term that is often used, recurs in their lives regularly, like tides in the ocean that shift intensity and scale in patterns of ebb and flow: bombings in Gaza, rockets on Tel Aviv, the violence of Israel's occupation in the West Bank, recurring killings on both sides, incitements, polarizing events, and the daily experience of stigmatization and estrangement. In all this, the Palestinian journeys in Tel Aviv are bounded in depth, possibility, and time. The Palestinian immersion in the city may be shallow but enduring, as with working-class Palestinian citizens who toil in the city for years but have little time and will to participate in its urban life. Many labor commuters from the West Bank have been in Tel Aviv for more than a decade, and yet the permit regime prevents them from any deeper engagement with the city. For others, though, the journey can be rather short but intense, as in the case of students who come and use the city only for a few years, while also exploring its social and leisure life.

Unlike a route or a path, a *journey* always entails the potential of individual transformation. The interaction between the Palestinians and Tel Aviv releases transformative energy through numerous urban encounters that the city's metaphoric bubble cannot contain or hide forever. In contrast to commonly held assumptions, we may say with some certainty that Palestinians make Tel Aviv, just like Tel Aviv remakes some Palestinians. The Palestinians and Palestinian citizens of Israel build the city's high-rises, staff its pharmacies and hospitals, drive its buses, and link its high-tech economy with the Arab world. They are the invisible cracks in the city's self-serving "Arab-free" utopia, but they also pose an opportunity to reimagine Tel Aviv and its relationship with Palestinians and the Arab world.

While this book has offered an ethnographic critique of Tel Aviv's self-proclaimed liberalism, it also calls for a reinforcement of liberalism's capacity to include and recognize its political Other. Cities may be unable to fully escape the national contexts within which they are placed, but, at the same time, they do not need to fall hostage to the delimiting political visions of the nation-state. Indeed, cities around the world often actively challenge national politics by promoting a more inclusive and progressive approach than the states they belong to would prefer. For all its flaws, Tel Aviv is still the city of residents who cast their votes further to the left on the political spectrum than the country as a whole. The individual journeys of Palestinian citizens and Palestinian labor commuters covered in this book may provide important starting points for the city's decision makers to address the many shortcomings and difficulties of their urban presence.

However, Tel Aviv remains at heart a settler-colonial city that was built in opposition to Palestine and the Palestinians. This historical legacy and the ongoing occupation and colonization of Palestinian territories restricts the city's capacity to be inclusive in a way that would overcome the antagonistic and hierarchical relations between "friends" and "enemies", between colonizers and colonized. Long after the mass displacement of Palestinians from Jaffa and other towns in 1948, which paved the way for Tel Aviv's rapid growth as a utopian Jewish-only city, a second kind of "exiling" may currently be underway: the forced invisibility and nonrecognition of those Palestinians in the city who are physically present but politically absent. They are rendered absent and invisible as they endure the exclusion and ambivalence of exiles despite still living on their homeland.

As parts of Palestine became Israel, and Tel Aviv encompassed Jaffa, the relationship between the Palestinians' cultural and political identity and the imposed ethnonational character of this space was forcibly reconfigured. People were displaced, cities were built, and a Jewish state violently immigrated to Palestine. The resulting contradiction between urban space and identity lies at the core of the Palestinian experience of Tel Aviv. However, the Palestinians who come to Tel Aviv do not necessarily want to reclaim this space as their own, in political terms, just like the students at Tel Aviv University are not there to avenge the displaced inhabitants of al-Sheikh Muwannis, the village that once stood where the university is now. They mostly want a fair chance, and they want access to a global vibrant city without the constant reminder that they are, by definition, outsiders in it. Tactics of immersive invisibility help them pierce the exclusive outer bubble of settler-colonial Tel Aviv to access the "liberal" city within, which harbors jobs, professional careers, and leisure spaces. But this analytical separation between the colonial and the liberal aspects of the city is, ultimately, flawed because today's liberalism is, in fact, an extension of the colonial logic of elimination of Palestinian identity and sovereignty. Such liberalism is the continuation of colonial elimination by means of conditional urban inclusion.

Against this backdrop, this book provides an opportunity for Tel Aviv to grasp the wider significance of the Palestinian presence and reconcile with its colonial past. As they staff many of Tel Aviv's offices, the Palestinian citizens are far more crucial to the city's relationship with the Arab world than is presently assumed. The students and young professionals who work on the Arabic service desks of the city's start-ups and corporations provide evidence for that, as Arab customers in the Gulf States and elsewhere are called on behalf of Israeli investment companies or foreign-exchange traders, and these customers usually think the companies are based in Cyprus or elsewhere. The Palestinians come under pressure not to disclose the fact that they sit in Tel Aviv. Usually pressured to keep their Palestinian identity invisible in a large number of everyday situations, these schemes demand the opposite from them: to conceal the Israeli-component of their identity and overstate the Arab one. This growing phenomenon shows that the liberal city and its globalized neoliberal economy need them more than the settler city would like to admit. A new set of "peace" agreements that normalized relations between Israel and the United Arab Emirates and Bahrain in 2020 underlines this significance of Palestinian citizens and Palestinian labor commuters at the heart of Israel's regional economy further.

Even outside of this regional domain, Palestinian citizens of Israel and Palestinian workers from the occupied territories already play an essential role in the city's economy. They are essentially much more than a readily available force of labor to fill niches in the economy. As they immerse themselves in the city to varying degrees, their lives and stories become implicated in Tel Aviv as much as Tel Aviv becomes a part of their lives. Politically, this mutual relationship has remained unaddressed for the many reasons I have outlined, including Tel Aviv's definition as an essentially Jewish Israeli city and the Palestinians' own tendency to look at the city as an illegitimate place of residence, while downplaying the Palestinian presence in Tel Aviv as an irrelevant political reality. This two-sided ignorance may already be changing with the gradual opening of the public discourse on this issue, exemplified by the impact of the groundbreaking 2016 film *Bar Bahar* (*In Between*) by Maysaloun Hamoud. The film explores the lives of three Palestinian women living in an apartment in Tel Aviv as they struggle to balance their life in the city with the expectations and pressures from their own community. This book aims to contribute to this gradual opening of the public discourse by making the complex reality and diversity of an emerging *Palestinian Tel Aviv* visible.

Granting recognition to the Palestinian presence in Tel Aviv and adopting urban policies that offer a sense of dignity, urban citizenship, and belonging would involve little risk for the city and, ultimately, benefit all. Barely a hundred years old, the story of Tel Aviv has only just begun. It seems that the Palestinian citizens will play an increasingly important part in this story, and the open question is whether this story will lead them into ever deeper marginalization and urban invisibility or to sustainable pathways toward urban equality and a sense of citizenship.

Tel Aviv is likely to remain the major urban center of Israel and continue to function as its economic core in any imaginable scenario: whether an independent Palestinian state becomes a de facto reality next to Israel, or a binational state subsumes Jewish and Arab citizens within a single polity, or even if the current "one-state condition" becomes a never-ending dystopia of differential Israeli rule.[10] As the urban heartland of a settler-colonial state that is responsible for the Palestinian people's past and ongoing dispossession, Tel Aviv has its own responsibility to remain open and inclusive toward Palestinian citizens and Palestinian laborers. As a first step, the city's liberal personality will have to recognize its evil settler-colonial twin. This requires an acknowledgment that a settler-colonial legacy continues to define and limit its liberalism, as the one becomes inherently implicated in the other. The ongoing erasure of Palestinian identity and sovereignty remains a core aspect of Tel Aviv's social and political character. Its self-proclaimed liberalism continues to implement this settler-colonial legacy of erasure through enforcing the marginality and invisibility of the indigenous Palestinian urban minority. In this sense, Tel Aviv is a liberal-colonial city in denial of its colonial kernel that does not live up to the unfulfilled ideal it promises to be: "An appealing city to live in for residents of all ages, characterized by quality education, equal opportunities, pluralism and communal solidarity."[11]

NOTES

1. Wolfe, "Settler Colonialism and Elimination of the Native."
2. Simpson, *Mohawk Interruptus*, 7.
3. Tatour, "Citzenship as Domination," 15.
4. Levine, *Overthrowing Geography*; Mann, *Place in History*.
5. Simpson, *Mohawk Interruptus*, 11.
6. Blokland et al., "Urban Citizenship and Right to the City."
7. Nunzio, "Marginality as a Politics of Limited Entitlements."
8. Tatour, "Citizenship as Domination," 11.
9. Lefebvre, *Urban Revolution*; Harvey, "Right to the City"; Rabinowitz, "Resistance and the City"; Feldman, "Refusing Invisibility"; Taylor, "Politics of Recognition."
10. Azoulay and Ophir, *One-State Condition*.
11. Municipality, "Tel Aviv Smart City," 7.

BIBLIOGRAPHY

Abu-Lughod, Ibrahim. "Palestinian Higher Education: National Identity, Liberation, and Globalization." *boundary 2* 27, no. 1 (2000): 75–95. https://doi.org /10.1215/01903659-27-1-75.

Abu-Lughod, Janet. "Tale of Two Cities: The Origins of Modern Cairo." *Comparative Studies in Society and History* 7, no. 4 (1965): 429–57. https://doi.org /10.1017/S0010417500003819.

Abu-Lughod, Lila. *Veiled Sentiments: Honor and Poetry in a Bedouin Society.* Berkeley: University of California Press, 1986.

Achilli, Luigi. "Disengagement from Politics: Nationalism, Political Identity, and the Everyday in a Palestinian Refugee Camp in Jordan." *Critique of Anthropology* 34, no. 2 (June 10, 2014): 234–57. https://doi.org/10.1177/0308275X13519276.

AFP. "Two MKs Charge Discrimination as Israeli Cities Bar Workers from Schools." *Times of Israel*, October 18, 2015. https://www.timesofisrael.com /discrimination-alleged-as-israeli-cities-bar-workers-from-schools/.

Agier, Michel. "Between War and City: Towards an Urban Anthropology of Refugee Camps." *Ethnography* 3, no. 3 (2002): 317–41. https://doi.org/10.1177 /146613802401092779.

Aleksandrowicz, Or. "The Camouflage of War: Planned Destruction in Jaffa and Tel Aviv, 1948." *Planning Perspectives* 32, no. 2 (April 3, 2017): 175–98. https://doi .org/10.1080/02665433.2016.1185962.

———. "Paper Boundaries: The Erased History of Neveh Shalom." *Theory and Criticism*, 41 (2013): 165–97. https://theory-and-criticism.vanleer.org.il/product /גבולות-של-נייר-ההיסטוריה-המחוקה-של-שכו/.

Al-Haj, Majid. "Higher Education among the Arabs in Israel: Formal Policy between Empowerment and Control." *Higher Education Policy* 16, no. 3 (September 2003): 351–68. https://doi.org/10.1057/palgrave.hep.8300025.

Al-Hayja', Muhammad Abu, and Rachel Leah Jones. "'Ayn Hawd and the 'Unrecognized Villages.'" *Journal of Palestine Studies* 31, no. 1 (2001): 39–49. https://doi.org/10.1525/jps.2001.31.1.39.

Ali, Nohad. "Representation of Arab Citizens in the Institutions of Higher Education in Israel." Haifa: Sikkuy, 2013. https://www.sikkuy.org.il/wp-content /uploads/2013/11/English_final-2014_representation_higher_education1.pdf.

Alkhateeb Shehada, Housni. "And Acre Will Remain in This Consciousness Forever . . . Anisa Ashkar and the Language of the Search for the Subjective." In *Anisa Ashkar: Zift*, edited by Michal Sapir, Sharbel Aboud, Ron Kuner, Jenifer Bar Lev, Sahar Shehada, and Anisa Ashkar, 126–38. Tel Aviv: N&N Aman Gallery, 2012.

al-Qaws. "About Us." alqaws.org. Accessed September 20, 2019. http://alqaws.org /about-us.

Althusser, Louis. "Ideology Interpellates Individuals as Subjects." In *Identity: A Reader*, edited by Paul DuGay, Jessica Evans, and Peter Redman, 31–38. London: SAGE, 2000.

Arieli, Tamar. "Israeli-Palestinian Border Enterprises Revisited." *Journal of Borderlands Studies* 24, no. 2 (2009): 1–14. https://doi.org/10.1080/08865655.2009.9695724.

Assaad, Ragui, and Melanie Arntz. "Constrained Geographical Mobility and Gendered Labor Market Outcomes under Structural Adjustment: Evidence from Egypt." *World Development* 33, no. 3 (2005): 431–54. https://doi.org /10.1016/j.worlddev.2004.08.007.

Aviv, Naomi. "Tsumud: On Anisa Ashkar and the Exhibition 'Zift,' Held at Nelly Aman Gallery in 2010." In *Anisa Ashkar: Zift*, edited by Michal Sapir, Sharbel Aboud, Ron Kuner, Jenifer Bar Lev, Sahar Shehada, and Anisa Ashkar, 140–56. Tel Aviv: N&N Aman Gallery, 2012.

Azaryahu, Maoz. *Tel Aviv: Mythography of a City*. Space, Place, and Society. New York: Syracuse University Press, 2007.

Azoulay, Ariella, and Adi Ophir. *The One-State Condition: Occupation and Democracy in Israel/Palestine*. Stanford, CA: Stanford University Press, 2012.

Babb, Florence E. "'Managua Is Nicaragua': The Making of a Neoliberal City." *City and Society* 11, nos. 1–2 (June 1999): 27–48. https://doi.org/10.1525/city.1999.11.1-2.27.

Babha, Homi. *The Location of Culture*. London: Routledge, 1984.

Bailey, Kerry A. "Indigenous Students: Resilient and Empowered in the Midst of Racism and Lateral Violence." *Ethnic and Racial Studies* 43, no. 6 (May 2, 2020): 1032–51. https://doi.org/10.1080/01419870.2019.1626015.

Baker, Beth. "Regime." In *Keywords of Mobility: Critical Engagements*, edited by Noel B. Salazar and Kiran Jayaram, 152–70. New York: Berghahn Books, 2016.

Baumer, Lilach. "Former Top Intel Executive Weighs In on Underrepresentation of Arabs in Israeli Tech." *CTech*, August 21, 2017, https://www.calcalistech.com /ctech/articles/0,7340,L-3720224,00.html.

Bayat, Asef. *Life as Politics: How Ordinary People Change the Middle East.* 2nd ed. Stanford, CA: Stanford University Press, 2013.

———. "Politics in the City-Inside-Out." *City and Society* 24, no. 2 (August 23, 2012): 110–28. https://doi.org/10.1111/j.1548-744X.2012.01071.x.

Bayoumi, Moustafa. *How Does It Feel to Be a Problem? Being Young and Arab in America.* New York: Penguin, 2009.

BBC. "Gaza Crisis: Toll of Operations in Gaza." BBC.co.uk, 2014. Accessed August 15, 2015. https://www.bbc.co.uk/news/world-middle-east-28439404.

Belkind, Nili. "A Message for Peace or a Tool for Oppression? Israeli Jewish-Arab Duo Achinoam Nini and Mira Awad's Representation of Israel at Eurovision 2009." *Current Musicology* 89 (2010): 7–35. https://doi.org/10.7916/D82F7M07.

Bell, Duncan. "The Dream Machine: On Liberalism and Empire." In *Reordering the World: Essays on Liberalism and Empire,* edited by Duncan Bell, 19–61. Princeton, NJ: Princeton University Press, 2016.

Ben-Ze'ev, Efrat. *Remembering Palestine in 1948: Beyond National Narratives.* Cambridge: Cambridge University Press, 2011.

Berda, Yael. *Living Emergency: Israel's Permit Regime in the Occupied West Bank.* Stanford, CA: Stanford University Press, 2018.

Bizawe Sagui, Eyal. "The Jaffa Bar That Takes a Leap Beyond Coexistence." Haaretz, February 8, 2016. https://www.haaretz.com/israel-news/culture/.premium.MAGAZINE-a-bar-beyond-coexistence-1.5401348.

Blatman-Thomas, Naama. "Commuting for Rights: Circular Mobilities and Regional Identities of Palestinians in a Jewish-Israeli Town." *Geoforum* 78 (January 2017): 22–32. https://doi.org/http://dx.doi.org/10.1016/j.geoforum.2016.11.007.

Blokland, Talja, Christine Hentschel, Andrej Holm, Henrik Lebuhn, and Talia Margalit. "Urban Citizenship and Right to the City: The Fragmentation of Claims." *International Journal of Urban and Regional Research* 39, no. 4 (2015): 655–65. https://doi.org/10.1111/1468-2427.12259.

Boullata, Kamal. "Artists Re-Member Palestine in Beirut." *Journal of Palestine Studies* 32, no. 4 (2003): 22–38. https://doi.org/10.1525/jps.2003.32.4.22.

Brighenti, Andrea Mubi. *Visibility in Social Theory and Social Research.* Basingstoke, UK: Palgrave Macmillan, 2010.

Brighenti, Andrea Mubi, and Alessandro Castelli. "Social Camouflage: Functions, Logic, Paradoxes." *Distinktion: Journal of Social Theory* 17, no. 2 (September 2016): 228–49. https://doi.org/10.1080/1600910X.2016.1217552.

Calhoun, Cheshire. "The Virtue of Civility." *Philosophy and Public Affairs* 29, no. 3 (2000): 251–75. https://doi.org/10.1111/j.1088-4963.2000.00251.x.

Canepari, Eleonora, and Elisabetta Rosa. "A Quiet Claim to Citizenship: Mobility, Urban Spaces and City Practices over Time." *Citizenship Studies* 21, no. 6 (August 18, 2017): 657–74. https://doi.org/10.1080/13621025.2017.1341654.

Christmann, Holger. "Nahum Gutman aus Tel Aviv—Der maler, der die Araber liebte." *FAZ*, October 28, 2001. https://www.faz.net/aktuell/feuilleton/israelisches -tagebuch-nahum-gutman-aus-tel-aviv-der-maler-der-die-araber-liebte-137501.html.

Cohen, Hillel. *Good Arabs: The Israeli Security Agencies and the Israeli Arabs, 1948– 1967*. Berkeley: University of California Press, 2011.

Coleman, Simon, and Tamara Kohn. *The Discipline of Leisure: Embodying Cultures of "Recreation."* New York: Berghahn Books, 2007.

Collier, Jane F., Bill Maurer, and Liliana Suarez-Navaz. "Sanctioned Identities: Legal Constructions of Modern Personhood." *Identities: Global Studies in Culture and Power* 2, nos. 1–2 (1996): 1–27. https://doi.org/10.1080/1070289X.1997.9962524.

Cook, Jonathan. "Israel aims to silence growing international criticism with Texas A&M deal in Nazareth." Mondoweiss, January 3, 2014. https://mondoweiss .net/2014/01/international-criticism-nazareth/

Coulthard, Glen Sean. *Red Skin, White Masks: Rejecting the Colonial Politics of Recognition*. Edited by Gerald R. Alfred. Minneapolis: University of Minnesota Press, 2014.

Coutin, Susan Bibler. "Being En Route." *American Anthropologist* 107, no. 2 (2005): 195–206.

Dacca, Amer. "What It's Really Like Being Arab in the 'Liberal' City of Tel Aviv." *Haaretz*, May 24, 2016. https://www.haaretz.com/opinion/.premium-what-it -s-really-like-being-arab-in-tel-aviv-1.5386657.

Davetian, Benet. *Civility: A Cultural History*. Toronto: University of Toronto Press, 2009.

DeCerteau, Michel. *The Practice of Everyday Life*. Berkeley: University of California Press, 2011.

Deeb, Lara, and Mona Harb. *Leisurely Islam: Negotiating Geography and Morality in Shi'ite South Beirut*. Princeton, NJ: Princeton University Press, 2013.

Dirasat. "An Uphill Climb: Toward Meaningful Integration of Arab Citizens in Institutes of Higher Education in Israel." Nazareth: Dirasat, 2013.

Du Bois, W. E. B. "Strivings of the Negro People." *The Atlantic*, August 1897. https://www.theatlantic.com/magazine/archive/1897/08/strivings-of-the -negro-people/305446/.

Economist. "Israel's Arab Labour Force—Out of Work: Arabs Remain Disproportionately Unemployed Compared to Jews." *The Economist*, February 5, 2014. https://www.economist.com/pomegranate/2014/02/05/out-of-work.

Edmonds, Penelope. "Unpacking Settler Colonialism's Urban Strategies: Indigenous Peoples in Victoria, British Columbia, and the Transition to a Settler-Colonial City." *Urban History Review* 38, no. 2 (2010): 4. https://doi.org /10.7202/039671ar.

Elia, Nada. "Gay Rights with a Side of Apartheid." *Settler Colonial Studies* 2, no. 2 (2012): 49–68. https://doi.org/10.1080/2201473X.2012.10648841.

Elias, Norbert. "Power and Civilisation." *Journal of Power* 1, no. 2 (August 1, 2008): 135–42. https://doi.org/10.1080/17540290802309540.

El-Kazaz, Sarah, and Kevin Mazur. "Introduction to Special Section: The Un-Exceptional Middle Eastern City." *City and Society* 29, no. 1 (April 10, 2017): 148–61. https://doi.org/10.1111/ciso.12116.

Eqeiq, Amal. "Louder Than the Blue ID: Palestinian Hip-Hop in Israel." In *Displaced at Home: Ethnicity and Gender among Palestinians in Israel*, edited by Rhoda Ann Kanaaneh and Isis Nusair, 53–73. New York: State University of New York Press, 2010.

Fanon, Frantz. *Black Skin, White Masks*. London: Pluto, 1986.

Farsakh, Leila. *Palestinian Labour Migration to Israel: Labour, Land and Occupation*. London: Routledge, 2005.

Feldman, Ilana. "Refusing Invisibility: Documentation and Memorialization in Palestinian Refugee Claims." *Journal of Refugee Studies* 21, no. 4 (2008): 498–516. https://doi.org/10.1093/jrs/fen044.

Fincham, Ben. *The Sociology of Fun*. London: Palgrave Macmillan, 2016.

Firro, Kais M. "Reshaping Druze Particularism in Israel." *Journal of Palestine Studies* 30, no. 3 (2001): 40–53. https://doi.org/10.1525/jps.2001.30.3.40.

Foucault, Michel. "Two Lectures." In *Power/Knowledge: Selected Interviews and Other Writings, 1972–1977*, edited by Colin Gordon, 78–108. New York: Pantheon Books, 1980.

Fraser, Nancy. "Social Justice in the Age of Identity Politics: Redistribution, Recognition, and Participation." In *Redistribution or Recognition? A Political-Philosophical Exchange*, edited by Nancy Fraser and Axel Honneth, 7–109. London: Verso, 2003.

Freeman, Victoria Jane. "'Toronto Has No History!' Indigeneity, Settler Colonialism, and Historical Memory in Canada's Largest City." *Urban History Review* 38, no. 2 (2010): 21–35. https://doi.org/10.7202/039672ar.

Freud, Sigmund. "Beyond the Pleasure Principle." In *The Standard Edition of the Complete Psychological Works of Sigmund Freud*, Vol. 18, edited by James Strachey. London: Hogarth, 1955.

Gagné, Natacha, and Benoît Trépied. "Introduction to Special Issue Colonialism, Law, and the City: The Politics of Urban Indigeneity." *City and Society* 28, no. 1 (2016): 8–22. https://doi.org/10.1111/ciso.12071.

Gately, Iain. *Rush Hour: How 500 Million Commuters Survive the Daily Journey to Work*. London: Head of Zeus, 2014.

Gerner, Deborah J., and Philip A. Schrodt. "Into the New Millenium: Challenges Facing Palestinian Higher Education in the Twenty-First Century." *Arab Studies Quarterly* 21, no. 4 (1999): 19–34.

Ghanem, As'ad. "Israel's Second-Class Citizens: Arabs in Israel and the Struggle for Equal Rights." *Foreign Affairs* 95, no. 4 (2016): 37–42.

Ghorashi, Halleh. "From Absolute Invisibility to Extreme Visibility: Emancipation Trajectory of Migrant Women in the Netherlands." *Feminist Review*, no. 94 (2010): 75–92.

Goffman, Erving. *The Presentation of Self in Everyday Life*. London: Penguin, 1990.

Golan, Arnon. "Jewish Settlement of Former Arab Towns and Their Incorporation into the Israeli Urban System (1948–50)." In *The Israeli Palestinians: An Arab Minority in the Jewish State*, edited by Alexander Bligh, 145–60. London: Frank Cass, 2003.

Goldstein, Daniel M. "Dancing on the Margins: Transforming Urban Marginality through Popular Performance." *City and Society* 9, no. 1 (1997): 201–15.

Gordon, Neve. *Israel's Occupation*. Berkeley: University of California Press, 2008.

Grandinetti, Tina. "The Palestinian Middle Class in Rawabi: Depoliticizing the Occupation." *Alternatives* 40, no. 1 (2015): 63–78. https://doi.org/10.1177/0304375 415581259.

Grazia, Sebastian de. *Of Time, Work and Leisure*. New York: Twentieth Century Fund, 1962.

Gutman, Yifat. *Memory Activism: Reimagining the Past for the Future in Israel-Palestine*. Nashville, TN: Vanderbilt University Press, 2017.

Hackl, Andreas. "Address Inequalities Facing Arabs, Says ICG." *New Humanitarian*, March 19, 2012. https://www.thenewhumanitarian.org/report/95095 /israel-address-inequalities-facing-arabs-says-icg.

———. "The Good Arab: Conditional Inclusion and Settler Colonial Citizenship among Palestinian Citizens of Israel in Jewish Tel Aviv." *Journal of the Royal Anthropological Institute* 26, no. 3 (2020): 594–611. https://doi.org/10.1111 /1467-9655.13316.

———. "Immersive Invisibility in the Settler-Colonial City: The Conditional Inclusion of Palestinians in Tel Aviv." *American Ethnologist* 45, no. 3 (2018): 1–13.

———. "Key Figure of Mobility: The Exile." *Social Anthropology* 25, no. 1 (2017): 55–68.

———. "Mobility Equity in a Globalized World: Reducing Inequalities in the Sustainable Development Agenda." *World Development* 112 (2018): 150–62.

———. "An Orchestra of Civil Resistance: Privilege, Diversity, and Identification among Cross-Border Activists in a Palestinian Village." *Peace and Change* 41, no. 2 (2016): 167–93. https://doi.org/10.1111/pech.12186

Hage, Ghassan. "The Affective Politics of Racial Mis-interpellation." *Theory, Culture and Society* 27, nos. 7–8 (2011): 112–29. https://doi.org/10.1177 /0263276410383713.

———. *Alter-Politics: Critical Anthropology and the Radical Imagination*. Melbourne: MUP Academic, 2015.

Halbfinger, David. "Israel Faces a Defining Question: How Much Democracy Should Arabs Get?" *New York Times*, March 12, 2020. https://www.nytimes.com /2020/03/12/world/middleeast/israel-arabs-vote.html.

Handelman, Don. *Models and Mirrors: Towards an Anthropology of Public Events.* Oxford: Berghahn Books, 1998.

Hanieh, Adam. *Lineages of Revolt: Issues of Contemporary Capitalism in the Middle East.* London: Haymarket Books, 2013.

Harms, Erik. "The Boss: Conspicuous Invisibility in Ho Chi Minh City." *City and Society* 25, no. 2 (2013): 195–215. https://doi.org/10.1111/ciso.12016.

Harvey, David. *Rebel Cities: From the Right to the City to the Urban Revolution.* London: Verso, 2012.

———. "The Right to the City." *New Left Review* 53 (2008): 23–40.

Hasisi, Badi, and David Weisburd. "Going beyond Ascribed Identities: The Importance of Procedural Justice in Airport Security Screening in Israel." *Law and Society Review* 45, no. 4 (2011): 867–92. https://doi.org/10.1111/j.1540-5893 .2011.00459.x.

Herzog, Hanna. "Choice as Everyday Politics: Female Palestinian Citizens of Israel in Mixed Cities." *International Journal of Politics, Culture, and Society* 22, no. 1 (2009): 5–21. https://doi.org/10.1007/s10767-009-9045-0.

Hilmy, Salman. "'ID Card' by Mahmoud Darwish: A Translation and Commentary." Washington Report on Middle East Affairs, vol. 36, no. 7 (2017): pp. 65–6. https://www.wrmea.org/017-november-december/id-card-by -mahmoud-darwish-a-translation-and-commentary.html.

Hirose, Akihiko, and Kay Kei-Ho Pih. "'No Asians Working Here': Racialized Otherness and Authenticity in Gastronomical Orientalism." *Ethnic and Racial Studies* 34, no. 9 (September 1, 2011): 1482–1501. https://doi.org/10.1080/0141987 0.2010.550929.

Hobbs, Allyson. *A Chosen Exile: A History of Racial Passing in American Life.* Cambridge, MA: Harvard University Press, 2014.

Holmes, Oliver, and Quique Kierszenbaum. "Far-Right Jewish Groups and Arab Youths Claim Streets of Lod as Israel Loses Control." *The Guardian,* May 15, 2021, https://www.theguardian.com/world/2021/may/15/far-right-jewish -groups-arab-youths-claim-streets-lod-israel-loses-control.

Holston, James, and Arjun Appadurai. "Introduction: Cities and Citizenship." In *Cities and Citizenship,* edited by James Holston, 1–18. Durham, NC: Duke University Press, 1999.

Hugill, David. "What Is a Settler-Colonial City?" *Geography Compass* 11, no. 5 (May 10, 2017): e12315. https://doi.org/10.1111/gec3.12315.

Ibrahim, Ibtisam. "Emigration Patterns among Palestinian Women in Israel." In *Displaced at Home: Ethnicity and Gender among Palestinians in Israel,* edited by Roda Ann Kanaaneh and Isis Nusair, 207–22. New York: State University of New York Press, 2010.

ILO. "The Situation of Workers of the Occupied Arab Territories." Geneva, 2017.

———. "The Situation of Workers of the Occupied Arab Territories." Geneva, 2018.

———. "The Situation of Workers of the Occupied Arab Territories." Geneva, 2019.

Jackman, Michael Connors, and Nishant Upadhyay. "Pinkwatching Israel, Whitewashing Canada: Queer (Settler) Politics and Indigenous Colonization in Canada." *WSQ: Women's Studies Quarterly* 42, nos. 3–4 (2014): 195–210. https://doi.org/10.1353/wsq.2014.0044.

Jamal, Amal. *Arab Minority Nationalism in Israel: The Politics of Indigeneity.* Routledge Studies on the Arab-Israeli Conflict. London: Routledge, 2011.

Jean-Klein, Iris. "Nationalism and Resistance: The Two Faces of Everyday Activism in Palestine during the Intifada." *Cultural Anthropology* 16, no. 1 (February 2001): 83–126. https://doi.org/10.1525/can.2001.16.1.83.

Jenkins, Richard. "Categorization: Identity, Social Process and Epistemology." *Current Sociology* 48, no. 3 (2000): 7–25. https://doi.org/10.1177/0011392100048003003.

Jonsson, Hjorleifur. "Serious Fun: Minority Cultural Dynamics and National Integration in Thailand." *American Ethnologist* 28, no. 1 (2001): 151–78. https://doi.org/10.1525/ae.2001.28.1.151.

Joronen, Mikko. "Spaces of Waiting: Politics of Precarious Recognition in the Occupied West Bank." *Environment and Planning D: Society and Space* 35, no. 6 (May 9, 2017): 994–1011. https://doi.org/10.1177/0263775817708789.

Kanaaneh, Rhoda Ann. *Surrounded: Palestinian Soldiers in the Israeli Military.* Stanford, CA: Stanford University Press, 2009.

Karkabi, Nadeem. "How and Why Haifa Has Become the 'Palestinian Cultural Capital' in Israel." *City and Community* 17, no. 4 (December 1, 2018): 1168–88. https://doi.org/10.1111/cico.12341.

———. "Staging Particular Difference: Politics of Space in the Palestinian Alternative Music Scene." *Middle East Journal of Culture and Communication* 6, no. 3 (2013): 308–28. https://doi.org/10.1163/18739865-00603004.

Kaufmann, Vincent, Manfred Max Bergman, and Dominique Joye. "Motility: Mobility as Capital." *International Journal of Urban and Regional Research* 28, no. 4 (2004): 745–56.

Kelly, Tobias. "'Jurisdictional Politics' in the Occupied West Bank: Territory, Community, and Economic Dependency in the Formation of Legal Subjects." *Law and Social Inquiry* 31, no. 1 (2006): 39–74.

Khalili, Laleh. "The Politics of Pleasure: Promenading on the Corniche and Beachgoing." *Environment and Planning D: Society and Space* 34, no. 4 (August 2016): 583–600. https://doi.org/10.1177/0263775815623538.

Khattab, Nabil, and Sami Miaari. *Palestinians in the Israeli Labor Market: A Multi-Disciplinary Approach.* London: Palgrave Macmillan, 2013.

Kimmerling, Baruch. "Zionism and Territory: The Socio-Territorial Dimensions of Zionist Politics." Berkeley International and Area Studies, Vol. 51. Berkeley: University of California Press, 1983.

King, Mary Elizabeth. *A Quiet Revolution: The First Palestinian Intifada and Nonviolent Resistance*. New York: Nation Books, 2007.

Koefoed, Lasse, and Kirsten Simonsen. "(Re)scaling Identities: Embodied Others and Alternative Spaces of Identification." *Ethnicities* 12, no. 5 (March 18, 2012): 623–42. https://doi.org/10.1177/1468796811434487.

Kohlberg, Etan. "Some Imāmī-Shīʿī Views on Taqiyya." *Journal of the American Oriental Society* 95, no. 3 (1975): 395–402. https://doi.org/10.2307/599351.

Koning, Anouk de. *Global Dreams: Class, Gender, and Public Space in Cosmopolitan Cairo*. Cairo: American University in Cairo Press, 2009.

Lacan, Jacques. *The Four Fundamental Concepts of Psychoanalysis*. New York: W. W. Norton, 1981.

Lamont, Michèle. "Addressing Recognition Gaps: Destigmatization and the Reduction of Inequality." *American Sociological Review* 83, no. 3 (2018): 419–44. https://doi.org/10.1177/0003122418773775.

Lamont, Michèle, and Nissim Mizrachi. *Responses to Stigmatization in Comparative Perspective*. New York: Routledge, 2012.

Lamont, Michèle, Graziella Moraes Silva, Jessica S. Welburn, Joshua Guetzkow, Nissim Mizrachi, Hanna Herzog, and Elisa Reis. *Getting Respect: Responding to Stigma and Discrimination in the United States, Brazil, and Israel*. Princeton, NJ: Princeton University Press, 2016.

Lee, Doreen. "'Anybody Can Do It': Aesthetic Empowerment, Urban Citizenship, and the Naturalization of Indonesian Graffiti and Street Art." *City and Society* 25, no. 3 (2013): 304–27. https://doi.org/10.1111/ciso.12024.

Lefebvre, Henri. *The Urban Revolution*. Minneapolis: University of Minnesota Press, 2003.

LeFevre, Tate A. "Representation, Resistance and the Logics of Difference: Indigenous Culture as Political Resource in the Settler-State." *Settler Colonial Studies* 3, no. 2 (April 1, 2013): 136–40. https://doi.org/10.1080/2201473X.2013 .781926.

Leivestad, Hege Hoyer. "Chapter 7—Motility." In *Keywords of Mobility: Critical Engagements*, edited by Noel B. Salazar and Kiran Jayaram, 133–51. New York: Berghahn Books, 2016.

Levine, Mark. *Overthrowing Geography: Jaffa, Tel Aviv, and the Struggle for Palestine, 1880–1948*. Berkeley: University of California Press, 2005.

Levy, Gideon. "The Jewish State Has No More Room for 'Good Arabs.'" *Haaretz*, June 10, 2015. Accessed May 19, 2020. https://www.haaretz.com/opinion /.premium-israel-has-no-more-room-for-good-arabs-1.5370900.

Lis, Jonathan, and Talila Nesher. "Israeli Students and MKs Clash over Controversial Nakba Day Ceremony in TA University." *Haaretz*, March 14, 2015. http://www.haaretz.com/news/diplomacy-defense/israeli-students-and-mks -clash-over-controversial-nakba-day-ceremony-in-ta-university-1.430418.

Littman, Shany. "There's a War Zone in South Tel Aviv, but Jewish Residents Don't See It." *Haaretz*, June 23, 2018. https://www.haaretz.com/magazine/.premium .MAGAZINE-a-tel-aviv-favela-jaffa-residents-tell-of-life-in-a-cycle-of-violence -1.6198495.

Locker-Biletzki, Amir. "Rethinking Settler Colonialism: A Marxist Critique of Gershon Shafir." *Rethinking Marxism* 30, no. 3 (July 3, 2018): 441–61. https://doi .org/10.1080/08935696.2018.1525969.

Malik, Fareesa, Brian Nicholson, and Richard Heeks. "Understanding the Development Implications of Online Outsourcing." In *IFIP Advances in Information and Communication Technology* 504 (2017): 425–36. https://doi.org /10.1007/978-3-319-59111-7_35.

Maltz, Judy. "The Gaza Effect: In Shaky Economy, Arab Businesses Hit Hardest." *Haaretz*, August 7, 2014. http://www.haaretz.com/news/national/.premium-1 .609299.

Mann, Barbara E. *A Place in History: Modernism, Tel Aviv, and the Creation of Jewish Urban Space.* Stanford, CA: Stanford University Press, 2006.

McDonald, David A. *My Voice Is My Weapon: Music, Nationalism and the Poetics of Palestinian Resistance.* Durham, NC: Duke University Press, 2013.

McFarlane, Colin. "The City as Assemblage: Dwelling and Urban Space." *Environment and Planning D: Society and Space* 29, no. 4 (2011): 649–71. https:// doi.org/10.1068/d4710.

Meghji, Ali, and Rima Saini. "Rationalising Racial Inequality: Ideology, Hegemony and Post-Racialism among the Black and South Asian Middle-Classes." *Sociology* 52, no. 4 (September 4, 2017): 671–87. https://doi.org/10.1177 /0038038517726645.

Mehta, Uday Singh. *Liberalism and Empire: A Study in Nineteenth-Century British Liberal Thought.* Chicago: University of Chicago Press, 1999.

Mendel, Yonatan. *The Creation of Israeli Arabic.* Basingstoke, UK: Palgrave Macmillan, 2014.

———. "Fantasising Israel." *London Review of Books* 31, no. 12 (2009): 28–29.

Monterescu, Daniel. *Jaffa: Shared and Shattered.* Bloomington: Indiana University Press, 2015.

Monterescu, Daniel, and Haim Hazan. *Twilight Nationalism: Politics of Existence at Life's End.* Stanford, CA: Stanford University Press, 2018.

Monterescu, Daniel, and Miriam Schickler. "Creative Marginality: Jews, Palestinians and the Alternative Cultural Scene in Tel Aviv-Jaffa." *Ethnologie Française* 45, no. 2 (2015): 293–308. https://doi.org/10.3917/ethn.152.0293.

Morris, Benny. *The Birth of the Palestinian Refugee Problem, 1947–1949.* Cambridge: Cambridge University Press, 1989.

Mouffe, Chantal. *On the Political.* London: Routledge, 2015.

Municipality, Tel Aviv-Yafo. "Tel Aviv Smart City: Tel Aviv Nonstop City." Tel Aviv, 2015.

Naciri, M. "Regards sur l'évolution de la citadinité au Maroc." In *Citadins, villes, urbanisation dans le monde Arabe aujourd'hui: Algérie, Émirats du golfe, Liban, Maroc, Syrie, Tunisie.* Tours., 37–59. URBAMA, no. hors série des Fascicules de Recherches, 1985.

Nawajaa, Mahmoud. "Palestinian Dabkeh in the Middle of Occupied Tel Aviv." Youtube, 2011. Accessed April 12, 2016. https://www.youtube.com/watch?v=hSoCssEoPhg.

NPR. "Arab Singer Joins Israeli in Song Contest." *NPR*, May 9, 2009. https://www.npr.org/templates/story/story.php?storyId=103980225&t=1600780745538.

Nunzio, Marco Di. "Marginality as a Politics of Limited Entitlements: Street Life and the Dilemma of Inclusion in Urban Ethiopia." *American Ethnologist* 44, no. 1 (2017): 91–103. https://doi.org/10.1111/amet.12428.

Ortner, Sherry B. *Anthropology and Social Theory: Culture, Power, and the Acting Subject.* Durham, NC: Duke University Press, 2006.

Palm, Michael. "Outsourcing, Self-Service and the Telemobility of Work." *Anthropology of Work Review* 27, no. 2 (2006): 1–9. https://doi.org/10.1525/awr.2006.27.2.1.

Pappé, Ilan. *The Forgotten Palestinians: A History of the Palestinians in Israel.* New Haven, CT: Yale University Press, 2011.

Pasquetti, Silvia. "Legal Emotions: An Ethnography of Distrust and Fear in the Arab Districts of an Israeli City." *Law and Society Review* 47, no. 3 (2013): 461–92.

Peteet, Julie. "Problematizing a Palestinian Diaspora." *International Journal of Middle East Studies* 39, no. 4 (2007): 627–46.

———. *Space and Mobility in Palestine.* Bloomington: Indiana University Press, 2017.

———. "Unsettling the Categories of Displacement." *Middle East Report*, no. 244 (2007): 2–9. https://doi.org/10.2307/25164796.

Peters, Stephen K. H. "Loaded Speech: Between Voices in Indigenous Public Speaking Events." *Journal of Linguistic Anthropology* 26, no. 3 (December 20, 2016): 315–34. https://doi.org/10.1111/jola.12130.

Petryna, Adriana. "Experimentality: On the Global Mobility and Regulation of Human Subjects Research." *PoLAR: Political and Legal Anthropology Review* 30, no. 2 (November 2007): 288–304. https://doi.org/10.1525/pol.2007.30.2.288.

Plonski, Sharri. *Palestinian Citizens of Israel: Power, Resistance and the Struggle for Space.* London: I. B. Tauris, 2018.

Porter, Libby, and Oren Yiftachel. "Urbanizing Settler-Colonial Studies: Introduction to the Special Issue." *Settler Colonial Studies* 9, no. 2 (2019): 177–86. https://doi.org/10.1080/2201473X.2017.1409394.

Portugali, Juval. *Implicate Relations: Society and Space in the Israeli-Palestinian Conflict*. Dordrecht: Kluwer Academic, 1993.

Prochaska, David. *Making Algeria French: Colonialism in Bône, 1870–1920*. Cambridge: Cambridge University Press, 2004.

Puar, Jasbir. "Rethinking Homonationalism." *International Journal of Middle East Studies* 45, no. 2 (2013): 336–39. https://doi.org/10.1017/S002074381300007X.

Pugh, Jeffrey D. "Negotiating Identity and Belonging through the Invisibility Bargain: Colombian Forced Migrants in Ecuador." *International Migration Review* 54, no. 4 (2018): 978–1010. https://doi.org/10.1111/imre.12344.

Rabinowitz, Dan. *Overlooking Nazareth: The Ethnography of Exclusion in Galilee*. Cambridge: Cambridge University Press, 1997. http://dx.doi.org/10.1017/CBO 9780511621819.

———. "Resistance and the City." *History and Anthropology* 25 (August 2014): 472–87. https://doi.org/10.1080/02757206.2014.930457.

Rabinowitz, Dan, and Khawla Abu-Baker. *Coffins on Our Shoulders: The Experience of the Palestinian Citizens of Israel*. Berkeley: University of California Press, 2005.

Rabinowitz, Dan, and Daniel Monterescu. "Reconfiguring the 'Mixed Town': Urban Transformations of Ethnonational Relations in Palestine and Israel." *International Journal of Middle East Studies* 40, no. 2 (2008): 195–226. https://doi .org/10.1017/S0020743808080513.

Ram, Mori. "White but Not Quite: Normalizing Colonial Conquests through Spatial Mimicry." *Antipode* 46, no. 3 (2014): 736–53. https://doi.org/10.1111/anti .12071.

Redden, Elizabeth. "Dream Deferred or Dashed in Israel." Inside Higher Ed, August 27, 2015. https://www.insidehighered.com/news/2015/08/27/what -happened-texas-ams-plan-open-branch-campus-nazareth.

Regev, Motti. "Present Absentee: Arab Music in Israeli Culture." *Public Culture* 7, no. 2 (May 1, 1995): 433–45. https://doi.org/10.1215/08992363-7-2-433.

Ritchie, Jason. "How Do You Say 'Come out of the Closet' in Arabic? Queer Activism and the Politics of Visibility in Israel-Palestine." *GLQ: Journal of Lesbian and Gay Studies* 16, no. 4 (2010): 557–75. https://doi.org/10.1215 /10642684-2010-004.

———. "Pinkwashing, Homonationalism, and Israel–Palestine: The Conceits of Queer Theory and the Politics of the Ordinary." *Antipode* 47, no. 3 (June 1, 2015): 616–34. https://doi.org/10.1111/anti.12100.

Robinson, Shira. *Citizen Strangers: Palestinians and the Birth of Israel's Liberal Settler State*. Stanford, CA: Stanford University Press, 2013.

Rotbard, Sharon. *White City, Black City: Architecture and War in Tel Aviv and Jaffa*. London: Pluto, 2015.

Sa'ar, Amalia. "Carefully on the Margins: Christian Palestinians in Haifa between Nation and State." *American Ethnologist* 25, no. 2 (1998): 215–39. https://doi.org /10.1525/ae.1998.25.2.215.

———. *Economic Citizenship: Neoliberal Paradoxes of Empowerment.* Oxford: Berghahn, 2016.

———. "Lonely in Your Firm Grip: Women in Israeli-Palestinian Families." *Journal of the Royal Anthropological Institute* 7, no. 4 (2001): 723–39. https://doi.org /10.1111/1467-9655.00086.

Salazar, Noel B. "The Power of Imagination in Transnational Mobilities." *Identities: Global Studies in Culture and Power* 18, no. 6 (2011): 576–98. https://doi .org/10.1080/1070289X.2011.672859.

Sassen, Saskia. "The Global City: Introducing a Concept." *Brown Journal of World Affairs* 11, no. 2 (2005): 27–40.

———. *The Mobility of Labor and Capital: A Study in International Investment and Labor Flow.* Cambridge: Cambridge University Press, 1988.

———. "Urban Capabilities: An Essay on Our Challenges and Differences." *Journal of International Affairs* 65, no. 2 (2012): 85–96. https://doi.org/10.1080/147 47731.2014.951206.

Saunders, Doug. *Arrival City: How the Largest Migration in History Is Reshaping Our World.* New York: Vintage Books, 2011.

Sela, Rona. *Effervescene—Housing, Language, History: A New Generation of Jewish-Arab Cities.* Tel Aviv: Nachum Gutman Museum of Art, 2013.

———. "Fawaran—Effervescence (Unrest)—Housing, Language, History: A New Generation in Jewish-Arab Cities." Ronasela.com, 2013. Accessed September 20, 2017. http://www.ronasela.com/en/details.asp?listid=63.

Sennett, Richard. "The Culture of Work." In *The SAGE Handbook of Sociology,* edited by Craig Calhoun, Chris Rojek, and Bryan S. Turner, 129–34. London: SAGE, 2005.

———. *The Fall of Public Man.* London: Penguin, 2002.

Shamir, Ronen. "Without Borders? Notes on Globalization as a Mobility Regime." *Sociological Theory* 23, no. 2 (2005): 197–217. https://doi.org/10.1111/j.0735 -2751.2005.00250.x.

Sherwood, Harriet. "Mira Awad: Israel's Palestinian Singing Star Caught between Worlds." *The Guardian,* October 9, 2010. https://www.theguardian.com/world /2010/oct/09/mira-awad-israel-palestinian-star.

Shtull-Trauring, Asaf. "Head to Head—Why Are So Few Arabs in Higher Education? An Interview with Haifa Professor Majid Al-Haj." *Haaretz,* June 28, 2011. http://www.haaretz.com/print-edition/features/head-to-head-why-are -so-few-arabs-in-higher-education-1.369967.

Sikkuy. "Equality Zones: Promoting Partnership between Jewish and Arab Municipal Authorities. Lessons and Insights." Jerusalem: Sikkuy, 2014. https:// www.sikkuy.org.il/wp-content/uploads/2014/12/equality-zones-en.pdf.

———. "Sikkuy Boosts Public Transportation for Galilee Arabs." nif.org, 2017. https://www.nif.org/stories/palestinian-society/sikkuy-boosts-public -transportation-for-galilee-arabs/.

Sikkuy, Dirasat, and Van Leer. "Arabic and Arab Culture on Israeli Campuses: An Updated Look (Executive Summary)." Sikkuy, 2014. http://www.sikkuy.org.il /wp-content/uploads/2014/12/present-yet-absent_internet_eng.pdf.

Simmel, Georg. "The Metropolis and Mental Life." In *The Sociology of Georg Simmel*, edited by Kurt Wolff, 11–19. New York: Free Press, 2011 [1903].

Simpson, Audra. *Mohawk Interruptus: Political Life across the Borders of Settler States*. Durham, NC: Duke University Press, 2014.

Skeggs, Beverley. *Class, Self, Culture*. London: Routledge, 2003.

Slyomovics, Susan. "Who and What Is Native to Israel? On Marcel Janco's Settler Art and Jacqueline Shohet Kahanoff's 'Levantinism.'" *Settler Colonial Studies* 4, no. 1 (January 2, 2014): 27–47. https://doi.org/10.1080/22014 73X.2013.784238.

Smith, Andrea. "Settler Sites of Memory and the Work of Mourning." *French Politics, Culture and Society* 31, no. 3 (2013): 65. https://doi.org/10.3167/fpcs .2013.310304.

Smith, Sandra Susan. *Lone Pursuit: Distrust and Defensive Individualism among the Black Poor*. New York: Russell Sage Foundation, 2007.

Sözer, Hande. *Managing Invisibility: Dissimulation and Identity Maintenance among Alevi Bulgarian Turks*. Leiden: Brill, 2014.

Spencer, Jonathan. *Anthropology, Politics, and the State: Democracy and Violence in South Asia*. Cambridge: Cambridge University Press, 2007. http://dx.doi.org /10.1017/CBO9780511801853.

Strohm, Kiven. "Impossible Identification: Contemporary Art, Politics and the Palestinians in Israel." PhD diss., Université de Montréal, 2013.

Sylvain, Renée. "Essentialism and the Indigenous Politics of Recognition in Southern Africa." *American Anthropologist* 116, no. 2 (2014): 251–64. https://doi .org/10.1111/aman.12087.

Tatour, Lana. "Citzenship as Domination: Settler Colonialism and the Making of Palestinian Citizenship in Israel." *Arab Studies Journal* 27, no. 2 (2019): 8–39. https://search.proquest.com/docview/2385748777?accountid=10673.

Tawil-Souri, Helga. "Uneven Borders, Coloured (Im)mobilities: ID Cards in Palestine/Israel." *Geopolitics* 17, no. 1 (January 1, 2012): 153–76. https://doi.org/10 .1080/14650045.2011.562944.

———. "Where Is the Political in Cultural Studies? In Palestine." *International Journal of Cultural Studies* 16, no. 1 (2011): 1–16. https://doi.org/10.1177 /1367877911408656.

Taylor, Charles. "The Politics of Recognition." In *Multiculturalism: Examining the Politics of Recognition*, edited by Amy Gutmann, 25–73. Princeton, NJ: Princeton University Press, 1994. http://press.princeton.edu/titles/5554.html.

Tel Aviv University. "History: The Evolution of Tel Aviv University." tau.ac.il. Accessed June 2, 2016. https://english.tau.ac.il/tau_history.

Thomas, Nicholas, and Diane Losche. *Double Vision: Art Histories and Colonial Histories in the Pacific*. Cambridge: Cambridge University Press, 1999.

Tirosh, Noam. "INakba, Mobile Media and Society's Memory." *Mobile Media and Communication* 6, no. 3 (April 9, 2018): 350–66. https://doi.org/10.1177/2050157 918758130.

Torpey, John. "Coming and Going: On the State Monopolization of the Legitimate 'Means of Movement.'" *Sociological Theory* 16, no. 3 (1998): 239–59. https://doi .org/10.1111/0735-2751.00055.

Torstrick, Rebecca L. *The Limits of Coexistence: Identity Politics in Israel*. Ann Arbor: University of Michigan Press, 2000.

UN. "Report of the Independent Commission of Inquiry Established Pursuant to Human Rights Council Resolution S-21/1." New York, 2015. https://reliefweb.int /sites/reliefweb.int/files/resources/A-HRC-29-52_en.pdf.

Veracini, Lorenzo. *Settler Colonialism: A Theoretical Overview*. London: Palgrave Macmillan, 2010. https://doi.org/10.1057/9780230299191.

Vigh, Henrik. "Motion Squared: A Second Look at the Concept of Social Navigation." *Anthropological Theory* 9, no. 4 (2009): 419–38.

Virani, Shafique N. "Taqiyya and Identity in a South Asian Community." *Journal of Asian Studies* 70, no. 1 (2011): 99–139. https://doi.org/10.1017/S0021911810002974.

Wacquant, Loïc. "Revisiting Territories of Relegation: Class, Ethnicity and State in the Making of Advanced Marginality." *Urban Studies* 53, no. 6 (December 17, 2015): 1077–88. https://doi.org/10.1177/0042098015613259.

Wacquant, Loïc J. D. *Urban Outcasts: A Comparative Sociology of Advanced Marginality*. Cambridge: Polity, 2008.

Weizman, Eyal. *Hollow Land: Israel's Architecture of Occupation*. London: Verso Books, 2012.

Wesley, David. *State Practices and Zionist Images: Shaping Economic Development in Arab Towns in Israel*. Oxford: Berghahn Books, 2013.

White, Melanie. "An Ambivalent Civility." *Canadian Journal of Sociology* 31, no. 4 (January 8, 2006): 445–60.

Wolfe, Patrick. "Settler Colonialism and the Elimination of the Native." *Journal of Genocide Research* 8, no. 4 (2006): 387–409. https://doi.org/10.1080/14623520 601056240.

World Bank. "Area C and the Future of the Palestinian Economy." Washington, DC, 2014. http://dx.doi.org/10.1596/978-1-4648-0193-8.

Yahav, Galia. "An Intifada Substitute in the Heart of Tel Aviv." *Haaretz*, July 1, 2013. https://www.haaretz.com/israel-news/culture/.premium-intifada-substitute -in-tel-aviv-1.5289303.

Yan, Grace, and Carla Almeida Santos. "'China, Forever': Tourism Discourse and Self-Orientalism." *Annals of Tourism Research* 36, no. 2 (2009): 295–315. https:// doi.org/https://doi.org/10.1016/j.annals.2009.01.003.

Yashiv, Eran, and Nitsa Katsir. "The Labour Market of Israeli Arabs: Key Features and Policy Solutions." *Tel Aviv University (Policy Paper)*. Tel Aviv, 2014.

Yazbak, Mahmoud. "The Islamic Waqf in Yaffa and the Urban Space: From the Ottoman State to the State of Israel." *Makan* 2 (2010): 23–45.

Yiftachel, Oren. "Centralized Power and Divided Space: 'Fractured Regions' in the Israeli 'Ethnocracy.'" *GeoJournal* 53, no. 3 (2001): 283–93.

———. "The Shrinking Space of Citizenship: Ethnocratic Politics in Israel." *Middle East Report*, no. 223 (2002): 38–45. https://doi.org/10.2307/1559463.

Zikri, Almog Ben, and Yaniv Kubovich. "Arab Worker Freed to House Arrest Hours after Barbaric Police Beating in Tel Aviv." *Haaretz*, May 23, 2016. https://www.haaretz.com/israel-news/arab-beaten-by-police-in-tel-aviv-released-to-house-arrest-1.5386545.

Ziv, Amalia. "Performative Politics in Israeli Queer Anti-Occupation Activism." *GLQ: Journal of Lesbian and Gay Studies* 16, no. 4 (2010): 537–56. https://doi.org/10.1215/10642684-2010-003.

Ziv, Amitai. "'Coming in Droves': Number of Arabs in Israeli High-Tech Soars." *Haaretz*, September 12, 2019. https://www.haaretz.com/israel-news/business/.premium-coming-in-droves-number-of-arabs-in-israeli-high-tech-soars-1.7834716.

Zochrot. "Remembering Hittin." Zochrot.org, 2007.

Zur, Yarden. "Survey: Half of Arabs in Israeli Universities Suffer Racism." *Haaretz*, July 5, 2017. https://www.haaretz.com/israel-news/.premium-survey-half-of-arabs-in-israeli-universities-suffer-racism-1.5491861.

INDEX

Page numbers in italics refer to figures.

ANDREAS HACKL is Lecturer in Anthropology of Development at the University of Edinburgh, a former newspaper correspondent for Israel/Palestine, and a research consultant for the International Labour Organization. His academic research has been published in leading journals such as *World Development*, *American Ethnologist*, and *Social Anthropology*.

www.ingramcontent.com/pod-product-compliance
Lightning Source LLC
Chambersburg PA
CBHW030818270326
41928CB00007B/783